W9-BEX-936

COASTWISE
NAVIGATION

Displaying the watchword by which he sailed solo across the Atlantic, navigation student William Fitz, Jr., is aboard the 26-foot sloop LADY BLUE he successfully navigated from Mylor Creek, Falmouth, Eng., to Mattapoisett, Buzzards Bay, Mass., via the Azores and Bermuda.

COASTWISE NAVIGATION

Frances W. Wright

CORNELL MARITIME PRESS

CENTREVILLE   MARYLAND

Copyright © 1980 by Cornell Maritime Press, Inc.

All Rights Reserved

No part of this book may be reproduced in any manner whatsoever without prior written permission of the publisher except in the case of brief quotations embodied in critical articles and reviews. Inquiries should be addressed to Cornell Maritime Press, Inc., Centreville, Maryland 21617.

Library of Congress Cataloging in Publication Data

Wright, Frances Woodworth.
    Coastwise navigation.

    "Companion to Celestial navigation."
    Bibliography: p.
    Includes index.
    1. Navigation I. Title.
VK559.W74   623.89′2   79-23452
ISBN 0—87033—260-0

Printed and Bound in the United States of America

Contents

Dedicated to Students of Astronomy 91-r, Harvard

Acknowledgments

This book is dedicated to all my students; to Astronomy 91-r at Harvard and to former students acknowledged in *Celestial Navigation* and *Particularized Navigation*—they all have provided encouragement, stimulus and material aid in critical reading with suggestions and comments.

More directly, I appreciate the critical checking by Leon Nawrocki, James Jackson, Jr., Dean Spencer, and William Blair. Leon read the first draft of the book and began the first draft of the Index. James, an experienced navigator, read the last half of the book, Dean read a second draft of the book and Index, while William contributed excellent comments on the final draft of *Coastwise Navigation*.

Peter Gill assisted with valuable comments and suggestions for Chapter 5. For Chapter 6 Nick Everett and Clem Wood contributed two of the maneuvering board problems when they were undergraduates.

I am especially appreciative of all the figures drawn by two former students, Steve Diskin and Quentin Danser. Steve, a graduate of the Harvard School of Design, produced more than half of them, and Quentin finished the remainder and plotted the cruises on Chart 116-SC Tr.

Special gratitude goes to Prof. Paul W. Hodge of the University of Washington for his encouragement and advice, and most of all to Prof. Bart J. Bok, who initiated my interest in navigation.

I wish to express appreciation and gratitude for all the cooperation received from the heads of several government agencies. Thanks are due for permission to reproduce illustrative data from the *Tide Tables* and *Tidal Current Tables, Coast Pilots,* and *Radio Navigation Aids (Pub. 117).* I appreciate cooperation from the Defense Mapping Agency Hydrographic/Topographic Center, the National Ocean Survey, the National Oceanic & Atmospheric Administration and the U.S. Coast Guard.

In particular, I thank Richard L. Branham of the U.S. Naval Observatory for special aid at various times, and also thanks to Allen L. Powell, Rear Admiral, NOAA, Director of the National Ocean Survey, for his help with publications.

To George Field, Director, Harvard College Observatory and Smithsonian Astrophysical Observatory, I express appreciation for his encouragement.

Most of all, for their inspiration, I thank the students who sailed around the world. Thanks especially to Andy Burnes, Bill Fitz, Brad Ives, Phineas Sprague and John Barnes.

Particularly, I value all the thought and art involved in producing the "spirit and freedom" of the sea, a symbol originated by Robert Perkins, Jr., and associated with all my students in navigation. Finally, I am grateful to Mary Twomey for her careful typing and arrangement of the manuscript.

—F.W.W.

Preface

This book, provided with a copy of training Chart 116-SC Tr and a do-it-yourself cutout for a compass rose, has been designed as an explanatory manual emphasizing the importance of actual on-land practice for learning the art of coastwise navigation, in sight of land or not too far from shore. In this text written for yachtsmen, the navigator-yachtsman sees how he should plot his course and keep track of his D.R. or "deduced" position, from estimating his speed, time and distance. He learns how to check this position by handling the tides and coping with the currents, as well as by practicing all the appropriate piloting techniques. He finds a rather full explanation of the magnetic compass and deviation. He can enjoy a few "paper" cruises and solve some nautical problems, with answers to help or check. He can always keep track of his *position*.

Both beginning and limited-experienced mariners should be stimulated by setting up a chart table at home. And one can certainly carry a small compass outdoors and find a place to "swing ship" to obtain deviations on different headings. The very best place though would be on a high roof, from which objects can be sighted. The second best place is a spot on land with a view of known objects, preferably one to three miles away, but even a backyard is better than setting up equipment indoors where there may be much metal close at hand.

With a little imagination one can simulate a ship's hull with a wooden table and rather large piece of particle board placed on it for the deck of the ship, and the compass taped on the board, so that the ship can be rotated on different headings, by hand. A pelorus can be added, and after experience with the compass, a radio direction finder (RDF) is in order, to be used on land usually with aeronautical beacons. Ultimately, one will want to add a sextant so that all kinds of angles may be measured.

I have written this manual as a companion to my *Celestial Navigation*, so that with the two aids (which includes the small third, *Particularized Navigation*, for emergencies) the mariner may keep track of his position in sailing or cruising, providing he learns the art *before* taking his departure.

My three books, *Celestial Navigation, Particularized Navigation* and *Coastwise Navigation* (See references in Appendix III) have provided and can offer the groundwork for a one-term course in navigation for undergraduates, such as at Harvard. The emphasis has been on celestial navigation, and several of my Harvard students have proved their capabilities by sailing around the world on their own voyages! Andy Burnes was the first to circle the globe in two to three years from Cape Cod. Phineas Sprague was my second student to achieve an adventure all the way around, departing from Maine, while Bill Fitz has the distinction of having sailed solo across the Atlantic from England. Several other students have taken long ocean voyages, including Ricky Cowen across the Atlantic; Mike Jacker in a 30-foot boat from the Gulf of Mexico to several Pacific Islands on his way to Tahiti and Hawaii with two other crew members, and around the world sailor, Brad Ives, departed in 1970 from Copenhagen with a crew of fourteen aboard SS SOFIA, formerly a Baltic trader rerigged by Brad as a topsail schooner. Brad is almost a second Bowditch in teaching navigation to others now that he too has circumnavigated the earth; he has given to several a new skill or a new way of life.

A celestial navigator has to be experienced in coastwise navigation in order to reach an ocean without disaster. Whenever he wants to land, he must achieve this landing safely and skillfully. The emphasis in all this navigating has been on "Constant Vigilance", the watchword for successful navigation, and so in *Coastwise Navigation* an effort has been exerted to give a *second* solution or technique as much as possible for checking purposes.

The navigator can never forget "Constant Vigilance" if he is to come safely home. Many of my students who have been vigilant around the world navigators have inspired others. Faithful readers of *Coastwise Navigation* may enjoy the thought that most of the Problem Sets in this text, along with Problem Sets in *Celestial Navigation*, are the same or similar to those once worked out by my students who successfully sailed around the world. As well as at Harvard, many of these problems have been worked out by members of the navigation courses at the Boston Museum of Science's Hayden Planetarium.

Happy navigating!

Frances W. Wright
Cambridge, Massachusetts

"There is a tide in the affairs of men,
Which, taken at the flood, leads on to fortune;"

Shakespeare
Julius Caesar

Chapter 1

Directions, Bearings and Headings

Coastwise Navigation is concerned with keeping track of your position in sight of land, although sometimes, in certain places, fog may prevent the mariner from seeing the land. At all times, however, in fog, rain or sunshine, you want to know where you are. Especially under sail, or in case of power failure, the most dangerous regions at sea are often those in sight of land, where you may be close to rocks, reefs, shallow water or strong currents. Hence, as a rule, coastwise should be mastered before celestial navigation, which is usually needed far away from many of these dangers. At least a mariner has to depart from the land, and return to the land—with safety, and hence should be experienced in both types of navigation.

DIRECTIONS

Direction is important in finding out where you are, or in keeping track of where you are. Picture yourself aboard a vessel at the center of an imaginary circle of 360°. You might be headed in the direction of the North Pole, on a course of 000° true (according to the definition of *true*), but let us assume that you are headed in the opposite direction, of 180° true (*t*), as pictured in Fig. 1-1, or due South. Any object in the same direction as the vessel's keel, but exactly in front, would be said to be *dead ahead*; any object behind, but along the vessel's keel, would be *dead astern*, or in the direction of 0° true (*t*) or North. The direction of 090° t would be abeam, and direction of 270° t would also be abeam, each direction making an angle of 90° with the vessel's keel.

   Face the bow, or front of your vessel. One direction is on your right or starboard, while a direction on your left is said to be on the port side of your vessel. Note that *right* or *starboard* are longer words than the words *left* or *port*. It is not absolutely necessary today to employ the older words starboard and port. Right and left are actually in use at the present time, but it is more fun to be able to understand either set of words, and also more important to realize that in this particular picture and sketch, 90° and 270° denote the true directions, *East* and *West* respectively. Note that if you turn and face true North on your vessel, East is on your right, while West is on your left, an important relationship to remember, wherever you are.

BEARINGS

Directions and Relative Bearings. It is always wise, in dealing with directions, to place yourself on your vessel at the center of a circle of directions (as you did in Fig. 1-1) even if you use only two or three of these. Suppose that you are still on a course of 180° true. If you sighted a light 45° to the right of your bow, this particular type of angle is called a *relative bearing*. Unless there is a statement to the contrary, a relative bearing is always measured *clockwise* from the keel, Fig. 1-2. For example, a relative bearing of 030° to port may also be described as a relative bearing of 330° (to starboard), Fig. 1-3.

True Directions and Bearings. A relative bearing-direction may also be described as a true direction measured clockwise from true North, or from 0°. In Fig. 1-2, the relative bearing of 045° is also a true bearing of 225°. In Fig. 1-3, the relative bearing of 330° of a light (measured clockwise from

1

the vessel's keel) may be described as a true bearing of 150° (measured clockwise from true North, the direction of the North Geographical Pole). The *direction* is the same, and this direction of a bearing line actually may give you a *line of position* on which you and your vessel are situated. Sometimes, in coastwise navigation, it is helpful to use relative bearings, and it is important to be able to handle either relative or true bearings.

PELORUS. Note that the measure of a bearing can be made in several ways, but the principle is the same in all. The number of degrees between the heading and the sighted object can be noted with a pelorus, an instrument specially made for this purpose (Fig. 1-4). This measurement is easily made if the pelorus can be rotated and set to go with the compass. The pelorus functions as a dummy compass. The zero point of the pelorus can also be set along the keel of the vessel so that the bearings of objects subsequently sighted will give relative bearings. A simple case of arithmetic is now in order. Look at Fig. 1-2 and note that the relative bearing of the Light (045°) plus the heading of your vessel (180° true) equals 225° (the true bearing of the light). Hence we have a rule: *If you add the relative bearing to the true heading of your vessel, you have the true bearing of the light.* This rule applies only when you use the relative bearing as defined, in the *clockwise* direction from the forward line of the keel. All of the above examples are merely simple arithmetic to the mariner, after he learns

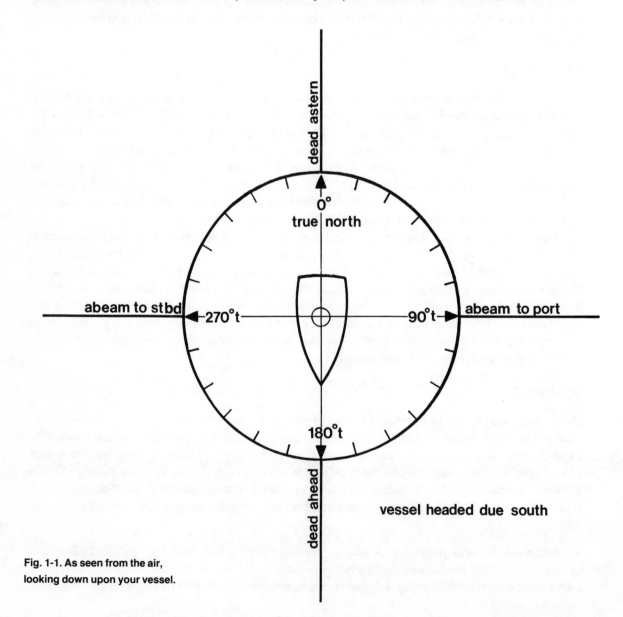

Fig. 1-1. As seen from the air,
looking down upon your vessel.

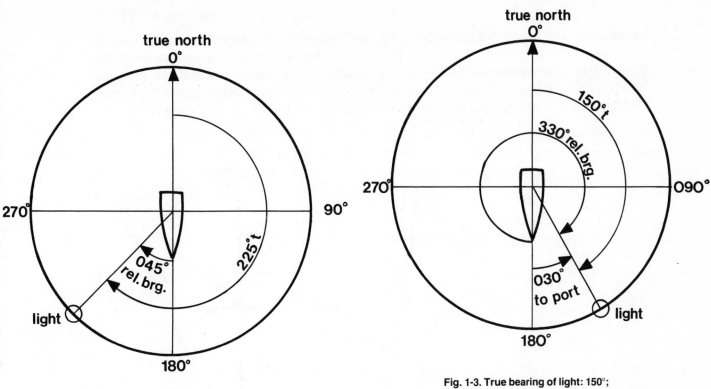

Fig. 1-2. True and relative bearings.

Fig. 1-3. True bearing of light: 150°;
relative bearing of light: 330°.

the meaning of the terms. In fact, most navigation demands nothing higher than simple arithmetic, but it should be stressed at this point that a simple mistake in arithmetic is no longer a simple mistake in navigation. It might cost you your life, or the life of a companion, and so the simple arithmetic and the simple terms must be mastered by the successful navigator right at the start.

Compass Bearing. In the case of relative bearings measured with a pelorus, some of the arithmetic is avoided if the pelorus can be rotated as mentioned and set with the compass heading on the lubber's line or keel-direction of the pelorus. With this pelorus setting, you can use the sighting vanes of the pelorus to sight a distant object. Note the direction of the object according to the position of the sighting vanes' center on the pelorus card of 360°. Remember that the latter has been set to go with

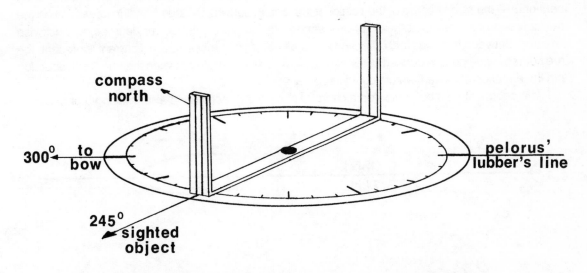

Fig. 1-4. A pelorus with 360° rotating card and vanes can be set to give compass directions.

the compass. This means that any reading of degrees on the pelorus card is the same as the reading of degrees on the compass. In other words, the number of degrees between the compass North and the direction of the distant object is the *compass bearing* of the object, measured from compass North on the compass card clockwise to the direction of the distant object, 245° in Fig. 1-4. Discussion of compass and magnetic bearings, in relation to true directions is continued in Chapter 2.

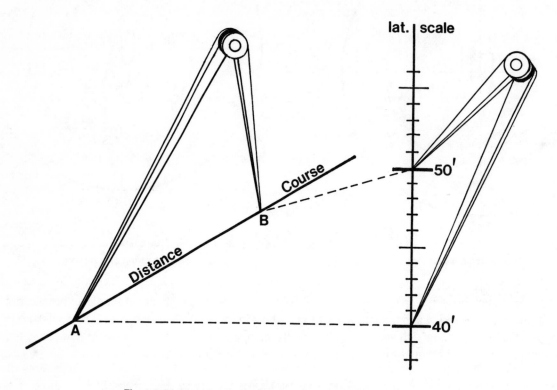

Fig. 1-5. Dividers, for measuring distances, ten miles in this case.

HEADINGS

True Courses and Headings. One direction to be emphasized at this point has already been mentioned—the true heading of the vessel. If there is no current, the true heading usually gives the true course, measured exactly as a true bearing—the angle or number of degrees, in clockwise direction, between the true North direction and the keel of your vessel. Even if current is present, the true course made good is defined in the same manner, as the angle between the true North direction and the direction of *movement* of your vessel.

The course should be plotted on a chart, to show the direction and also the length or *distance*

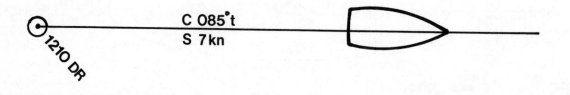

Fig. 1-6. Labeling a course.

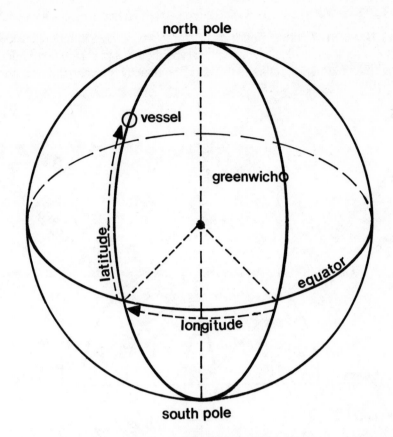

Fig. 1-7. Latitude and Longitude.

covered in *nautical miles.* A nautical mile is equal to a minute of arc of Latitude (Lat). This unit corresponds to 6076.1 feet or 1852 meters. In plotting the distance, the number of appropriate miles may be taken from the latitude scale by use of dividers, Fig. 1-5, indispensable in navigation for plotting any position or distance. By laying off the distance in this way, you can keep track of your Dead Reckoning (*DR,* from *deduced reckoning*) position.

Labeling of Course. The course should be properly labeled, as seen in Fig. 1-6. The direction should be indicated by three digits, written above and parallel to the direction of the course, while the speed S is designated in knots (*kn*) below and parallel to the course. For instance, *S7 kn* implies a speed of seven nautical miles per hour (*Never* say 7 kn per hour). Following the three digits, *t* is used for a true course, and *m* or *Mag.* for a magnetic course (discussed in Chapter 2). The sketched vessel in the figure is merely a help in understanding the terms and should not be entered on your chart, but you do want to enter on your chart the DR positions, with the time and the hours and minutes of time preceding the DR letters. (Seconds are not entered on charts, as a rule.)

Latitude and Longitude. The object of navigation is to keep track of your vessel as the latter moves from one position to another. Any position is defined by its Latitude and its Longitude. The Lat. is the number of degrees, minutes and tenths of minutes of arc between your position and the Earth's Equator (the circle halfway between the Poles, dividing the Earth into a Northern and a Southern hemisphere). The Lat. may then be North or South, according to the hemisphere, and is measured along a Meridian on the Earth, a circle through your position and also through the North and South Poles of the Earth. The Long. of a point is the angle between the local Meridian for that point and the Greenwich Meridian. It is measured East or West from Greenwich along the Earth's Equator, in degrees, minutes and tenths of minutes of arc, Fig. 1-7.

DEFINITIONS

Special Terms Used in Relative Bearings. Before leaving this introduction to the subject of directions and bearing lines, it adds to your nautical vocabulary if you learn two other definitions. The first is "broad on the bow" which refers to the direction exactly between the bow and abeam. If the

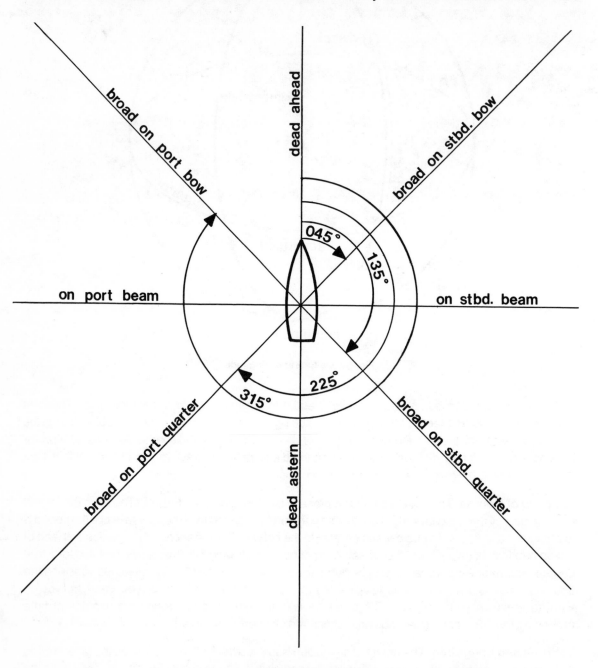

Fig. 1-8. Special relative bearings.

object is on the starboard side, the object will be said to be "broad on the starboard bow", and would then be on a relative bearing of 045° to starboard, Fig. 1-8. A similar situation exists on the port side of the vessel when an object is "broad on the port bow". The relative bearing in this case would be either 315°, or 045° to port. The second expression is "broad on the quarter" either to starboard or port, as the case may be. Any object "broad on the starboard quarter" would have a relative bearing of 135°, while an object "broad on the port quarter" would have a relative bearing of 225°, or a relative bearing of 135° to port. Fig. 1-8 shows these nautical terms and the relative bearings associated with the different terms. The wise mariner has these terms under control. An example is shown in Fig. 1-9 to clarify a situation, and the beginner should practice drawing other situations, and work out the answers, with sketches, of the problems in Problem Set 1, at the end of this chapter.

Examples: A ship is on a true heading of 030° (Fig. 1-9). A light A is observed to be broad on the starboard bow. What is the relative bearing and the true bearing of this light A?

    Ans: The relative bearing of A is 045°.
    Ans: The true bearing of A is 075°.

Another light B is abeam to starboard. What is the relative bearing and what is the true bearing of B?

    Ans: Relative bearing of B is 090°.
    Ans: True bearing of B is 120°.

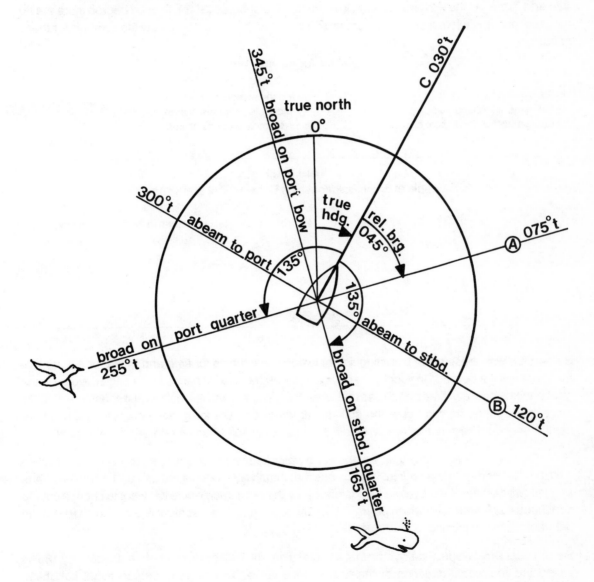

Fig. 1-9. Example clarifying relative and true bearings.

A whale is suddenly sighted broad on the starboard quarter. What is the relative bearing of the whale, and what is the true bearing?

> *Ans:* Relative bearing of whale is 135°.
> *Ans:* True bearing of whale is 165°.

A bird is sighted broad on the port quarter. Give the relative bearing and the true bearing of the bird.

> *Ans:* The relative bearing of the bird is 225° (or 135° to port).
> *Ans:* The true bearing of the bird is 225° (030° + 225°).

Another ship is sighted broad on the port bow. Give the relative bearing and the true bearing of the second ship.

> *Ans:* Relative bearing is 315°, or 045° to port.
> *Ans:* True bearing of other ship is 345° (030° + 315°).

Arc and Time. All the way around a circle there are 360 degrees (360°). In each degree there are 60 minutes, and in each minute of arc there are 60 seconds. It is useful to review the symbols for these units:

Symbols for Arc and Time

° is the symbol for degrees h is the symbol for hours of time
′ is the symbol for minutes of arc m denotes minutes of time
″ is the symbol for seconds of arc s denotes seconds of time

TABLE 1-1
Table of Basic Relationships Between Arc and Time

$$360° = 24^h \text{ (based on rotation of Earth in 24 hours or a day)}$$

$$15° = 1^h$$

$$1° = 60' = 4^m$$

$$1' = 60'' = 4^s$$

Be careful, with these units, to distinguish between the symbols for *time* and those for *arc*, so that mistakes will not be made in your future navigation. The *Nautical Almanac* has a page devoted to the relationships between time and arc, so that when the navigator wishes, he can just consult it—usually more quickly than he can figure the equivalents as given here for a few. However, the beginner navigator should be sure that he can obtain the figures himself when no reference is available.

Rhumb Line. A curve on the surface of the Earth which keeps a constant direction or course, is called a rhumb line or rhumb line course. It is obvious that rhumb line courses are usually laid out on charts and followed on the water by wise navigators, since the helmsman would not want to change course continuously. A projection which portrays a rhumb line course as a straight line on the chart is quite desirable for easy plotting.

Reciprocal Directions. Finally, note that any direction which differs from another direction by 180° is called the *reciprocal direction* of the first, or vice versa. The average person might call these "opposite" directions, but the mariner uses the term *reciprocal*. It does not change the value of a direction to add 360° to, or subtract 360° from, the original direction, Fig. 1-10.

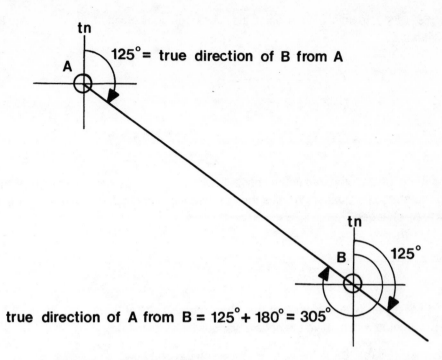

Fig. 1-10. Add 180° to the first direction of B from A, to obtain the reciprocal direction or direction of A from B.

PROBLEM SET 1

In Problems 1, 4 and 5 make a sketch which indicates (with labels) the North, the true course mentioned, the position of the vessel and any other object cited. Fill in answers.

1) VENUS is on a true course of 065°, speed 10 kn, when a freighter is sighted on the port beam, distant 7 miles.

 (a) What is the true bearing of the freighter from VENUS?

 Ans: True Brg. _____

 (b) What is the true bearing of VENUS from the freighter?

 Ans: True Brg. _____

 Sketch:

2) A ship at Lat. 02° 46.8′S; Long. 28° 01.2′W, sails on a true course due North, speed 21 kn, for 9 1/2 hours. Give the Lat. and Long. at the end of this run.

 Ans: Lat. _____ Long. _____

3) Express 189° 28′42″ in units of time, using the simple relations given above or on page 277 of *the Nautical Almanac.*

189° =

28′ =

42″ =

4) The navigator of SPICA, on a true course of 127°, wishes to change course when a certain light is broad on the starboard quarter. What is the true bearing of the light (from true North) when the course is to be changed?

Ans: _____

5) A sloop is sailing on a true course of 296° from Lat. 50° 25′N; Long. 15° 40′W. A school of porpoises is sighted with relative bearings at various times as follows:

(a) 016°;   (b) 106°;   (c) broad on the port bow

What are the corresponding true bearings (from North) of the school from the sloop?

Ans: (a)_____ (b)_____ (c)_____

Sketches:

If the sloop of this problem than changed course and headed for the school of porposises when the latter had the relative bearing of (b), what would be the true course of the sloop?

Ans: _____

Sketch:

6) At Lat. 14° 25′S, Long. 112° 37′W, a motor cruiser heads on a true course of 180°, with a speed of 12 knots, and no current. What will be the DR position after two hours and ten minutes?

Ans: _____

Chapter 2

The Magnetic Compass and Its Errors

As stated in 1976 at the International Navigational Congress, Boston Museum of Science, the magnetic compass is one of the few navigational instruments in common use today quite independent of electrical power (See Appendix III, #20 of titles under recommended publications). Compared with gyrocompasses, it is simple to manufacture and contains a comparatively small number of parts, Fig. 2-1.

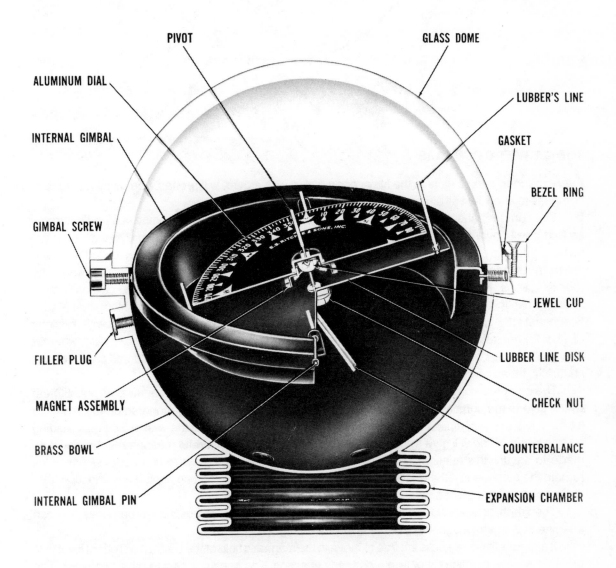

Fig. 2-1. Magnetic compass. (Courtesy of E.S. Ritchie & Sons.)

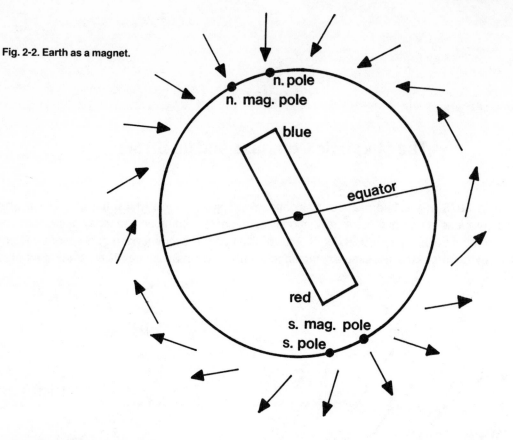

Fig. 2-2. Earth as a magnet.

THE MAGNETIC COMPASS

Every mariner, unless he is in the Navy or on a ship with a gyro, will probably be using a magnetic compass to show him all directions at sea.

The compass should be of good quality—the product of a well-known compass manufacturer—so that it will never fail the mariner, who should understand a few facts in regard to this important instrument. Many parts are self-explanatory. The best *compass card* (sometimes called an aluminum dial) is made of light, nonmagnetic material and is graduated in 360°, increasing clockwise. The four directions: North (0° or 360°), East (090°), South (180°) and West (270°) are called *cardinal points*, while the directions midway between these are four intercardinal points at Northeast (045°), Southeast (135°), Southwest (225°), and Northwest (315°). It is wise to have a compass with divisions of 1° or 2°, because no mistake may be made in reading directions from the compass card, whether they are bearings or headings. Often, on small boats, there are compasses graduated only every 5°. Naturally, these compasses do not give the same accuracy!

The compass card carries underneath it two or six magnetic needles (or equivalent substitutes) which give to the compass its directive properties. When the compass is mounted on the vessel, a lubber's line of the compass should be aligned carefully with the keel of the vessel, so that a reading on this lubber's line will give the compass heading of the vessel. Careful measurements should be made to assure this relationship. Style in compasses varies from time to time, but the principles remain the same, and if the mariner understands these principles, he can handle any variation from the procedures mentioned.

The Earth acts as though it were a giant magnet, and so, for descriptive purposes, we can imagine that a giant magnet exists inside the Earth, Fig. 2-2.

If a magnetized needle is left free to move in the magnetic field of the Earth, it will orient itself with one end always pointing roughly in a northerly direction. The needle is said to have two poles. The one that points in the northerly direction is called the North-seeking or *red pole*, while the opposite pole is called the South-seeking or *blue pole*. In navigational practice, the terms *red* and *blue* are used universally for indicating North- and South-seeking poles, respectively, and bar magnets and magnetic needles are painted accordingly.

It is easy to take any two magnets and observe that *unlike poles attract, while like poles repel each other.* It is important to remember this relationship. The North Magnetic Pole of the Earth, which by definition is a blue pole, lies some 10° North of the Hudson Bay region, while the South Magnetic Pole is west of the area discovered by the French navigator d'Urville in 1840. They have changed in position over a few years, see Table 2-1.

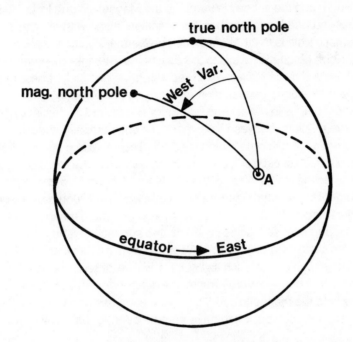

Fig. 2-3. West variation on the Earth.

Note that the North Magnetic Pole is called by this North designation because of its geographical location. It has South magnetism. A free magnetized needle will orient itself according to the local magnetic field. At the surface of the Earth such a needle will not assume a horizontal position generally, but instead will made a considerable angle with a horizontal plane. This angle is called *dip*, and has been measured carefully at a great many places on the Earth. It is tabulated on special charts. It is greatest directly above the Earth's magnetic poles, where the free magnetic needle will stand vertically. Somewhere halfway between the two magnetic poles, along the *Magnetic Equator*,

TABLE 2-1

North Magnetic Pole		South Magnetic Pole
Lat. 71° N		Lat. 72° S
Long. 96° W	1940	Long. 156° E
Lat. 74.9° N		Lat. 67.1° S
Long. 101° W	1960	Long. 142° E
Lat. 76° N		Lat. 66° S
Long. 101° W	1970	Long. 139° E

the magnetic lines of force are horizontal, and only on the Magnetic Equator will the free needle be horizontal. In the standard marine compass the *directive force* on the needle is the horizontal component of the local Earth's magnetic force. The directive force along any Meridian is greatest at the Magnetic Equator. It becomes gradually smaller away from the Equator, and the horizontal component vanishes directly over the poles. Regular magnetic compasses are therefore ineffective at high geomagnetic latitudes, and special techniques in navigation are used here. Most mariners do not navigate in polar regions, and so do not have to worry about these special techniques.

Variation. At any position A on the Earth, there is an angle between two directions from A. The first is the direction to true North, and the second is from A to the Magnetic North Pole. This angle is called *variation*. As a mariner you need to remember this definition, along with all others, usually in italics here. If the North Magnetic Pole is to the West of the true North Pole, the variation is said to be *West* (Fig. 2-3), while if the North Magnetic Pole is to the East of the true pole, the variation is called *East*.

With this book there are three circles which represent, respectively, true directions, magnetic directions and compass directions (explanation follows), and all three increase clockwise through 360°. This is the appropriate time to put at hand the yellow and the red circles, and use them to help in an understanding of the relations between true, magnetic and compass directions as you read on. First, assume that the variation for some region is 15° W. Second, place the smaller magnetic circle (yellow) over the true direction circle (red), and make the centers of the circles coincide, but with the North Magnetic Pole 15° to the left, or West, of the true North. A pin or pivot through the centers of the circles will aid in alignment for various cases—a technique which will soon be quite unnecessary, but which will help in understanding for the beginner. It will also give more meaning to some mnemonics conceived for the same purpose, as a guide in adding and subtracting, and when to do which.

If the two circles are set in this position, with West variation, as shown in Fig. 2-4, it is easily seen that the magnetic bearing of an object, such as L (Light), will be larger, measured clockwise from the magnetic North, than the true bearing. Furthermore, the *difference* between the two bearings is equal to the variation. If you read the magnetic bearing on your compass with the latter free of errors, and then subtract the variation West, you would have the true bearing. Similarly, if you started with the

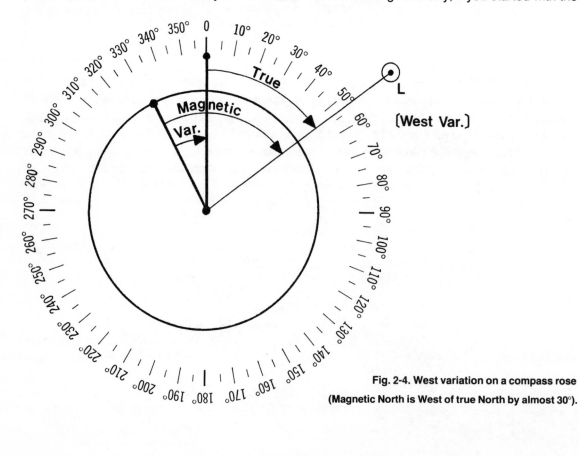

Fig. 2-4. West variation on a compass rose
(Magnetic North is West of true North by almost 30°).

true bearing of L, and wanted the magnetic bearing of the same L, you would merely *add* the variation 15° W. Sometimes on the water, or preparing for a cruise, you start with one of these bearings, and want the other. As you can see, it is just a case of adding or subtracting the variation, but you have to be *sure* about adding or subtracting, since the error will be doubled if you add when you should subtract, or vice versa. It is best, at first, to work with the two circles of Fig. 2-4, until you feel sure about adding or subtracting. Then you can use mnemonics to obtain the answer more quickly. This aid will be given after a later discussion of deviation in the compass, since the mnemonics suggested at the end of this discussion will serve in two capacities—to take care of both variation and deviation.

Examples in Applying Variation

1. If the variation for the region is 8° E, and the magnetic heading of your vessel is 146°, what is the corresponding true heading?

    Ans:

Note: Answers are given in Appendix II. For your answers, fill in the blanks here, and then compare results.

2. If you were at a different position, where the variation is 20° W, and your heading was 146° magnetic, what would be the corresponding true heading?

    Ans:

3. If you knew that the true heading of your vessel was 215°, and the variation was 17° W, what would be the magnetic heading?

    Ans:

4. Given: True heading of the yacht VENUS is 316° in a region with variation 22° E, what is the magnetic heading of VENUS?

    Ans:

5. In Example 1, on magnetic heading given there, if the magnetic bearing of a water tank was 203°, give the true bearing of the tank.

    Ans:

6. In Example 2, if you observed a light with a magnetic bearing of 030°, what would you know about the true bearing of the light?

    Ans:

7. In Example 3, give the true bearing of a cupola with a 197° magnetic bearing.

   Ans:

8. In Example 4, if another ship has a magnetic bearing of 085° from VENUS, what is the corresponding true bearing of VENUS from the other ship?

   Ans:

Variation figures depend upon the geographical position of your vessel. These figures are usually given on every chart which you might be carrying for plotting purposes. In addition, they are shown on a Magnetic Variation Chart of the World, Epoch 1975.0 (WOBZC42), and also in *Particularized Navigation* (See Appendix III.). These figures do not depend at all on the heading of your vessel. On a cruise, a wise mariner will check the chart values of the variation at frequent intervals. Over a hundred miles there may well be a change of two or three degrees in the value of the variation. Also, it is well to note that in some places, especially close to shore, submerged magnetic ore deposits may lead to local fluctuations in the value of the variation. These points are noted on a chart, and a navigator will always be aware of them if he just inspects the chart carefully.

COMPASS ERRORS

A modern vessel with a metal hull and fittings is a giant magnet in itself. Also, the metal in or around the vessel may cause magnetic disturbances which may lead to incorrect compass readings if they are neglected.

The nature of a vessel's *permanent magnetic* qualities is mostly determined by the magnetic heading on which the vessel was built. Steel plates of a metal vessel contain a large number of very small elementary magnets. Each of these elementary magnets has its own tiny red (North-seeking) and blue (South-seeking) pole. The steel plates in the vessel are so disturbed by the hammering and riveting during the construction that the small elementary magnets in each section align themselves gradually according to the Earth's local magnetic field. Although inside the metal the effect of each elementary blue pole will be compensated by that of an adjacent red pole, there will be an excess of elementary red poles on the side towards magnetic North and an excess of elementary blue poles at the opposite end. All these aligned elementary magnets, then, combine to make one single giant magnet, with its red pole pointing in the direction of magnetic North, and its blue pole pointed in the opposite direction. A metal vessel built on a North magnetic heading will have a red pole at its bow, and a blue pole at its stern (Fig. 2-5). On the other hand, for a vessel built on a South magnetic heading, the red pole will be at the stern, the blue pole at the bow. A vessel constructed on an East magnetic heading will have the red pole on the port side, and the blue pole on the starboard side. For vessels built on an intercardinal heading, the magnet which represents the vessel will assume a position broad on the bow or quarter, as the case may be.

The attraction by the magnetized hull is not the only source of a magnetic disturbance. The superstructure of the vessel will contribute and also the cargo or any piece of magnetized metal left near the compass. Loose objects, such as jack-knives, keys, bracelets, or watch cases, should be removed from the vicinity of the compass unless their effect on the compass has been tested. Certainly the helmsman should watch the contents of his pockets!

All electrical currents have a magnetic field associated with them. Although all wires leading to the binnacle may be twisted in order to neutralize incoming and outgoing currents, all possibilities of electrical troubles may not be eliminated necessarily.

In addition, this so-called permanent magnetism is more appropriately called *subpermanent* magnetism, as a reminder that there is nothing absolutely permanent about the permanent magnetism. Changes of cargo or the position of the boom, changes in the use of electrical currents, and changes in magnetic headings of the vessel, even as the latter is placed on different magnetic headings, may change the magnetic properties of the compass.

Deviation. You are now ready for the definition of deviation: *Deviation is also defined as a difference in directions, but in this case one direction is from the vessel to Magnetic North, and the other direction is from the vessel to Compass North. If the Compass North Pole is to the West of the Magnetic North Pole, the Deviation is called West, while if the Compass North Pole is to the East of the Magnetic North Pole, the Deviation is called East.*

CARDINAL HEADINGS. As a result of the facts just described, the wise mariner will proceed to find the deviations of his magnetic compass, if there are any, and he must find these deviations on different headings, since the above discussion should bring forth the most important relation on this subject—that *deviation depends upon the heading of your vessel.* Since you have already found that deviation is a difference between magnetic and compass directions, it seems clear that you must have at least *one* magnetic direction whenever you want to find the deviation. Let us now investigate the procedure which you can use to obtain a magnetic direction. The easiest way is to head your vessel, in turn, on the four cardinal headings 000°, 090°, 180°, and 270°. Consider the first in detail.

On the compass heading of 000°, for instance, if you have a rotatable pelorus (the most helpful type) you can set 000° of the pelorus' card on the pelorus' lubber line so that the pelorus will function as a dummy compass. The vanes of the pelorus can then be rotated so as to sight a distant object through the vanes. The helmsman should call, "Mark," as long as he is on the 000° heading by the compass and the pelorus has been set to agree with the compass. The pelorus man should call, "Mark," as soon as he sights the distant object (preferably four miles away, unless the vessel is pivoting at anchor, or proceeding around a very small circle). Your *height of eye* above the water also is a factor in the desired distance of the object, as you want to *sight* it! If the distant object is too near, a parallax effect will be present and cause errors in the compass bearing which the mariner is trying to find.

Similarly, on 090° compass heading, with the helmsman calling, "Mark, mark," the pelorus man can set the pelorus to go with the compass, and then, after rotating the vanes of the pelorus, he can read the compass bearing of the distant object on the compass heading of 090°. This operation must be repeated on the other two cardinal headings of 180° and 270°. There will then be four compass

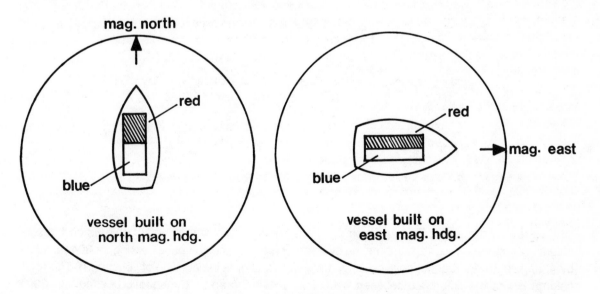

Fig. 2-5. Metal vessel represented by a magnet in different positions according to heading on which vessel was built.

bearings. If they differ, you know at once that your compass has deviations, since in the absence of deviation, all four compass bearings would be the same, or equal. Now comes an important fact for the mariner. Since under ordinary circumstances and with symmetrical conditions, all the West deviation balances the East deviation, the average or mean of the four compass bearings obtained will give just what the mariner needs—the magnetic bearing of the distant object, which can be charted or uncharted. It might even be a tree off the coast, if you can see it!

If you do not have time to compensate the compass, you can obtain further deviation figures on more headings by repeating the procedure above—on all 24 compass headings 15° apart:

TABLE 2-2

Compass Headings	Compass Headings
015°	195°
030°	210°
045°	225°
060°	240°
075°	255°
090°	270°
105°	285°
120°	300°
135°	315°
150°	330°
165°	345°
180°	360°

On each of these compass headings find the compass bearing of the distant object, as explained, and then on each heading find the difference between the compass bearing and the magnetic bearing of the object. The magnetic bearing can be obtained most easily *first*, as already described, as the average of the four cardinal bearings on the four cardinal compass headings, and does not have to be the average of 24 compass headings.

For an example, suppose you obtained figures on the compass cardinal headings, as follows:

TABLE 2-3

(1)	(2)	(3)	(4)
Compass Heading	Compass Bearing	Magnetic Bearing	Deviation
000°	060°	076°	16°E
090°	070°	076°	6°E
180°	090°	076°	14°W
270°	084°	076°	8°W
	4/304°		
	76°		

To review the steps: First, on each compass heading sight with vanes of pelorus and obtain column (2) figures. Second, compute the average or mean of the compass bearing, or 304° divided by 4, to give 76° for the magnetic bearing, and enter this figure in each line of column (3). The final column is just the difference between the compass bearing and the magnetic bearing. On 000° compass heading, the compass bearing is smaller than the magnetic bearing. If your blue circle of compass directions is now placed on the magnetic circle, in order to have the compass bearing smaller than the magnetic bearing (060° is less than 076°) the compass North at 000° would have to be to the East of the magnetic North. The beginner should experiment with all three circles and pivot them to different values for compass bearings and corresponding magnetic bearings, until thoroughly understanding the theory behind any rules used.

MNEMONICS FOR DEVIATION WEST OR EAST. Some mariners use handy mnemonics to tell at once whether the deviation is East or West. The following can usually be remembered:

"True Virgins Make Dull Company At Weddings"

T stands for True
V for Variation
M for Magnetic
D for Deviation
C for Compass
A for Add
W for West

This means that if you start with a true bearing or heading (at left in the mnemonics) and want the corresponding magnetic or compass bearing or heading, *add* any *West* error, whether it is variation or deviation, and similarly *subtract* any *East* error. On the other hand, if you start with a compass bearing or heading at right in the mnemonics, and want the corresponding true bearing or heading, you do just the opposite—*add* an *East* variation or deviation, and *subtract* a *West* error.

A Second Rule for Determination of East or West When Finding Deviation:

At the compass, when working with compass and magnetic bearings

If Compass is Best, Error is West

If Compass is Least, Error is East

Example. Return to Table 2-3 and see how it works. In Table 2-3, on a compass heading of 000°, the compass bearing of the distant object was 060°, while the magnetic bearing was 076°. Hence, the deviation is East (because the compass is *least*, in value of the degrees, with 60° less than 76°. Next, on a compass heading of 090°, the compass bearing was 70°, while the magnetic bearing was still 76°. According to the rule again, the compass is least, and the deviation 6°E. On the third compass heading (180°) the compass bearing (090°) is greater or best, as compared with the magnetic bearing of 076°. Hence, the deviation is 14°W. A similar case exists for the 270° compass heading. 84° is greater or *best* as compared with 76°, and so you have a deviation of 8°W. Use this rule when the compass is involved, but I do not advise it when the compass is not involved. The "True Virgins" rule is much better and safer to use when variation is used to obtain true directions. These few mnemonics can replace any supposed need for acquiring a plastic gadget to help with the adding and subtracting. It is really safer to carry a rule in your head rather than in your pocket! However, find your favorite method—and *avoid a mistake*. In general, a wise navigator checks any results by two different techniques. The best are (1) rules and mnemonics, and (2) continuous thinking of relationships and meanings or an understanding of the subject. Example of Table 2-3 is now continued:

It is good practice to continue with the example of Table 2-3, and assume that on all the other headings 15° apart, you obtained the following compass bearings of the same distant object, with a magnetic bearing of 076°, already found. The results can be presented in Table 2-4 as shown.

A similar table of deviations obtained by you should be fixed to the wall near your own magnetic compass, so that you will always remember to consult it and have it convenient to use. Note, however, that in its present form you must enter it with a compass heading. It is very easy, however, to add another column to give the corresponding magnetic headings, as seen in Table 2-4 for only the first three magnetic headings (for illustration). You can easily fill in the other values for practice. If the deviation figures are small, you can interpolate between the values given. If, however, the deviation figures are rather large, as in the case of our example (Table 2-4), a *Napier diagram* is convenient for plotting the *curve of deviations*, as shown in Fig. 2-6. The figures on the vertical lines represent headings, either compass or magnetic. If you enter the diagram with a heading, find it on a vertical line. At that point travel off along the *dotted* line if you entered with a *compass* heading, but along the *solid* line if you entered with a *magnetic* heading. Note also that *East* deviation is laid off to the *right* and *West* deviation to the *left* of the vertical lines. Do the traveling by counting dots (the space between two adjacent dots being equal to 1°) and place a pencil dot of your own at the numbered dot which corresponds to the number of degrees in your deviation. It would be good practice to check that the dots of the deviation curve of your example are plotted correctly. Note that the curve of deviations has been drawn right through these plotted dots.

For reading interpolated deviation values after the curve is plotted, dividers are convenient (Fig. 1-5). Work with them. Hold the divider-tips parallel to the dotted lines or to the solid lines, depending on whether the curve is entered with compass or with magnetic headings. *The number of dots between the vertical lines and the curve give the interpolated and desired deviations for any headings.* With the deviation curve you may even find the corresponding magnetic headings. After counting the dots from the vertical line to your curve (as already explained), return to the vertical line,

TABLE 2-4
Deviations for the Compass

First Method of Finding Deviations on Every 15° Headings

psc Compass Hdg.	psc Compass Brg.	Mag. Brg.	Deviation	Mag. Hdg.
000°	060°	076°	16°E	016°
015°	053°	076°	23°E	038°
030°	050°	076°	26°E	056°
045°	049°	076°	27°E	
060°	053°	076°	23°E	
075°	061°	076°	15°E	
090°	070°	076°	6°E	
105°	079°	076°	3°W	
120°	087°	076°	11°W	
135°	093°	076°	17°W	
150°	095°	076°	19°W	
165°	093°	076°	17°W	
180°	090°	076°	14°W	
195°	086°	076°	10°W	
210°	082°	076°	6°W	
225°	081°	076°	5°W	
240°	081°	076°	5°W	
255°	082°	076°	6°W	
270°	084°	076°	8°W	
285°	085°	076°	9°W	
300°	085°	076°	9°W	
315°	081°	076°	5°W	
330°	076°	076°	0°	
345°	068°	076°	8°E	

Note: psc = per standard compass.

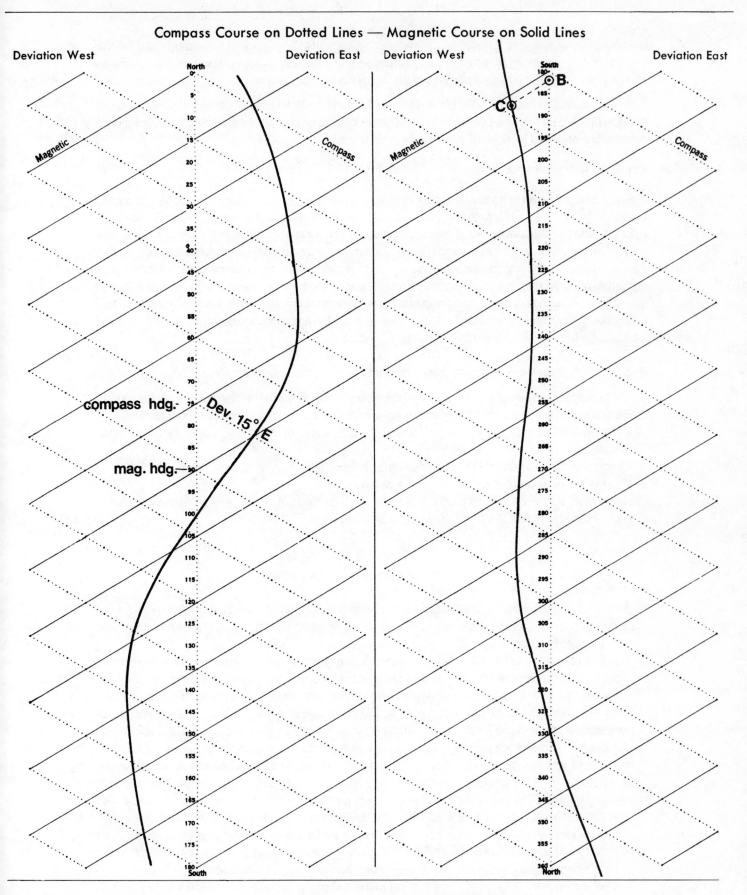

Fig. 2-6. Deviation curve plotted on a Napier diagram.

holding your divider-tips parallel to the magnetic directions. The magnetic heading read on the vertical line at your point of return is *your* corresponding magnetic heading. This can be a check on your arithmetic, and the helpful phrases at the top of the Napier diagram:

"Compass Course on Dotted Lines; Magnetic Course on Solid Lines," should remind you about the use of the dots and lines of the Napier diagram. With large deviations a curve for interpolation is much more accurate than linear interpolation with figures.

COMPASS COMPENSATION

You are now prepared to handle your own compass deviations—to find them and to apply the correct figures in going from compass to magnetic, and to true or vice versa, either with bearings or headings. *Applying the proper corrections is the most important aspect in handling a magnetic compass.* You may, however, wish to go further and remove the errors (or deviations) in the compass, especially if they are large. Removing the errors in the compass is called *compass compensation*. Under usual circumstances compass compensation can be accomplished rather easily if you have the time to swing your vessel on different headings and place compensating magnets or adjust screws in your compass. If you have the latter (a N-S screw and an E-W screw), found on many of the small compasses today, you can use the following procedure:

Preparation. (In general, have conditions similar to those when underway.)

1. Great care should be taken to be sure that the lubber's line marks the direction of the vessel's keel.
2. Remove all loose metal in the immediate vicinity, including any metal objects in your clothing.
3. Compensate with engine running (if possible), and with any radio on, if it is to be on when underway.
4. *Swing ship* to make certain the compass is not *stuck*. (Use magnets to unstick.)
5. Use the same distant object, which can be called A.
6. Remember that the compensation is most effective if carried out on magnetic headings.
7. Enter in a table (Table 2-5 here) the steps in procedure.

Compensation on Magnetic Headings

1. Bind or clamp the vanes of the pelorus at the magnetic bearing of A and keep them there for the rest of the compensation. Note that with the same distant object sighted in line with its magnetic direction, all directions on the pelorus are now magnetic.
2. Place or clamp 90° of the pelorus on its lubber's line. Instruct the helmsman *right rudder* or *left rudder* until you can sight A through the vanes. At that moment your vessel must be headed East magnetic. At that very same moment the helmsman can read the compass heading on the compass. Deviation is thus obtained here as the difference between the magnetic and compass headings, and this value for deviation can be entered in the Compensation Table 2-5, where you can keep a record of the proceedings. You now want to remove this deviation, or make it zero in value, and you can accomplish this by turning the E-W screw by hand or with a non-magnetic screwdriver, until the compass heading is also 090°, giving no deviation now on this magnetic heading of 090°. You can tell by trial and error which way to turn the E screw to obtain the desired 090°. If you should have screws which are not labeled, the E-W screws are probably in fore and aft direction, while the N-S screws are probably in athwartship position. With or without screws, you may find more deviation on E-W headings than on N-S headings because of vertical soft iron which is handled effectively on ships with the Flinders Bar, named for Capt. Matthew Flinders. This English navigator (1774-1814) was the first to think of using vertical bars of soft iron in this way. Yachts and small vessels do not carry a Flinders Bar, as a rule.

3. Place or clamp 270° of the pelorus on the lubber's line. Instruct the helmsman, "port", or, "starboard", until you sight throught the vanes at A. Exactly at that moment the heading of your vessel must be *West* magnetic. With the same non-magnetic screwdriver turn the E-W screw again, but only enough to remove *half of the deviation* which you find here. If, for instance, the compass heading was now 274°, you would turn the E-W screw so as to make the compass heading read 272°. It is well to have any residual deviation well distributed, and here, if you removed the whole 4° of the deviation first noted, you would be throwing deviation back on the East heading if you turned the screw to make the compass heading 270°. That is why you remove only half of what you find on the 270° magnetic heading.

4. Go through similar procedures on North and South headings, again magnetic. First, with 000° clamped to the lubber's line of the pelorus, instruct the helmsman, "right rudder," or, "left rudder," until you can sight A through the vanes. Find the deviation again as the difference between the magnetic heading of 000° and the compass heading which the helmsman reads after you have instructed him about steering so that you can see A.

5. After removing all the deviation found on 000° magnetic heading, place your vessel on a 180° magnetic heading, by clamping or setting 180° of the pelorus on its lubber's line. Again, instruct the helmsman, "right rudder," or, "left rudder," until you can sight A through the vanes. At that moment the helmsman can read the compass heading, and deviation will be the difference between the compass and the magnetic headings. Next, remove only half of the deviation found here, so that you will distribute a residual deviation on both N and S headings.

6. You have now done all you can about deviation unless you have quadrantal spheres, necessary on steel boats, and which can compensate for horizontal soft iron which affects the compass. They can be used on intercardinal headings. On a Northeast heading (magnetic) you would find any possible deviation with the same techniques used on the cardinal headings. To remove East deviation on this heading, move the quadrantal spheres in, or closer to the compass. If the deviation were West on a Northeast Heading, move the quadrantal spheres out, or away from the compass. (Keep symmetrical conditions, and never move one sphere alone.)

7. You would then swing to a Southeast heading (magnetic) and remove half of any deviation found there.

For those more interested in the rotary system now used in most small compasses with compensating magnets, you will enjoy inspecting the accompanying diagram of the interior magnets affected by the screws mentioned. The diagram shows the magnets in the neutral position (Fig. 2-7).

8. In case you do not have a compass with compensating magnets, or even in case you were not able to remove all the deviation with the compensating screws, you are wise if you always carry four or

TABLE 2-5

Compensation

Before Compensation			After Compensation	
Vessel's Hdg. Mag.	Vessel's Hdg. psc	Dev.	Vessel's Hdg. psc	Dev. (final)
090°				
270°				
000°				
180°				
045°				
135°				
225°				
315°				

Note: psc stands for *per standard compass* and can be used as an abbreviation for *compass,* used in tables of this text.

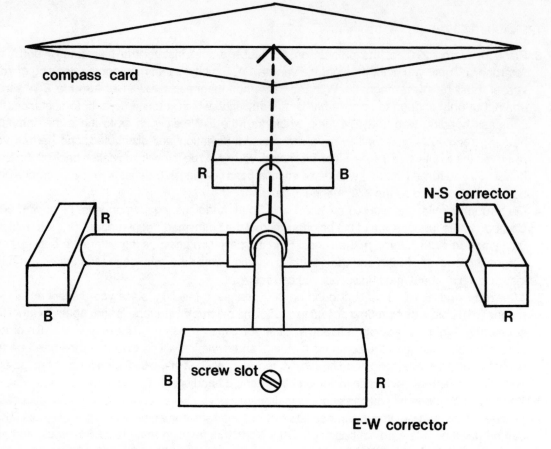

Fig. 2-7. Magnets in neutral position. (Courtesy of Kielhorn and *Sail Magazine*, **Oct., 1976.)**

five extra compensating magnets of your own. They are usually sold in pairs, with the North-seeking end painted red, and the South-seeking end blue so that you can distinguish easily the identity of the poles. You can use these magnets (which vary in size, to go with different compasses) only on cardinal headings, as a rule. Table 2-6 will help:

TABLE 2-6
Procedure with Athwartship and Fore/Aft
Compensating Magnets

Compensation with:	Headings on Which To Correct	Rules:
Fore and Aft (along or parallel to keel) Compensating Magnets	E or W	Place red end of magnet *forward* for E Deviation on E Magnetic Heading and for W Deviation on W Magnetic Heading
Athwartship (at right angle to keel) Compensating Magnets	N or S	Place red end of magnet to *starboard* for E Deviation on N Magnetic Heading and for W Deviation on S Magnetic Heading

Note: In placing any of these compensating magnets, it is most effective to align the center of the magnet with the center of the compass.

If quadrantal spheres are available, move them *in* with E deviation on NE magnetic heading and *out* (or even off) with W deviation on NE magnetic heading.

If you look at this Fig. 2-8 of two magnets, it may seem evident to you that a compensating magnet Y will have greatest effect on another magnet X if magnet Y is placed at *right angles* to the other magnet X. Consider the effect of the nearest pole R of magnet Y on the two poles of magnet X. The R pole of Y will repel the R pole of X and also attract the B pole of magnet X, and so change the direction of magnet X more than if magnet Y were not at right angles to X. This fact will help the beginner understand the preceding rules or Table 2-6, Procedure with Athwartship and Fore and Aft Compensating Magnets. The X magnet can represent the compass magnet or magnets, while the Y magnet can represent the compensating magnet which you might want to use if your compass lacked compensating screws, or just needed more magnetic strength than given by the screws.

DEVIATION

Semicircular Deviation. Another interesting relationship to notice in understanding the simple procedure of compensation outlined is the fact that if we consider *only* the effect of horizontal subpermanent magnetism, it will give zero deviations on two opposite headings. The values on these two headings will depend on the magnetic properties of the vessel and the *position of the compass on the vessel*. East deviations will be shown for all headings in one of the semicircles of headings on one side of the zero-deviation headings, while West deviations will appear on the other semicircle of headings, as shown in Fig. 2-9. The figure shows a metal vessel built on a NE magnetic heading.

Quadrantal Deviation. Transient, rather than subpermanent magnetism, occurs in soft iron. When not in a magnetic field, the elementary magnets in a soft iron bar will be oriented at random with their axes pointing in all directions. These magnets retain considerable mobility, with the result that they align themselves the instant that the bar is placed in a magnetic field—a phenomenon called *induction*. Soft iron is found in abundance on most large vessels in the hull, bulkheads, etc. For most vessels, the induced magnetism caused by the soft iron, at about the same level as that of the compass, produces the most pronounced disturbance of the compass. If this soft iron is distributed symmetrically with respect to the vessel's keel, a centrally placed compass will show no deviation on the cardinal magnetic headings. When the vessel is headed on one of the intercardinal magnetic headings, most of the red magnetism will be on one side of the compass needle, and most of the blue on the other side. The result is a marked deflection of the needle from the direction of magnetic North. Fig. 2-10 shows what usually happens if the compass is placed amidships.

As already stated, the most important thing for you to do on this subject of deviation is to find the deviation by swinging your vessel on different headings to find any deviation on each heading, which may be residual after compensation or which may exist because conditions have changed on your vessel. You have already read about First Method of Finding Deviations on Every 15° Headings (Table 2-4) and accompanying description. There is another way which you should know. It can be called Second Method For Finding Deviations, and the steps of the procedure are:

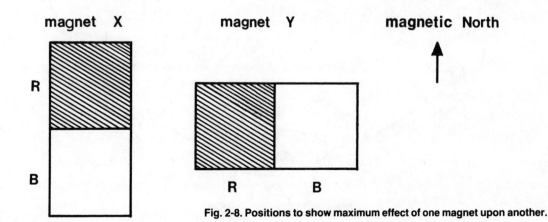

Fig. 2-8. Positions to show maximum effect of one magnet upon another.

1. Clamp the vanes of your pelorus at the magnetic bearing of your distant object, and keep them clamped (or taped) for the rest of the procedure.

2. Steer by the compass, on the different headings 15° apart. On each heading, such as 000° compass, sight your distant object.

3. The *reading* on the lubber's line of your pelorus will give you your magnetic heading, which can then be compared with your compass heading. Note that in this technique, you are finding the deviation by a difference in headings, whereas in the first method described (Table 2-4) you found the deviation from a difference in bearings. One method is as accurate as the other, but the last described saves time because the magnetic bearing remains *clamped* and does not have to be changed. If you should prefer the first method, with a model shown (Table 2-8), use it. Blank Tables 2-7 and 2-8 are included here for models. Often, your equipment will dictate the techniques which you will choose, or prompt you to acquire more or better equipment before departing.

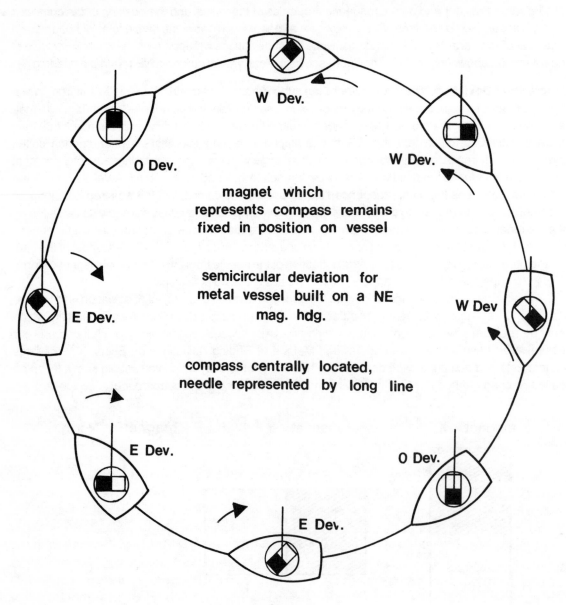

W Dev.

O Dev.

W Dev.

magnet which
represents compass remains
fixed in position on vessel

semicircular deviation for
metal vessel built on a NE
mag. hdg.

W Dev

E Dev.

compass centrally located,
needle represented by long line

E Dev.

O Dev.

E Dev.

Fig. 2-9. Semicircular deviation.

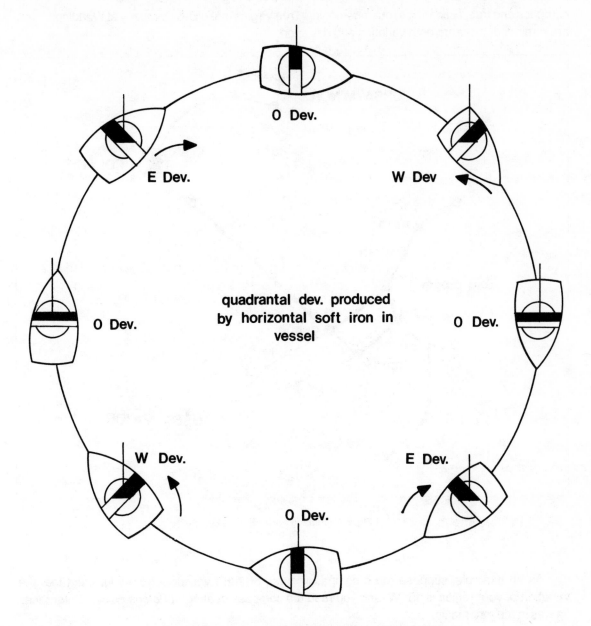

O Dev.

E Dev.

W Dev

quadrantal dev. produced
by horizontal soft iron in
vessel

O Dev.

O Dev.

W Dev.

E Dev.

O Dev.

Fig. 2-10. Quadrantal deviation due to horizontal soft iron in a vessel.

Checking Deviation on One Heading as You Sail. Before completing the subject of compass deviation, here is a simple way of checking the deviation while you are sailing or cruising on a compass course. You might want to check for deviation just on one leg while you are cruising on this leg, and you might like to do it quickly without much effort. This easiest method depends upon the star *Polaris,* the *North Star,* so-called because it gives you the direction of true North to within a degree, which is quite satisfactory. (Consider true North as 000°, or 360°, and use the value nearest the compass direction.) First, you find *Polaris* in the sky. To achieve this, find the *Big Dipper* (Fig. 2-11) towards the North, and use the *Pointers* to identify *Polaris*. This *North Star* is on the line of the *Pointers,* and about five times as far from the *Dipper* as the distance between the *Pointers*. *Polaris,* as seen over your compass, or through the vanes of your pelorus (if you set the pelorus to agree with the compass), will probably have a different direction or bearing as read from the compass card or from the pelorus card, because this last direction is, of course, a compass direction. Between compass and true, according to our mnemonic, "True Virgins make Dull Company at Weddings," you are reminded, there are both variation and deviation.

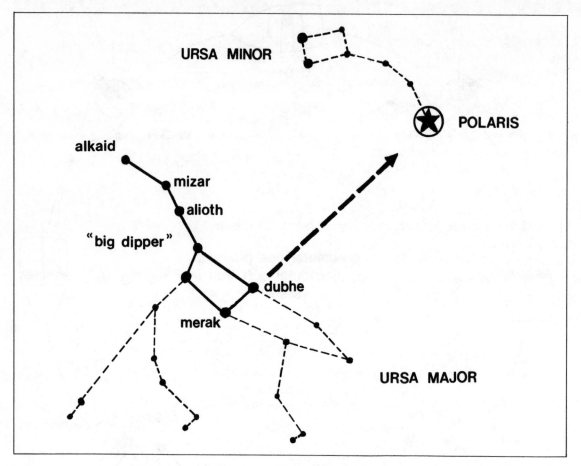

Fig. 2-11. Finding *Polaris* **in the sky.**

As an example, suppose (on a compass course of 286°) you note from your chart that the variation of your region is 15° W, and you read the compass bearing of *Polaris* as 37°. Enter these figures in the mnemonic:

Bearings

T	V	M	D	C	a	W
000°	15°W			037°		

and perform the simple arithmetic:

T	V	M	D	C	a	W
000°	15°W	015°		037°		

You can be sure at once that the total error is 37°W (compass "best"). You also know that the sum of variation and deviation = total error, and so you could write:

15°W = Var.
_____Dev. ?
37°W = Total Error

You see that the deviation must be 22°W to make this sum come out right. Often you may not be interested in the deviation. You just might want a check on your heading, and to be safe, you would fill in the mnemonic again:

Headings

T	V	M	D	C	a	W
249°	15°W	264°	22°W	286°		

and for another check, apply the total error, 37°W, to the compass heading and obtain 249° true. Note that you can use the mnemonic either with headings or with bearings, but you do not want to mix the two in the same mnemonic. The T, M, and C values in any one mnemonic must apply either to headings *or* to bearings.

TABLE 2-7

For Finding Deviations

(Model for some future cruise)
(Second and Preferred Method)

Vessel's Hdg. psc	Vessel's Hdg. Mag.	Dev.	Vessel's Hdg. psc	Vessel's Hdg. Mag.	Dev.
000°			180°		
015°			195°		
030°			210°		
045°			225°		
060°			240°		
075°			255°		
090°			270°		
105°			285°		
120°			300°		
135°			315°		
150°			330°		
165°			345°		

If you should lack a pelorus, your hand held in a vertical position over the compass will give the same direction to within 5°, depending upon the thickness of your hand!

For another example, suppose that you are on a small yacht and wish to check your compass heading by *Polaris* at evening twilight. Your compass heading reads 110°, and the variation for the region is 25°E. You read the compass bearing of *Polaris* as 020°.

(a) What is the true heading of the yacht on this heading?

Ans: Difference between psc bearing (020°) and 000° for *Polaris* = 20°W
(W because *Polaris* is "best") = Total Error

psc Hdg. 110°
<u>20° W</u>
True Hdg. 090° *Ans.*

(b) What is the approximate deviation on this heading?

Ans: 25°E Var.
<u>_____ Dev. ?</u>
20°W Total Error

It is obvious that the deviation must be 45°W, to make the sum add up correctly. Hence, *answer* is 45°W.

In this example, the mnemonic was not used, but if the beginner has any difficulty in understanding the procedure above, fill in the mnemonic as in the first example, until all the steps are clear.

Another example:

Compass course is 195° in a region where Var. = 20°W
Compass bearing of *Polaris* = 335°.
(a) What is the corresponding true course?
(b) What is the deviation on this heading?

Ans: (a) Total Error = 360° − 335° = 25°E
and 195° psc
<u>+   25° E</u>
220° True Course *Ans.*

(b) You can write   20°W = Var.
<u>_____   Dev. ?</u>
25°E = Total Error

Inspection shows that Dev. must = 45°E *Ans.*

SUMMARY

If you should be having any difficulty remembering when to add and when to subtract, the only solution is to *write the mnemonic each time:*

T   V   M   D   C   a   W

The "a" and "W" at the end tell you that if you go from left to right in the mnemonic, *add* any West error, whether it is variation or deviation, while you *subtract* an East error. On the other hand, if you go from right to left, do just the opposite: *subtract* West and *add* East errors. The mnemonic can be your guide!

The above information is sufficient for you to find any deviation errors which you may have in your compass, and you can even remove most of the deviation if you wish. The teacher or advanced mariner who wants to make a deviation curve of his own at any time, for teaching purposes or just from theory, should add one more fact to his compass compensation knowledge, and that is the formula or equation for deviation:

$$\text{Dev.} = A + B \sin Z' + C \cos Z' + D \sin 2 Z' + E \cos 2 Z'$$

where Z' represents the compass heading of the vessel.

A represents the constant error of the compass.

It can be caused by an error in the position of the lubber's line or by unsymmetrically placed soft iron.

B represents a correction which is maximum on headings East or West by the compass.

C represents a correction which is maximum for headings North or South by the compass.

D determines the effect of the horizontal soft iron, which usually has its greatest value on intercardinal headings, where the quadrantal spheres can compensate for it.

E, the last term, is usually very small and may be caused by unsymmetrically distributed soft iron or by

---

TABLE 2-8
(blank)
(Method used in Tables 2-3 and 2-4)
Swinging Your Vessel for Deviations (First Method)

---

1. Use the distant object A. Let the vanes of your pelorus swing freely.
2. On psc heading 15° apart (one at a time), instruct the pelorus man to sight A over the pelorus vanes.
3. Read the psc bearing of A at this moment, and enter it in Table 2-8.
4. Magnetic bearing of A = mean of psc bearings of A on the four cardinal headings.

Vessel's Hdg. psc	Compass Brg. of A	Mag. Brg. of A	Deviation
000°			
015°			
030°			
045°			
060°			
075°			
090°			
105°			
120°			
135°			
150°			
165°			
180°			
195°			
210°			
225°			
240°			
255°			
270°			
285°			
300°			
315°			
330°			
345°			

the fact that the compass is not placed midships. In the deviation curve of the Napier diagram (Fig. 2-6)

$$A = 0°; B = 7°; C = 15°; D = 11°; \text{ and } E = 1°.$$

By assigning different values to these constants, you can obtain different deviation curves, easily found by substitution in the deviation formula. Usually, on your own vessel, you will not be interested in these constants, but merely in the deviation on each heading, remembering that *deviation depends upon the heading of the vessel.*

PROBLEM SET 2

1) On a Napier diagram (Fig. 2-12) draw a deviation curve from the following data:

Vessel's Hdg. psc	Dev.	Vessel's Hdg. psc	Dev.
000°	16°E	180°	14°W
015°	23°E	195°	10°W
030°	26°E	210°	6°W
045°	27°E	225°	5°W
060°	23°E	240°	5°W
075°	15°E	255°	6°W
090°	6°E	270°	8°W
105°	3°W	285°	9°W
120°	11°W	300°	9°W
135°	17°W	315°	5°W
150°	19°W	330°	0
165°	17°W	345°	8°E

This is the same curve of deviations as shown in Fig. 2-6. You will use it for your deviation curve throughout this text whenever one is needed.

2) Complete the data in the following array, assuming for your compass the deviation curve already given. If you are in regions with variations as shown, use your deviation curve of Napier diagram and find, in each case, the missing values of the compass course, the magnetic course, or the true course to be plotted, as the case may be. *In each case check your arithmetic by finding the total compass error.*

	Compass Course	Dev.	Magnetic Course	Variation	True Course	Total Compass Error
1.	066°			29°W		
2.	080°			28°W		
3.	278°			15°E		
4.			085°	10°W		
5.			032°	20°E		
6.			290°	30°W		
7.				15°W	147°	
8.				08°E	026°	
9.				13°W	207°	
10.	110°			20°E		

Compass Course on Dotted Lines — Magnetic Course on Solid Lines

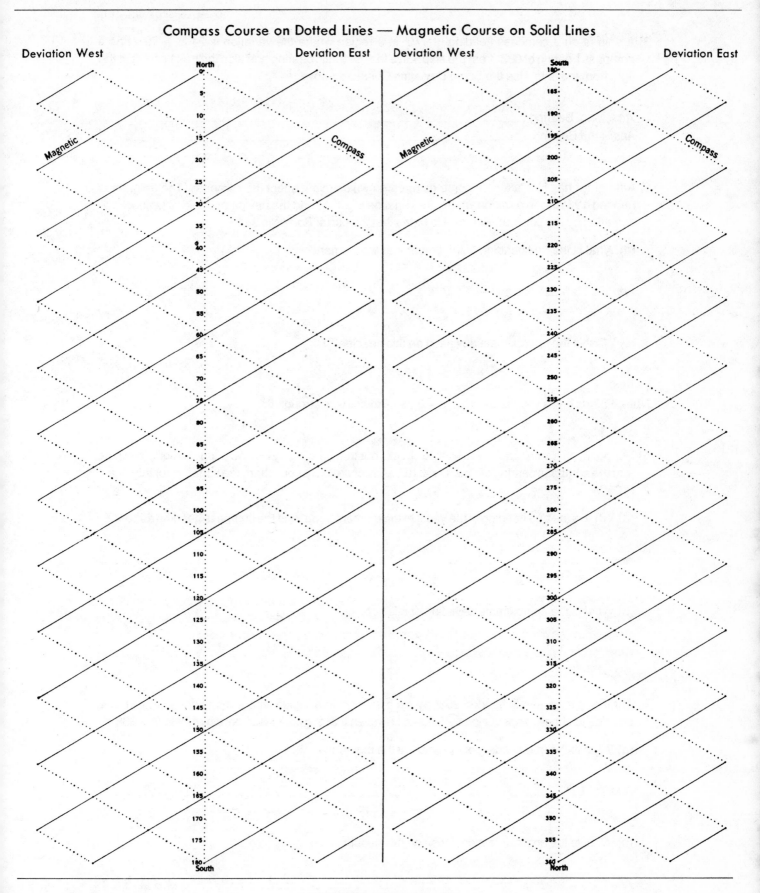

Fig. 2-12. Blank Napier diagram.

3) A ship is on a compass heading of 170° in a region where the variation is 24°E. A light has a compass bearing of 063° from the ship. Give the magnetic bearing and also the true bearing of the light from the ship. Use the Same Deviation Curve As Above.

Ans: Mag. Bearing _____

Ans: True Bearing _____

4) A freighter has just taken on some extra cargo which might affect the compass. The freighter is headed 193° psc in a region where the variation is 20°W, and the navigator decides to check the deviation by the polestar, *Polaris.* He notes that the psc of *Polaris* is 351°.

(a) What is the true heading of the freighter at the moment?

Ans: _____

(b) What is the approximate deviation on this heading?

Ans: _____

Note: *Polaris* gives you the deviations in these Problems, 4 through 6.

5) Suppose, on a small yacht, you wish to check your true heading by *Polaris* during twilight. You note that the compass bearing of *Polaris* is 016°, and according to your chart, the variation for the region is 25°W.

(a) What is the true heading of the yacht at the moment if you read the compass heading as 184°?

Ans: _____

(b) What is the approximate deviation of this heading?

Ans: _____

6) Another yachtsman is headed 203° by his compass, in a region where the variation is 20°E. He decides to check the deviation by *Polaris.* He notes that the compass bearing of *Polaris* is 338°.

(a) What is the true heading of the yacht at the moment?

Ans: _____

(b) What is the approximate deviation on this heading?

Ans: _____

Note: The deviations are rather large, to show the great error which would result from a mistake in arithmetic, or from adding instead of subtracting, etc.

Chapter 3

Charts, Plotting and Symbols

An essential part of most coastwise navigation is the plotting in advance of the vessel's cruise. If you want to arrive at your destination without mishap, you are wise to have the complete legs of your cruise all plotted out on navigational charts, with headings, bearings and times all worked out in advance. In this way, if the fog comes in or some other unexpected circumstance arises, you'll be ready for it. There is nothing more pathetic than the vessel that has to send out a radio message saying, "Where am I?", unless it is the grinding crunch that occurs when your craft unexpectedly discovers a reef that you hadn't noticed on the chart when you glanced at it earlier. According to a disaster described by the U.S. Navy Hydrographic Office on the back of Pilot Chart 1400 for August, 1963, a large ore carrier was passing through Serpent's Mouth, South of Trinidad. The vessel's radar, course recorder, fathometer and fathometer recorder were all in operation. However, as often happens even with the most advanced electronics, little was done to check the position of the carrier, except for the misidentification of a light! Even then, the misidentification of the light would have been noticed *if the estimated course had been plotted*. It then would have been evident that the vessel was on, or had passed over, Icacos Point! The subsequent grounding was quite unnecessary and due to utter negligence. Plotting is one safety device which you should always use.

Most navigators don't mind plotting their courses; in fact, it's half the fun of the voyage. This chapter gives you a chance to learn how to do it, and helps you through some of the enjoyable practice cruises. The emphasis here is on *plotting*. Chapter 5 emphasizes how you *check* your position on the plotted courses—the techniques of piloting.

CHARTS

Navigational Charts. There are four main types of charts in general use in coastwise navigation, and they are distinguished by their *scales*, as adopted by the Defense Mapping Agency Hydrographic Topographic Center (DMAHTC):

1. LARGEST SCALE CHARTS are for entering and leaving harbors where considerable detail is needed. The area covered is so small that the *same* scale holds over the chart. (For small scale ocean going charts, the Earth's curvature leads to the application of a different scale on different parts of the chart.) The scale is presented horizontally so that you can use it conveniently in measuring distances and plotting points. It is also given as a ratio, such as 1:10,000 which means that one inch on the chart represents 10,000 inches on the Earth's surface; or one centimeter represents 10,000 cm; or one of any unit represents 10,000 of the same units on the Earth's surface. For largest scale charts the scales are usually larger than 1:50,000 (with a scale number smaller than 50,000).

2. COAST CHARTS, with scale 1:50,000 to 1:150,000, are for inshore navigation, for entering bays and harbors of considerable width. Because of limited coverage the same scale may be used all over this chart.

3. GENERAL CHARTS, with scale 1:150,000 to 1:600,000, are for coastwise navigation outside reefs and shoals.

4. SAILING CHARTS, for ocean sailing and cruising, have scales 1:600,000 and smaller.
In addition there are special *Intracoastal Waterway* charts covering, for example, the partially protected waterways from New Jersey to Mexico, with scale usually 1:40,000.

It is not necessary to remember exact scale numbers, but you should be able to tell from the particular number whether it is *large* or *small* scale. It is helpful to know this fact when ordering charts for a cruise. They are published by, and may be procured through, government agents (See Appendix III).

With this book you will find a copy of Chart 116-SC Tr, a large scale chart (1:40,000) printed for small craft and for training (Tr) purposes. On it you can practice plotting a cruise, and inspect and learn the many chart symbols and useful information given there. The mariner who does not avail himself of all this important information is sailing blindfolded quite needlessly. Let him be wise and use both eyes!

Simple Mercator Chart Construction. First, however, since this chart is a Mercator projection, you may want to know what that term means. The Earth is round and your chart is flat, so some kind of approximation must be made in representing the Earth's surface as a flat plane. The Mercator projection is one of the most common ways of doing this. You will understand the projection best if you make a simple Mercator chart of your own, as you may want to do anyway, at various times in the future. Here are the directions:

1. Draw a horizontal base line at the bottom of a sheet of paper.

2. Erect three vertical lines at equal intervals. These lines will function as three meridians of the chart. You can consider them one degree apart, according to the region you desire. They might be, for instance, at 66°W, 67°W and 68°W, as pictured in Fig. 3-1.

3. The next step involves choosing the Latitude for your chart. For instance, if you want your chart to cover 41°N Lat. (which can be called the middle Latitude Lm, use a circular protractor to draw a diagonal at a 41° angle to the horizontal line at A, as shown in Fig. 3-1. If you mark as B (in the figure) the intersection of the 67° meridian with the diagonal, then use your dividers so that one tip is at A and the other tip at B. Without changing the distance between the tips, swing arc AB over from A onto the 68° meridian, and call the intersection with the 68° meridian D. In other words, you have marked off AD on the 68°meridian, and made AD = AB. The point D is important. It tells you that Lat. 41° is represented on your chart by the line DE (parallel to the base line). You can find the 42° North Lat. line in the same way. Swinging the line AC over to give AF, note that AD = DF, and that your first horizontal line drawn will represent 40°N. (The horizontal lines at 40°, 41° and 42° are called *Parallels of Latitude*.)

You have now made a simple Mercator chart, with the same scale all over the four degrees. You can go a little further, to obtain 1′ of Latitude and 1′ of Longitude, as follows:

Using dividers (Fig. 1-5), simply bisect 1° (which is 60′) to obtain 30′ of Latitude, then bisect 30′ to obtain 15′, trisect 15′ to obtain 5′, and then divide 5′ into five parts by eye. You can do the same with 1° of Longitude, so that you can plot positions (Lat. and Long.) of any position which you may desire in the region of the chart with an accuracy of around 1′. Note that this accuracy is not good enough for harbor charts. If you want to construct a Mercator projection chart of large scale, simply choose a smaller area, say 10′ width in Long.

DISTANCE. The Latitude scale also gives a scale of nautical miles, since one nautical mile = 1′ of Lat. from the Equator to the poles. Remember that 1′ of Long. = 1′ of Lat. (or 1 n.m.) only at the Equator, so that the *Latitude scale always gives the distance scale on a Mercator chart*.

If you will look at Fig. 3-1 carefully, you will note that AD is greater than AH. This difference would be even more noticeable at higher Latitudes, as it is the result of the Earth's curvature. To understand

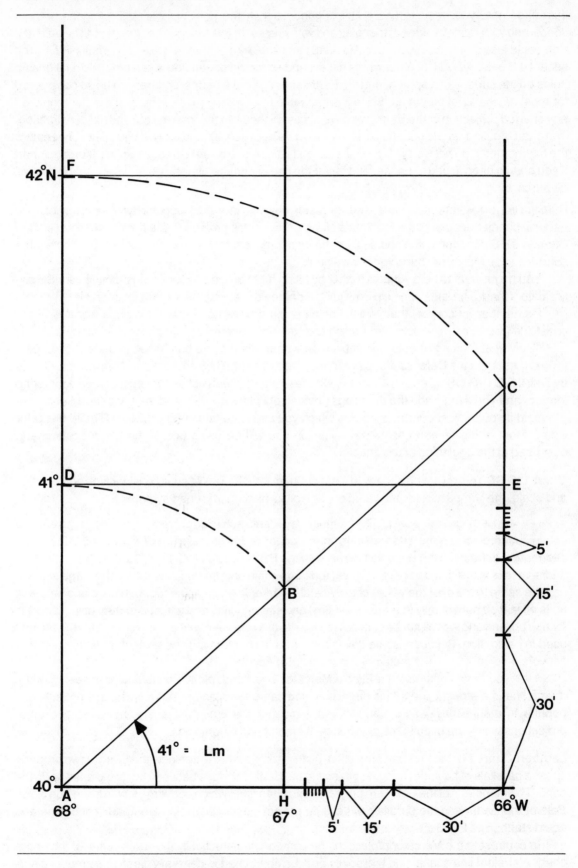

Fig. 3-1. Construction of a Simple Mercator Chart at Lm = 41°N.

this difference, you need to use a little trigonometry in the right triangle AHB. Trigonometry is concerned with ratios of sides of triangles and with angles. In this triangle the secant of 41° = AB/AH. You could also say (since you made AD = AB) that linearly 1° of Lat. = 1° of Long. multiplied by the secant 41° or by AB/AH. In other words the expanding factor for Latitude is *sec Lm*. This relationship holds on the surface of a sphere, and the Earth, although not a perfect sphere, can be so considered for most navigational problems. Since it is desirable to have any relationships on the Earth hold on any charted projection of the Earth, we have accomplished it in this case by our special construction. The chart is called *simple* because of a uniform scale between 40° and 42°N. If you do not understand the trigonometry, do not worry about it; the essential point is to be able to construct this Mercator chart if you should need it, and to understand better the use of commercial and government charts you will be purchasing.

RHUMB LINE ON MERCATOR CHART. The Mercator chart is the most popular type of projection for nautical charts because of the fact that a straight line on this projection is a rhumb line course (See Chapter 1). Since rhumb line courses are the most practical for the mariner, ease in plotting such a course makes Mercator charts very convenient.

You might want to help yourself further by using ruled or lined paper in constructing your Simple Mercator Chart. The lines can help in dividing a degree of Lat. into 30′ or smaller intervals.

Remember, of course, that your homemade chart does not show the various features of the coast line (rocks, reefs, wrecks, etc.) which are noted on government charts for your safety.

"Universal Plotting Sheets" of simple Mercator charts may be purchased in pads of 50 sheets (100 charts) from the Defense Mapping Agency Department. They are listed as Aeronautical Charts by DMAHTC (VP-OS) (See Appendix III). On these charts much of the construction has been done for you, and you simply add the meridians (instead of Latitude lines), and the *Longitude Scale* is of great aid if you think about the principles which you use in constructing your own Simple Mercator Chart. Most of the time in coastwise navigation you will be using one of the larger scale charts described at the beginning of this chapter.

Chart 116-SC Tr. You are now ready to inspect Chart 116-SC Tr. We shall consider type of projection and scale, the compass rose and variation, as well as plotting and chart symbols.

TYPE OF PROJECTION AND SCALE. The number, type and scale of projection is always given in a conspicuous place on the chart, usually in the upper or lower margin. For Chart 116-SC Tr, this information appears in the upper left corner of page B. The scale (1:40,000) is larger than 1:50,000, and so it falls in the first category—among the large scale charts. Because it is such a large scale, it has the same scale over the whole chart. A scale marker is given at the top, with units and tenths of units all laid off horizontally in terms of nautical and statute miles and yards. A statute mile (5280′) is for use on land and we will not be concerned with it in this book. A nautical mile (6076.1 feet) is the unit used in navigation. Because, some day in the future, navigators may be using the metric system, a conversion of miles into the metric system is given in Appendix IV.

After you have constructed a Simple Mercator Chart and, plotted on it, and after seeing that a rhumb line is a straight line in this projection, you can understand quite well why this projection is popular in marine navigation. You will use it most of the time. There are, however, two other projections which are used some of the time—Lambert and Gnomonic.

Lambert Chart. For the Lambert projection, picture a cone which intersects the Earth at two properly chosen parallels of Latitude. Imagine projecting the Earth's surface between the two planes upon the cone. The meridians of the Earth are projected into chart lines which converge towards the true North Pole of the Earth, and the parallels of Latitude project into circles which are nearly concentric and equidistant. (See Fig. 3-7)

In contrast to the Mercator projection, the Lambert has practically the same scale for the entire chart. A straight line connecting two points on a Lambert chart is generally close to a great circle. A rhumb line is curved. To measure a rhumb line course between two points, connect them with a straight line (which becomes the course), and then read the course near the halfway mark. For large distances you can break the intended track into several legs, and measure the course for each leg separately. The Lambert chart is the most popular chart in air navigation. The Aircraft Chart 3071 is very useful for mariners who sail across the Atlantic. It is covered with Loran lines for additional help. If you should happen to be off-course, another great circle course can be constructed quite easily because the latter is a straight line, for practical purposes. As you might expect, the course is the angle between a meridian near the middle of a leg and the straight line which represents the course.

Gnomonic Chart. A Gnomonic chart does not play much of a role in coastwise navigation. You can remember that a *straight line in this projection is precisely a great circle*, and so the projection is of paramount use in great circle sailing, when the navigator may prefer drawing straight lines to computing numerical values. Since it is used mostly in transoceanic sailing, it will not be considered further here, except to state that it is the projection of the Earth upon a plane tangent to the Earth at a point near the center of the region where the chart will be used. You can obtain great circle courses from it, but it is not practical to use as a *plotting* chart.

Compass Rose, Variation and Date of Chart. A very important symbol on every marine chart is the compass rose, which is double on large scale charts. The outer circle displays true directions, while the inner rose shows magnetic directions. These are similar to the do-it-yourself compass circles provided with this book, except that those on the chart are set relative to each other by the variation of the region of this chart. You can read the value of the variation near the center of the compass rose nearest the desired position. For the West end of Chart 116-SC Tr, for instance, the variation is 13° 30'W for the year 1970, and the annual increase in variation is also stated there (2' in this case). This increase is trivial for a few years, since you are usually interested in variation only to the nearest degree, but in other regions the annual increase could be greater, and your chart so old that you would need to take this difference into account. Hence, you are wise to read its value always. The date of your chart is usually given in a lower margin (1970 for Chart 116-SC Tr), and you can easily subtract or add the necessary correction for a later year than the chart date.

PLOTTING

It is easiest, and it usually gives sufficient accuracy, to plot your courses in terms of miles and tenths of miles, as given in the top horizontal scale on Chart 116-SC Tr. Near the Bartlett Reef light, towards the West end of the chart, another scale is presented with the smallest division equal to 5", which is about 0.1'. For the navigator who prefers seconds to tenths of Longitude, note that

$$6'' = 0.1'$$
$$12'' (2 \times 6'') = 0.2'$$
$$18'' (3 \times 6'') = 0.3'$$

These relations always hold, but you will probably use them for Longitude only on the training chart and on others of similar scale.

Chart 116-SC Tr. The parallel lines marked 41°18', 41°20', etc., represent parallels of Lat. (2' or 2 n.m. apart), while 71°52' and 71°54' represent parallels of Long. (2' of Long. apart). The latter are also called *meridians*. By measuring with your dividers, you can see at once that 1' of Lat. is greater than 1' of Long. in linear measure, and so, remember, never use the Longitude scale for a distance scale; use the Latitude scale. This is an easy mistake for a beginner to make, and it cannot be emphasized too much. In the majority of charts the meridians run vertically (and the parallels of Latitude horizontally), but sometimes, as here, more water can be shown if the lines are tilted, still at right angles to each other. Further on in this chapter, symbols will be discussed in connection with the following cruise.

You are now ready to try out a practice cruise on your chart. You are navigating VEGA along the

Connecticut shore. You decided that you would like to cruise out of New London Harbor southward and then West, beyond and South of Bartlett Reef light. Next you want to change course to East, to finally reach a point about 0.4 miles South of Groton Long Pt. Thus, you decide on the following Log for your VEGA cruise.

TABLE 3-1

Cruise of VEGA

Pt. of Dep.: Lat. 41°18′N, Long. 72°05′05″W or 72°05.1′W
(SW of New London Harbor)

LOG

Legs	True	Mag.	Compass	Speed	Dist. N.M.	Time Beg. Leg	End of Leg Position Lat.	Long.
1	168°	_____	_____	10kn	1.46	0736	41°16.6′N	72°04.7′W
2	256°	_____	_____	10kn	4.00	0745	41°15.6′N	72°09.8′W
3	091°	_____	_____	10kn	4.00	0809		
4	050°	_____	_____	10kn	3.73	0833	41°18.0′N	72°00.7′W
				Total	13.19	0855 ETA		

Directions follow, after list of necessary plotting tools:

1. dividers, Fig. 1-5
2. parallel rulers, Fig. 3-2, available in different lengths; 12″ recommended, depending upon plotting space
3. chart table; smooth, flat surface necessary

Note: Two similar triangles can be used instead of parallel rulers. Some navigators prefer them, since they are less apt to slip, but they require more practice initially. For some experienced navigators the plotter-protractor identified as Weems Mark II (Federal Stock Catalog No. FSN 6605-693-8388) is a favorite. To date, most of my students have preferred parallel rulers, in the classsoom at least.

First, plot *Point of Departure* (Pt. of Dep.) as in the Log. The Latitude of this point is easy, since it is right on parallel of Lat. at 41°18′N, already printed as a line on the chart. The next step is to plot Longitude, from nearest meridian, 72°06′W. Whenever possible use dividers instead of parallel rulers to gain speed. For plotting correct Longitude, for instance, take dividers and place 55″ (60″ − 5″) between tips by using the scale near Bartlett Reef light. Next, holding 55″ on your dividers, place one tip on the 72°06′W Long. line at latter's intersection with the 41°18′ Lat. line, and mark where the other tip lies, which is your Pt. of Dep. accurately plotted. Label it with correct time (given in Log) and circle it with a small circle, so it will stand out. Write Pt. of Dep. after the time, and you are now ready to begin plotting the cruise.

True Courses. Since your courses or legs are true, you should align your parallel rulers with the center of the rose and also with the true direction (outer circle) of 168° (See Fig. 3-2). The work will be easier in this particular case if you align the *left* ruler along these two points, since in general, the less you move parallel rulers, the less danger of their slipping. Bear down heavily on the left ruler and move the right one, in this case toward the Pt. of Dep., to the East, as far as you can do so comfortably. Now *hold the right ruler down firmly*, and move the left ruler to join the right ruler again. One further move of the right will cause it to pass through the Pt. of Dep., where you want to be careful about letting it go exactly through this point. In this movement try to keep both rulers as far as possible North, especially if you have 12″ rulers.

Draw a *course* line, through your plotted Pt. of Dep., in the direction of 168° (which you have found with your parallel rulers) and label it correctly, with 168°t above, and *S 10 kn* (for speed 10 knots) below the course. Three figures in Chapter 5 show a reduced scale of the VEGA cruise already

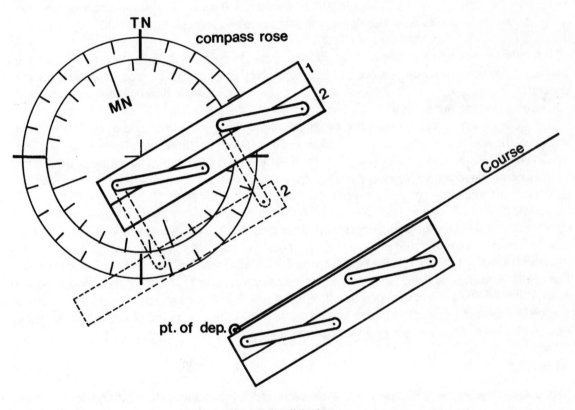

Fig. 3-2. Parallel rulers.

plotted, as a guide for you (Figs. 5-16, 13, 15). You can check as you plot on Chart 116-SC Tr. Generally use a number three pencil, to eliminate smudges and ridges on your chart, and every navigator also needs a large eraser!

Measuring Distances. Measuring the distance of leg 1 is the next task. On leg 1 of the VEGA cruise the distance covered is to be 1.46 miles, according to the Log. Remember that the horizontal line near the top of your chart gives distance in nautical miles (n.m.). To lay off a distance of 1.46 n.m., place the right tip of your dividers exactly above the "1". Place the left tip to the left, beyond the "0". Its position would be between .4 and .5, just before the "1/2" (or 0.5 n.m.). The divider tip should touch a point a little more than halfway between .4 and .5 (estimated by eye). Hold this distance on the dividers (by not altering the distance between tips), and transfer the dividers to leg 1. Press one tip lightly on Pt. of Dep. The other tip, along the course, will mark the end of leg 1, which should then be labeled with a small circle and correct time, followed by DR (deduced reckoning). This time is found by simple arithmetic, from the fundamental *formula for the relation between distance, speed and time:*

(a) Distance (n.m.) = Time (hrs.) x Speed (knots)

or

(b) Distance (kilometers) = Time (hrs.) x Speed (kilometers/hr.)

In the cruise you are using nautical miles and knots, and on leg 1 the Distance =1.46 n.m., Speed = 10 knots, and you want the time. The preceding formula can be rearranged to state:

(c) Time (hrs.) $= \dfrac{\text{Distance}}{\text{Speed}} = \dfrac{1.46}{10} = .146$

and .146 hrs. = .146 x 60 minutes = 8.76 minutes = 9 minutes to nearest minute, which is usually the accuracy required. Hence, the time at the beginning of leg 2 is 0736 + 9 = 0745.

A time-speed-distance table is a help and also a check on time or distance, when you have one and want the other. A short table of that nature is given in Appendix IV. You can use it (or the preceding formula) whenever you have two of the three (time, speed or distance) and want the third (See Table IV-11 in Appendix IV).

Finally, on leg 1, you can mark the end of this leg with the small circle and 0745 DR, the time which you have just found. Similarly, you can proceed with the other three legs of this cruise, and find in addition the Estimated Time of Arrival (ETA) off Groton Long Pt. (0855). The details of this cruise have been displayed on your reduced chart and some figures have been entered in the Log with the positions (Lat. and Long.) given for checks. Fill in any blanks of the Log.

It will be a good review of Chapter 2 to fill in the correct magnetic courses which correspond to true courses given. Use the *deviation table or curve* (See Fig. 2-6) for VEGA's compass. For example, on leg 1 the true course of 168° will be a magnetic course of 168° + 14°W (Var.) or 182°. Entering the deviation curve at 182° (Pt. B in the figure) on the vertical line, hold your dividers parallel to the solid line at 180° and see that this direction intersects the deviation curve at C, making the deviation equal to BC or 11'W. The 11° is obtained by use of your dividers. Put BC between divider tips and measure this distance on the vertical line, obtaining 11'. Using the curve to the left of the vertical line, the deviation is West. (*Answers* are given in Appendix II.)

SYMBOLS

In general, there are over 760 chart symbols divided into different categories, including A for coastline features, B for coast features (abbreviations), C for land (natural features), D for control points, K for lights, L for buoys and beacons, M for radio and radar stations, N for fog signals, O for dangers, Q for soundings, and S for quality of the bottom.

Examples are shown in Figs. 3-3 to 6. The entire list is printed on Chart No. 1 of the Defense Mapping Agency (See Appendix III) and can also be purchased in pamphlet form. They have been prepared by the U.S. Government for your safety, and you should know some of these symbols as well as your know your own name. Chart No. 1 should be a part of your Navigation Kit. Many a disaster has happened because the mariner misidentified a buoy or misinterpreted a chart symbol. The importance of these symbols and knowledge about them cannot be overemphasized. The ore carrier, previously mentioned, probably would not have run aground if correct identification of the Pta Tolete light had been made.

We shall begin a study of chart symbols by looking at the Pt. of Dep. for VEGA, ask a few questions and work out answers.

1. QUESTION: Explain or describe the aids to navigation available to you just from Chart 116-SC Tr, within a radius of 0.6 n.m. from your Pt. of Dep.

ANSWER: The most important light on this chart (within the radius mentioned) is the New London

K. Lights

No.	Abbr.	Symbol — Description
†1		Position of light
2	Lt	Light
†(Ka)		Riprap surrounding light
3	Lt Ho	Lighthouse
†4	AERO	Aeronautical light (See F-22)
4u		Marine and air navigation light
†5	Bn	Light beacon
†6		Light vessel; Lightship
x		Lantern
9		Street lamp
10	REF	Reflector
†11	Ldg Lt	Leading light
†12		Sector light
†13		Directional light
14		Harbor light
15		Fishing light
16		Tidal light
†17	Priv maintd	Private light (maintained by private interests; to be used with caution)
21	F	Fixed light
22	Occ	Occulting light
23	Fl	Flashing light
23a	E Int	Isophase light (equal interval)
24	Qk Fl	Quick flashing (scintillating) light
25	Int Qk Fl / I Qk Fl	Interrupted quick flashing light
25a		Short flashing light
26	Alt	Alternating light
27	Gp Occ	Group occulting light
28	Gp Fl	Group flashing light
28a	S-L Fl	Short-long flashing light
28b		Group short flashing light
29	F Fl	Fixed and flashing light
30	F Gp Fl	Fixed and group flashing light
30a	Mo	Morse code light
31	Rot	Revolving or Rotating light
41		Period
42		Every
43		With
44		Visible (range)
(Kb)	M	Nautical mile (See E-11)
(Kc)	m; min	Minutes (See E-2)
(Kd)	sec	Seconds (See E-3)
45	Fl	Flash
46	Occ	Occultation
46a	Occ	Eclipse
47	Gp	Group
48	Occ	Intermittent light
49	SEC	Sector
50		Color of sector
51	Aux	Auxiliary light
52		Varied
61	Vi	Violet
62		Purple
63	Bu	Blue
64	G	Green
65	Or	Orange
66	R	Red
67	W	White
67a	Am	Amber
67b	Y	Yellow
68	OBSC	Obscured light
68a	Fog Det Lt	Fog detector light (See N-Nb)

Lights (continued)

No.	Abbr.	Description
69		Unwatched light
70	Occas	Occasional light
71	Irreg	Irregular light
72	Prov	Provisional light
73	Temp	Temporary light
(Ke)	D: Destr	Destroyed
74	Exting	Extinguished light
75		Faint light
76		Upper light
77		Lower light
78		Rear light
79		Front light
80	Vert	Vertical lights
81	Hor	Horizontal lights
(Kf)	VB	Vertical beam
(Kg)	RGE	Range
(Kh)	Exper	Experimental light
(Ki)	TRLB	Temporarily replaced by lighted buoy showing the same characteristics
(Kj)	TRUB	Temporarily replaced by unlighted buoy
(Kk)	TLB	Temporary lighted buoy
(Kl)	TUB	Temporary unlighted buoy

L. Buoys and Beacons
(see General Remarks)

No.	Abbr.	Description
†1		Position of buoy
†2		Light buoy
†3	BELL	Bell buoy
†3a	GONG	Gong buoy
†4	WHIS	Whistle buoy
†5	C	Can or Cylindrical buoy
†6	N	Nun or Conical buoy
†7	SP	Spherical buoy
†8	S	Spar buoy
†8a	P	Pillar or Spindle buoy
†9		Buoy with topmark (ball) (see L-70)
†10		Barrel or Ton buoy
(La)		Color unknown
(Lb)	FLOAT	Float
†12	FLOAT	Lightfloat
13		Outer or Landfall buoy
14	BW	Fairway buoy (BWVS)
14a	BW	Mid-channel buoy (BWVS)
15	R "2"	Starboard-hand buoy (entering from seaward)
16	"1"	Port-hand buoy (entering from seaward)
17	RB	Bifurcation buoy (RBHB)
18	RB	Junction buoy (RBHB)
19	RB	Isolated danger buoy (RBHB)
†20	RB / G	Wreck buoy (RBHB or G)
20a	RB / G	Obstruction buoy (RBHB or G)
21	Tel	Telegraph-cable buoy
†22		Mooring buoy (colors of mooring buoys never carried)
22a		Mooring
†22b	Tel	Mooring buoy with telegraphic communications
†22c	T	Mooring buoy with telephonic communications
23		Warping buoy
24	Y	Quarantine buoy
24a	Explos Anch	Practice area buoy
25		Explosive anchorage buoy
25a	AERO	Aeronautical anchorage buoy
26	Deviation	Compass adjustment buoy
27	BW	Fish trap (area) buoy (BWHB)
27a		Spoil ground buoy
28	W	Anchorage buoy (marks limits)
29	Priv maintd	Private aid to navigation (buoy) (maintained by private interests, use with caution)

Fig. 3-3. Section from K & L from back of 1210 Tr Chart. (Courtesy of NOS, U.S. Department of Commerce.)

L. Buoys and Beacons (continued)

No.	Abbr.	Description
†29 (cont.)	R	Starboard-hand buoy (entering from seaward)
	B	Port-hand buoy
30		Temporary buoy (See K i,j,k,l)
30a		Winter buoy
†31	HB	Horizontal stripes or bands
†32	VS	Vertical stripes
†33	Chec	Checkered
33a	Diag	Diagonal bands
41	W	White
42	B	Black
43	R	Red
44	Y	Yellow
45	G	Green
46	Br	Brown
47	Gy	Gray
48	Bu	Blue
48a	Am	Amber
48b	Or	Orange
†51		Floating beacon
†52	Bn	Fixed beacon (unlighted or daybeacon)
	▲ Bn	Black beacon
	△ Bn	Color unknown
(Lc)	MARKER	Private aid to navigation
53	Bn	Beacon, in general (See L-52)
54		Tower beacon
55		Cardinal marking system
56	Deviation Bn	Compass adjustment beacon
57		Topmarks (See L-9, 70)
58		Telegraph-cable (landing) beacon
	Piles	Piles (See O-30, H-9)
59	Stumps	Stakes
		Stumps (See O-30)
		Perches
61	CAIRN, Cairn	Cairn
62	TR	Painted patches
†63	TR	Landmark (position accurate) (See D-2)
†(Ld)	Tr	Landmark (position approximate)
64	REF	Reflector
65	MARKER	Range targets, markers
(Le)	W Or. Or.	Special-purpose buoys
†66		Oil installation buoy
†67		Drilling platform (See O-Ob, O-Oc)
70	Note:	TOPMARKS on buoys and beacons may be shown on charts of foreign waters. The abbreviation for black is not shown adjacent to buoys or beacons.
(Lf)	Ra Ref	Radar reflector (See M-13)

M. Radio and Radar Stations

No.	Abbr.	Description
1	R Sta	Radio telegraph station
2	R T	Radio telephone station
3	R Bn	Radiobeacon
4	R Bn	Circular radiobeacon
5	R D	Directional radiobeacon: Radio range
6		Rotating loop radiobeacon
7	R DF	Radio direction finding station
(Ma)	TELEM ANT	Telemetry antenna
(Mb)	R RELAY MAST	Radio relay mast
(Mc)	MICRO TR	Microwave tower
9	R MAST, R TR	Radio mast, Radio tower
9a	TV TR	Television mast; Television tower
†10	R TR (WBAL) 1090 kHz	Radio broadcasting station (commercial)
10a	R Sta	Q.T.G. Radio station
11	Ra	Radar station
12	Racon	Radar responder beacon
13	Ra Ref	Radar reflector (See L-Lf)
14	Ra (conspic)	Radar conspicuous object
14a		Ramark
15	D F S	Distance finding station (synchronized signals)
16	AERO R Bn 302	Aeronautical radiobeacon
17	Decca Sta	Decca station
18	Loran Sta Venice	Loran station (name)
†19	CONSOL Bn 190 kHz MMF	Consol (Consolan) station
(Md)	AERO R Rge 342	Aeronautical radio range
(Me)	Ra Ref Calibration Bn	Radar calibration beacon
(Mf)	LORAN TR SPRING ISLAND	Loran tower (name)
(Mg)	R TR F R Lt	Obstruction light

N. Fog Signals

No.	Abbr.	Description
1	Fog Sig	Fog-signal station
2		Radio fog-signal station
3	GUN	Explosive fog signal
4		Submarine fog signal
5	SUB-BELL	Submarine fog bell (action of waves)
6	SUB-BELL	Submarine fog bell (mechanical)
7	SUB-OSC	Submarine oscillator
8	NAUTO	Nautophone
9	DIA	Diaphone
10	GUN	Fog gun
11	SIREN	Fog siren
12	HORN	Fog trumpet
13	HORN	Fog horn
†13a	HORN	Electric fog horn
14	BELL	Fog bell
15	WHIS	Fog whistle
16	HORN	Reed horn
17	GONG	Fog gong
18		Submarine sound signal not connected to the shore (See N-5,6,7)
18a		Submarine sound signal connected to the shore (See N-5,6,7)
(Na)	HORN	Typhon
(Nb)	Fog Det Lt	Fog detector light (See K 68a)

Fig. 3-4. Section from L & M (and N in part) from back of 1210 Tr Chart. (Courtesy of NOS, U.S. Department of Commerce.)

O. Dangers

1 Rock which does not cover (height above MHW) (See General Remarks)
— *Uncov 2 ft *(2) ⚓ Uncov 2 ft ⚓(2)
11 Wreck showing any portion of hull or superstructure (above sounding datum)
(Oc) Obstruction (Fish haven) — Fish haven (fishing reef)
28 Wreck (See O-11 to 16)

12 Wreck with only masts visible (above sounding datum) — Masts — Wreckage (Wks)
29 Wreckage

13 Old symbols for wrecks
13a Wreck always partially submerged
29a Wreck remains (dangerous only for anchoring)

2 Rock which covers and uncovers, with height in feet above chart (sounding) datum
30 Submerged piling (See H-9, L-59) — Subm piles

†3 Rock awash at (near) level of chart (sounding) datum
Dotted line emphasizes danger to navigation
†14 Sunken wreck dangerous to surface navigation (less than 11 fathoms over wreck) (See O-6a)
30a Snags; Submerged stumps (See L-59) — Snags — Stumps

†(Oa) Rock awash (height unknown)
Dotted line emphasizes danger to navigation
15 Wreck over which depth is known — 5₁ Wk
31 Lesser depth possible

4 Sunken rock (depth unknown)
Dotted line emphasizes danger to navigation
15a Wreck with depth cleared by wire drag — 2₃ Wk
32 Uncov Dries (See A-10; O-2, 10)
33 Cov Covers (See A-10; O-2, 10)
34 Uncov Uncovers (See A-10; O-2, 10)

5 Shoal sounding on isolated rock — 5₁ Rk
16 Sunken wreck, not dangerous to surface navigation
(3) Rep (1958) Reported (with date) — *Eagle Rk (1958)

†6 Sunken rock not dangerous to surface navigation (See O-4)
17 Foul ground — Foul
46 Reported (with name and date) — *Hazel (rep 1958)

2₁ Rk 2₃ Wk 2₃ Obstr
6a Sunken danger with depth cleared by wire drag (in feet or fathoms)
18 Tide Rips — Overfalls or Tide rips
35 Discol Discolored (See O-9)

7 Reef — Reef of unknown extent
19 Eddies — Eddies (Symbol used only in small areas)
36 Discol Discolored (See O-9)
37 Isolated danger

8 Submarine volcano — Sub Vol
20 Kelp, Seaweed — Kelp (Symbol used only in small areas)
38 Limiting danger line

9 Discol Water — Discolored water
21 Bk Bank
22 Shl Shoal
23 Rf Reef (See A-11d, 11g; O-10)
23a Ridge
24 Le Ledge
39 Limit of rocky area — rky
41 PA Position approximate
42 PD Position doubtful
43 ED Existence doubtful
44 P Pos Position doubtful
45 D Doubtful
46 Unexamined
†(Od), LD Least Depth

2₁ Rk 2₃ Wk 2₃ Obstr
10 Coral reef, detached (uncovers at sounding datum)
25 Breakers (See A-12)
(Oe) Subm Crib — Crib (above water)
Platform (lighted) HORN

Coral — Co Co Co
†26 Sunken rock (See O-4)
(Of) Obstr
Hazel (lighted) HORN

Coral or Rocky reef, covered at sounding datum (See A-11d, 11g)
27 Obstruction
†(Oh) Submerged Well — Submerged Well (buoyed)
(Og) Offshore platform (named)

Reef Line

P. Various Limits, etc.

1 Leading line, Range line
2 Transit
3 In line with
4 Limit of sector
5 Channel, Course, Track recommended (marked by buoys or beacons) (See P-21)
(Pa) Alternate course
6 Radar guided track — Ra — Ra
7 Submarine cable (power, telegraph, telephone, etc.)
†7a Cable Area — Submarine cable area
7b Abandoned submarine cable (includes disused cable)
†8 Submarine pipeline
8a Pipeline Area — Submarine pipeline area
9 Maritime limit in general
(Pb) RESTRICTED AREA — Limit of restricted area
10 Limit of fishing zone (fish trap areas)
(Pc) U.S. Harbor Line
11 Limit of dumping ground, spoil ground (See P-9, G-13)
12 Anchorage limit
13 Limit of airport (See I-23, 24)
13a Limit of military practice areas
14 Limit of sovereignty (Territorial waters)
15 Customs boundary
16 International boundary (also State boundary)
17 Stream limit
18 Ice limit
19 Limit of tide
20 Limit of navigation
21 Course recommended (not marked by buoys or beacons) (See P-5)
22 District or province limit
23 Reservation line — (Options)
24 COURSE 053°00' TRUE — MARKERS MARKERS — Measured distance
25 PROHIBITED AREA — Prohibited area (See G-12,46)
(Pd) (Screen Optional)
(Pe) SAFETY FAIRWAY — Shipping safety fairway — Directed traffic lanes

Q. Soundings

No.	Symbol		Description
1	SD		Doubtful sounding
2	65		No bottom found
3			Out of position
4			Least depth in narrow channels
5	30 FEET APR 1972		Dredged channel (with controlling depth indicated)
6	24 FEET MAY 1972		Dredged area
7			Drying (or uncovering) heights; in feet above chart (sounding) datum
8	6₆		Swept channel (See Q-9)
†9			Swept area, not adequately sounded (shown by green tint)
†9a			Swept area adequately sounded (swept by wire drag to depth indicated)
10	8₂	19	Hair-line depth figures
10a	8₂	19	Figures for ordinary soundings
11	8₂	19	Soundings taken from foreign charts
12	8₂	19	Soundings taken from older surveys (or smaller scale chts)
13	8₂	19	Echo soundings
14	8₂	19	Sloping figures (See Q-12)
15	8₂	19	Upright figures (See Q-10a)
16	(25)	(2)	Bracketed figures (See O-1, 2)
17	6	6₁	Underlined sounding figures (See Q-8)
18	3₂	6₁	Soundings expressed in fathoms and feet
22	6—5—5—2ft		Unsounded area
(Qa)			Stream

Fig. 3-5. Section from O, P and Q from back of 1210 Tr Chart. (Courtesy of NOS, U.S. Department of Commerce.)

R. †Depth Contours and Tints (see General Remarks)

Feet	Fms/Meters		Feet	Fms/Meters
0	0		300	50
6	1		600	100
12	2		1,200	200
18	3		1,800	300
24	4		2,400	400
30	5		3,000	500
36	6		6,000	1,000
60	10		12,000	2,000
120	20		18,000	3,000
180	30		Or continuous lines, with values	
240	40			

————5———— (blue or black) ———100———

S. Quality of the Bottom

No.	Abbr.	Term		No.	Abbr.	Term		No.	Abbr.	Term
1	Grd	Ground		24	Oys	Oysters		50	spk	Speckled
2	S	Sand		25	Ms	Mussels		51	gty	Gritty
3	M	Mud; Muddy		26	Spg	Sponge		52	dec	Decayed
4	Oz	Ooze		27	K	Kelp		53	fly	Flinty
5	Ml	Marl		28	Wd	Sea-weed		54	glac	Glacial
6	Cl	Clay		28	Grs	Grass		55	ten	Tenacious
7	G	Gravel		29	Stg	Sea-tangle		56	wh	White
8	Sn	Shingle		31	Spi	Spicules		57	bk	Black
9	P	Pebbles		32	Fr	Foraminifera		58	vi	Violet
10	St	Stones		33	Gl	Globigerina		59	bu	Blue
11	Rk; rky	Rock; Rocky		34	Di	Diatoms		60	gn	Green
11a	Blds	Boulders		35	Rd	Radiolaria		61	yl	Yellow
12	Ck	Chalk		36	Pt	Pteropods		62	or	Orange
12a	Ca	Calcareous		37	Po	Polyzoa		63	rd	Red
13	Qz	Quartz		38	Cir	Cirripeda		64	br	Brown
13a	Sch	Schist		38a	Fu	Fucus		65	ch	Chocolate
14	Co	Coral		38b	Ma	Mattes		66	gy	Gray
(Sa)	Co Hd	Coral head		39	fne	Fine		67	lt	Light
15	Mds	Madrepores		40	crs	Coarse		68	dk	Dark
16	Vol	Volcanic		41	sft	Soft				
(Sb)	Vol Ash	Volcanic ash		42	hrd	Hard		70	vard	Varied
17	La	Lava		43	stf	Stiff		71	unev	Uneven
18	Pm	Pumice		44	sml	Small		(Sc)	S/M	Surface layer and Under layer
19	T	Tufa		45	lrg	Large				
20	Sc	Scoriae		46	stk	Sticky				
21	Cn	Cinders		47	brk	Broken				
21a		Ash		47a	grd	Ground (Shells)		76		Fresh water springs in sea-bed
22	Mn	Manganese		48	rt	Rotten				
23	Sh	Shells		49	str	Streaky				

T. Tides and Currents

No.	Abbr.	Term
1	HW	High water
1a	HHW	Higher high water
2	LW	Low water
(Ta)	LWD	Low water datum
2a	LLW	Lower low water
3	MTL	Mean tide level
4	MSL	Mean sea level
4a		Elevation of mean sea level above chart (sounding) datum
5		Chart datum (datum for sounding reduction)
6	Sp	Spring tide
7	Np	Neap tide
7a	MHW	Mean high water
8	MHWS	Mean high water springs
8a	MHWN	Mean high water neaps
8b	MHHW	Mean higher high water
8c	MLW	Mean low water
9	MLWS	Mean low water springs
9a	MLWN	Mean low water neaps
9b	MLLW	Mean lower low water
10	ISLW	Indian spring low water
11		High water full and change (vulgar establishment of the port)
12		Low water full and change
13		Mean establishment of the port
13a		Establishment of the port
14		Unit of height
15		Equinoctial
16		Quarter; Quadrature
17	Str	Stream
18		Current, general, with rate
19		Flood stream (current) with rate
20		Ebb stream (current) with rate
21		Tide gauge; Tidepole, Automatic tide gauge
23	vel	Velocity; Rate
24	kn	Knots
25	ht	Height
26		Tide
27		New moon
28		Full moon
29		Ordinary
30		Syzygy
31	fl	Flood
32		Ebb
33		Tidal stream diagram
34		Place for which tabulated tidal stream data are given
35		Range (of tide)
36		Phase lag
(Tb)		Current diagram, with explanatory note

Fig. 3-6. Sections from parts of R, S and T from back of 1210 Tr Chart. (Courtesy of NOS, U.S. Department of Commerce.)

Ledge light on the West side of Southwest Ledge. Its exact position is shown by the black dot, as for all lights and buoys. Note that the position of a light is more accurate than the position of a buoy, which can drift in a storm, as a buoy is only anchored and not fixed on the bottom. The newest symbol for a light is the balloon-shaped magenta figure near the dot (See Fig. 3-3 for this exact symbol). The characteristics of this light, from the chart, follow:

Light Characteristics. "Gp Fl W (3) Alt Fl R (1). 30 sec 58 ft. 13 M, Horn"   Inspection of these abbreviations under "K" and "L" gives the following information:

Gp Fl = Group flashing light (instead of a single flash, there will be more).
(3) indicates 3 flashes, and W implies a white light.
Fl R = flashing, and R is the abbreviation for red (color abbreviations are given under the category L, Fig. 3-4).
(1) indicates one flash.
"30 sec" means that you will see the three flashing white lights, followed by one red flashing light, all in the space of 30 seconds.

Then the sequence is repeated. (Sometimes, in critical cases, a stopwatch is most helpful in distinguishing between lights with similar characteristics.) The New London Ledge light (on Southwest Ledge) is 58 ft. high, as read from the chart, and the reference level is usually understood to be mean high water (explained in the next chapter) and always indicated (for safety) on the chart itself, usually under the title, page B on Chart 116-SC Tr.

Light List Information. The following is an example of further details in the *Light List,* for the New London Ledge light, in addition to the preceeding information from the chart:

$$0.3^S Wfl., \quad 4.7^S ec.$$
$$0.3^S Wfl., \quad 4.7^S ec.$$
$$0.3^S Wfl., \quad 9.7^S ec.$$
$$0.3^S Rfl., \quad 9.7^S ec.$$
$$3 W., 1R., \quad Flashes$$

This information adds the length of the flashes ($.3^S$ for W and R) while in between the flashes the light is *eclipsed* or is dark, for 4.7^S between the white flashes and for 9.7^S before and after the R flash. Additional information in the list reads:

"In 30 feet, on West side of Southwest Ledge,
East side of entrance to New London Harbor.
41°18.3′N   72°04.6′W   (confirms the position)
58 feet above water (confirms the height)
Red brick dwelling on square pier.
Horn: 2 blasts ev 20^S (2^S bl-2^Ssi-2^Sbl-14^Ssi)"

The last item of information tells the length of the horn blasts. *If you read all this information ahead of time, you cannot fail to identify this light correctly.*

Range of Light. One other piece of information should be added on the subject of light ranges, the distances at which lights may be seen. The 13 M on the training chart indicates the light is seen for 13 miles if your height of eye is 15 feet. If you were in swimming, your eye would be at the level of water, probably. If you were at a great height, for instance, you could see much further in the direction of the light, and even see beyond your swimming-horizon. For a height of eye of 15′, the distance to the horizon would be 4.4 miles, just from the geometry of the situation. In case you were much higher, you could subtract 4.4 miles from 13 in this case, and add the distance you see for your added height. In Appendix IV, Table IV-9 gives the range for different heights of eye, for future use. Another factor to take into consideration when you want exact distance at which lights can be seen is their luminosity, which depends upon the state of the atmosphere.

Luminous Ranges—Lights and Buoys. Distances which take this factor into account are called *luminous ranges* and *Light Lists* present a graph which enables you to find the luminous range when needed. Helpful explanations are given in the list for your region. The particular volume to cover your cruise of VEGA is Volume 1 (Atlantic Coast, St. Croix River, Maine to Little River, South Carolina). In foreign countries you sometimes have to rely on the charts themselves.

The first and most important step, always, in planning a cruise, is to study the chart of the region. Study each buoy and ask yourself why it was placed in the position given, and be sure that you can identify it when you see it. Note all characteristics and emphasize the reasons for locations; then you will have no worry about sayings like, "Red, right, returning," which means (in the U.S. "*lateral* system" of buoys) that red buoys are kept to the right of your vessel when you are returning to the land. "Returning to the land" implies "from seaward", and "from seaward" is considered to be in a *clockwise* direction around the country. In the other chief buoyage system ("*cardinal* system"), however, the rules are different, and your safest procedure is to study reasons for the positioning of lights and buoys, taking pains to be sure that you can identify the particular light or buoy when you see it on the water. Remember, finally, that changes are continually taking place, some due to man and some due to nature. When you encounter a change, stop and ponder as to the best action you should take. Do not rush ahead with blind faith that everything will come out all right, without your efforts.

In addition to the New London Ledge light, there are numerous buoys within the radius of 0.6 miles. These can be divided into two main categories:

One Type	Another Type
N "4"	"3" FL 4 sec
R	Ra Ref
C "5"	
R N "6"	"2" FL R 4 sec
	Ra Ref
	Sarah Ledge "1"
	FL G 4 sec
	Gong
	Ra Ref

These letters and figures were read from Chart 116-SC Tr near the diamonds which designate buoys on charts. Ra Ref indicates Radar Reflector. The main difference between these two types of buoys is that those in the left column are unlighted, while those in the right column have lights, denoted by magenta circles. The number enclosed in quotation marks appears on its buoy. Fl means "flashing", N stands for nun buoy, while C denotes a can buoy. Note that nun buoys have *even* numbers, and can buoys have *odd* numbers. Remember that numbers increase in the U.S. system as the vessel approaches land from seaward. It is important to remember these facts but crucial to study the buoys and lights that you will encounter on your plotted courses.

Another bit of helpful information about lights comes from *Basic Marine Navigation* (See Appendix III). The navigator should guard against being misled by the apparent absence of color in faint or distant lights. Our eyes, because of their peculiar nature, are not always capable of distinguishing color in a very faint light. The color which is recognized at the greatest distance is red. However, a green light (or a blue one) can be seen as a gray-white light from a much greater distance than a red light of the same strength, whereas green (or blue) *color* can be distinguished only when the green light is at one third the distance of the red light. The atmosphere can play some peculiar tricks. It has the property of scattering blue or green light more readily than a red light. A distant white light can therefore appear to be decidedly reddened. A cautious navigator will not put too much faith in color observations of faint or distant lights. It is a good precaution to check repeatedly on the apparent coloring of a light as your vessel draws gradually closer.

2. QUESTION: Why is there a need for C "5" buoy?

ANSWER: Look at the rocks around Cormorant Rock, look at Middle Rock and Shore Rock, and you will probably decide that C "5" buoy will protect you from striking these rocks. Also, there is the matter of depth of water at any point (called a *sounding*). Most numbers seen on the chart represent depth of water where the figure appears. Depths or *soundings* are usually given for times of *mean low water* (explained in next chapter). The unit used is always stated under the chart title, and on our chart this unit is *feet*. In the future, the unit may someday be metric. On ocean charts it is given in fathoms at present (1 fathom = 6 feet), but the mariner must always check this unit, especially as a *change to the metric system may appear at any moment*.

To return to C "5" buoy, it is very close to shallow spots, indicated by figures in feet there, and with curved lines representing the same depth as shown by the figure on the chart. Inspection of the region of C "5" buoy indicates that water to the West and North of this buoy is to be avoided, and the buoy is a mark on the water to give you this message. In coming down the New London channel you might have been swept over in that direction, and the buoy would alert you in this case.

Channel Buoys. Buoys "3" Fl W 4 sec and "2" Fl R 4 sec mark the entrance to the channel leading to New London Harbor, and if you were entering the channel, soon you would expect to pass between another pair which mark the channel, with larger numbers, as you can see—"5" and "6". Leg 1 of the VEGA cruise passes almost at once between Sarah Ledge buoy and the "3" Fl buoy at the channel entrance. You certainly have some checks on your leg 1, besides the "Storm Warnings" from Southwest Ledge, which you should always investigate before starting out on any cruise.

3. QUESTION: What is the purpose of Sarah Ledge buoy?

ANSWER: In case you wanted to reach the channel to New London Harbor, it will function as a guide to the entrance buoys mentioned previously, and it will also keep you away from the very shallow spot of 14 feet, which might be very important if you were on a freighter. *Groundings are usually due to human error, carelessness in looking at figures or failing to check with various techniques* (discussed later).

In general, your most helpful navigational aid in this circle of 0.6 miles is the New London Ledge light, because it is fixed on the bottom, and hence its position would not have changed. As seen under piloting techniques, bearing lines obtained from fixed objects which are also charted, offer good lines of position, and in a fog all these aids will help you tremendously in keeping track of your position. It is not enough, as some careless people think, to cruise from buoy to buoy. You would not, for instance, cruise to C buoy just because it is a buoy. You will stay away from this buoy, at least on the cruise of VEGA.

4. QUESTION: At the end of leg 1, on your chart, you can read "See Note A". What does "Note A" say?

ANSWER: Near the top margin of the chart it says: "*NAVAL ANCHORAGE*—for barges and small vessels drawing less than 12 feet. Navigation regulations are published in Chapter 2 of *Coast Pilot 2*, or in subsequent yearly supplements and weekly *Notices to Mariners*. Copies of the regulations may be obtained at the Office of the Division Engineer, Corps of Engineers, Waltham, MA 02154." This note also gives the address for obtaining *Anchorage Regulations*.

5. QUESTION: On your chart there is an abbreviation for a *quality of the bottom*, indicated within the Dumping Ground which encloses "Note A." What does "hrd" mean?

ANSWER: "hrd" means "hard", the abbreviation given as one of the many chart symbols in the "S" category. It used to be a popular custom at one time to cast out the line with a 14-pound or so standard lead at the end. The lead contained a hollow which could be filled with tallow or other grease. It should come up with a sample of the bottom, which in some sections of the coast could be very helpful in deciding on the most probable position of the vessel. According to a famous Nantucket story, one skipper vowed he could tell where he was by *tasting* a sample of the bottom. Whether he could or not is not absolutely clear, but it is certain that samples of the bottom proved a determining factor in many instances of finding where the position was. In this case, for instance, if the mariner found mud (M) or sand (S) on the bottom, when he was in this particular position where "hrd" is read, he should become very cautious, and find other immediate checks on his position. South and West of the Dumping Ground here, note M S Sh, which stands for mud, sand and shells. Altogether, about 40 chart symbols on the nature of the bottom are given for the mariner's use, and a good mariner should know how to interpret them, and be able to use them if the need should ever arise. Of all the methods given for checking a position, however, (See Chapter 5) this method of sampling the bottom might be placed low on the list today, in this age of electronics.

6. QUESTION: What can you say about the depth of water near the end of leg 2, around 1 1/2 tenths of a mile almost due South?

ANSWER: The sounding given on the chart at this position is 63′, and this implies a depth below the *mean low water* level here (See Chapter 4).

7. QUESTION: Can you find a light with protective riprap around it?

ANSWER: Race Rock light, off Race Pt. on Fishers Island. Vessels have been known to excel in "homing" to such an extent that they rammed the lightship which preceded the present automatic light structure, and they have even been known to ram a light. At any event, the riprap can function as some protection on all sides against wind, waves and collisions (See Fig. 3-3, K for symbol).

Common Symbols. Some of the most important and common chart symbols are shown in Figs. 3-3, 3-4, 3-5 and 3-6. They are reproduced in black and white only, and were reduced in size so as to fit on a page. They were taken from the back side of Chart 1210 Tr. The wise mariner will become familiar with most of these symbols before he takes departure.

Summary of Characteristics—Lights and Buoys. In the case of a light, or lighted buoy, the black dot shows the exact position of this aid to navigation. The larger black or grey areas are colored magenta on the charts.

Among the lights, F indicates a continuous fixed light which is *on* all the time, whereas a Fl lighted buoy flashes a light at certain periods indicated on the chart and in the *Light List*. The Fl light is off more than it is on. The number of flashes will usually not exceed 30 per minute. A F Fl light signifies fixed *and* flashing, and shows a steady light which is varied at regular intervals by a flash of greater brilliance. A Gp Fl light shows at regular intervals groups of two or more flashes. Qk Fl means quick flashing and shows not less than 60 flashes per minute. I Qk Fl means interrupted quick flashing and gives quick flashes for around four seconds followed for around four seconds by a dark period. S-L Fl is the symbol for a short flash of around 0.4 seconds followed by a long flash of about four times that duration. Remember that exact figures for any particular light are given in *Light Lists*. Occ stands for an occulting light, which is *on more than it is off, opposite of the Fl light,* and is eclipsed at regular intervals.

Again, correct identification of lights and buoys cannot be overemphasized. Failure to take this matter seriously has been the cause of numerous wrecks! As you can imagine, a lop (line of position/See Chapter 5) through the wrong light is not of much help.

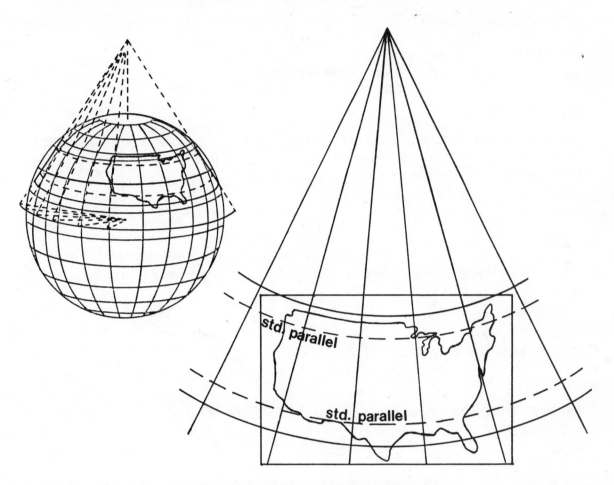

Fig. 3-7. Sketch to show the principles of a Lambert Chart.

WRECK DUE TO MISIDENTIFICATION OF LIGHT. Near the beginning of 1970, a large freighter departed Houston, Texas, for Southeast Asia via the Panama Canal. When, South of Cuba, the Third Mate sighted a light abaft port beam, the Master came to the bridge, and without a stopwatch timed the light twice and identified it as Cabo San Antonio light. A visual bearing of this light, along with a radar range of the same light, gave a fix, but the fix was fallacious because the light was misidentified and the error perpetuated for almost two days. The result was a grounding of the freighter on Farall Rocks off Banco Gorda. This disaster was analyzed on the back of Pilot Chart N.0.16, November, 1971.

In connection with the symbol for a buoy, note whether there are vertical or horizontal bands on the buoy. Remember that a vertical line is like a hand beckoning you on, while horizontal bands are more like a sign warning you away from a danger. That is why a midchannel buoy has vertical bands. Many of the symbols are self-explanatory. Take care in studying the "danger" symbols under 0. A dangerous sunken *wreck*, for instance, is denoted by the symbol shown on Fig. 3-5, number 14. The surrounding dots indicate danger. Without the dots, the wreck is not dangerous to navigation. A similar array of dots in a circle around a star or a cross again denotes danger in connection with a submerged rock.

A sounding denoted by a larger figure followed by a small subscript number shows that the depth is the number of fathoms denoted by the large figure plus the depth in feet shown by the subscript. You will find this symbol, probably, only on charts based on older surveys or on smaller scale charts. Under "Depth Contours", fms is an abbreviation for fathoms. Note the continuous series of dashes to give 100 fathoms.

PROBLEM SET 3

Cruise of ALGOL

Imagine you are interested in a cruise North of the Gull Islands. The Pt. of Dep. is 1/2 mile N of Little Gull Island light, at 41°12.9′N, 72°06.4′W; Speed — 5 kn. Time of Dep. 0536 EDT (Eastern Daylight Time). Use the deviation curve of Fig. 2-6.

LOG

Leg	True Course	Mag.	Compass Course	(n.m.) Distance	Time End of Leg	At End of Each Leg Lat.	Long.
1	057°	071°	_____	2.2	_____	_____	_____
2	291°	305°	_____	3.6	_____	_____	_____
3	270°	284°	_____	3.6	_____	_____	_____
4	024°	038°	_____	1.6	_____	_____	_____

You should fill in the log, as regards compass course, time and positions at end of legs. (*Answers* in Appendix II.)

HINT IN PLOTTING: To help yourself in plotting, extend the 41°12′ parallel of Lat. to the East, so that you can measure from it. Obtain distances to the nearest tenth of mile, and time to the nearest minute. Obtain positions to nearest tenth of a minute of Lat. and Long.

Chapter 4

Tides and Currents

As seen in Chapter 3, the soundings given on charts for coastwise navigation tell you the *depth* of the water at time of *mean low water* (if not stated otherwise under the chart's title). If you also know the *height* of the water *above* mean low water (height of the tide), you know how deep the water is at many points. Just remember the draft of your own vessel (depth to which the vessel is submerged), and you know what waters you can enter safely, without grounding. A grounding may be a disaster for your vessel, or for *both* you and your vessel. Hence, this situation must be avoided if you want to practice "Constant Vigilance" and come safely home. If you are still doubtful about this truth, it may stimulate you to read an exciting adventure book, such as the classic *The Riddle of the Sands* by Erskine Childers. At all events, to find out about the height or depth of the water, it is absolutely necessary to know more about tides, and with this knowledge you can enter more waters safely and have additional adventures.

TIDES

Moon. Now that man has actually landed on the Moon and even revisited the Moon, it may seem easier to appreciate the fact that the Moon has been the Earth's nearest neighbor in space

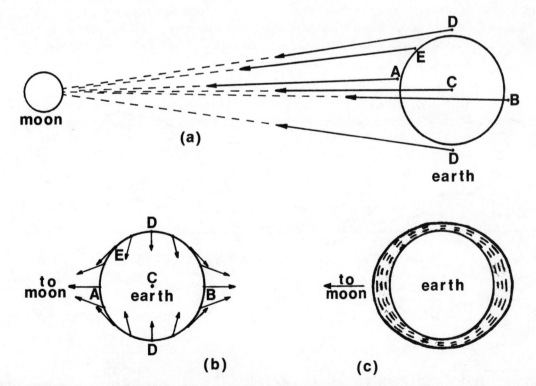

Fig. 4-1. Tidal forces produced by the Moon. Arrows in (a) represent the attractions by the Moon on various points at the surface of the Earth; arrows in (b) represent differences between the attraction on each point and the average attraction for the entire Earth; these arrows are the tide-producing forces. The forces directed horizontally, such as the force at E, produce the tides shown in (c).

throughout many millions of years. It makes one revolution Eastward around the Earth in about 29 1/2 days with respect to the Sun (basic period for the phases of the Moon), or at the rate of about 13° per day. The last fact affects the time of Moonrise each day, making it later as a rule. Because of its relative close distance to the Earth (about 240,000 miles) it seems reasonable to expect that it would have a greater effect than any other celestial body on the Earth's solid surface and its waters. In other words, the Moon produces tides on the Earth, and the tide-producing force is the difference between the force exerted by the Moon at a particular point on the Earth and the average force exerted by the Moon on the Earth as a whole. The latter force can be pictured as acting at the center of the Earth.

Tidal Forces. The force exerted by the Moon at each point on the Earth can be represented by an arrow, or by a vector with a definite direction and also with a length which depends upon the strength of the force. The differences between the forces at each point and the average force at the center of the Earth can also be represented by arrows or vectors. These arrows have been drawn in Fig. 4-1, which is an adaptation from a classical drawing by George H. Darwin.

It is not difficult to see that at A the force of attraction of the Moon is somewhat greater than at C, since A is closer to the Moon than C. At A the Moon is directly overhead for you as mariner, or at your Zenith, and is pulling up the waters of the Earth here. The effect of the pull of the Moon is to decrease slightly the effect of the Earth's gravitational attraction. At A the Moon is initiating a high tide. At B the attraction of the Moon is less than at C. We might say that the Moon is pulling the solid bottom of the ocean away from under the water. The result is a force directed upward. The force at B is almost equal to that at A. Neither force is very significant as a tide-raising force. However, a high tide is also being initiated at B. At D the Moon will be on the horizon. The amounts of the total forces exerted at D and C will also be almost equal, but since these directions differ slightly, the tidal forces will be pointing downward. The effect of the arrows at D on the tides is small. At D you have the beginning of low tides.

The more important tide-raising forces are found at intermediate points, such as at E, where the tidal force is directed horizontally. The horizontal component is never operating against gravity, and draws particles of water over the surface of the Earth, which of course is in the same horizontal plane. Hence, at E the tide-raising force is very important, while at other points between A and D, and between D and B the forces directed horizontally produce the tides shown in Fig. 4-2 and Fig. 4-3,

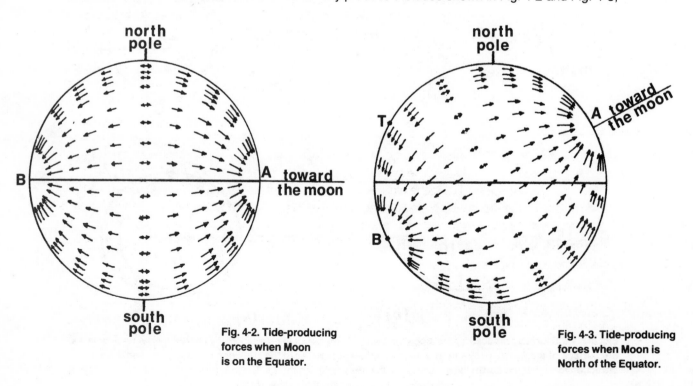

Fig. 4-2. Tide-producing forces when Moon is on the Equator.

Fig. 4-3. Tide-producing forces when Moon is North of the Equator.

taken essentially from *Basic Marine Navigation*, where they were reproduced from Marmer's *The Tides*. Fig. 4-2 shows the distribution of the horizontal force components on a day when the Moon is on the Celestial Equator, and when the mariner is also at the Equator at A. The Moon is overhead for this mariner. Think of the arrows as the differences noted in Fig. 4-1 above, and you can understand how the Moon has a tendency to pull the water to the level of a high tide at A and also at B, 180° from A in Longitude, since B is on the other side of the Earth from A. A mariner anywhere else on the meridian through A in Fig. 4-2 would also experience a high tide, which probably would not be as high as the high tide at A, but it still is the highest tide of the day for that mariner. The same reasoning holds for the second high tide on the opposite side of the Earth.

In the mathematical theory of the tides it is shown that the foregoing analysis is deficient mainly in not considering the rotation of the Earth on its axis. The distribution of the tidal forces is as shown in Fig. 4-2, but the difficulty is evident. Because of the Earth's rotation, these forces may not have enough time to build up the highs at A and B, with lows at both D's (Fig. 4-1).

The mathematical theory of the tides is quite complex. Enough has been given above to understand the *Tide Tables* which you must consult before you undertake a cruise, provided you note a few more facts.

Semidiurnal Tide. It is helpful to think of a tide as the veritcal rise and fall of the water which accompanies the tidal phenomenon as already explained. Usually there are two high tides each day (with 180' or 12^h between A and B approximately). More accurately, since the Moon is always moving Eastward at the rate of 13° per day (the equivalent of about 50^m in time) one high tide will be followed by the next high tide 12^h25^m later (with a low tide in between, 6^h13^m later than the first high tide). The mariner remembers that there are in general two high tides and two low tides each day, for a normal tide with the above time-interval in between. It is called, officially, a semidiurnal tide. Tides on the Atlantic Coast of the USA are usually semidiurnal.

However, there are a few other factors which complicate the above simple conditions for a normal tide. First, there can be a shallow ocean instead of a deep one. The shallow ocean can cause a delay in the rise of the water for a high tide, or the nature of the land nearby may also cause a delay with a different time interval. A lag in time can be expected.

Diurnal Tides. The tide may be daily or diurnal instead of semidiurnal. Inspection of Fig. 4-3 shows how a diurnal tide can arise. Here the Moon is not in the plane of the Earth's Equator, but North of the Equator, about 23°N. This figure resembles Fig. 4-2 except for this different position of the Moon, which can range from 0° to 18-29° from the Equator. Note that the point at the *same* Lat. but 180° from A in Long. is at T. The point T is no longer on the other side of the Earth from A, and also on the same line to the Moon. The point which more nearly fits this description is B, and at B you may expect a high tide similar to the high tide at A. As the axis of the Earth, on which the Earth rotates, is through the poles of the Earth, the point B will never pass through the point A. The point T is the point which in 12^h25^m will pass through A, and the high tide associated with T is probably quite different from the high tide at B. Hence, although usually there may be a high tide at T when there is a high tide at A and also at B, the high tide at T will not be symmetrical or similar to the high tide at A. In fact, the high tide at T may be quite asymmetrical to the high tide at A. A daily variation of the tide will be superposed on the customary variations with period of half a day. Technically, a tide with a period of a whole day is referred to as a *tropic* or *diurnal* tide, with only one high and one low per day. Along the Northern shore of the Gulf of Mexico, in the Java Sea, the Gulf of Tonkin, and in a few other places you would find a diurnal tide.

Mixed Tides. A third type of tide is called *mixed*. In this type, as the name implies, there is a mixture of the semidiurnal and diurnal tides. This means, for instance, that there may be a striking difference in the two highs for the day, and also in the two lows. It is customary to distinguish between *higher high water* and *lower high water* for the highs, and between *higher low water* and *lower low water for the lows (Fig. 4-4)*.

The response to the semidiurnal and diurnal tide components is not the same for the different oceans and for different points on the shores of one ocean. Some basins respond readily to the semidiurnal variations, but are not expecially adapted for the setting up of a diurnal vibration. The North Atlantic is an example of this type of basin. The Gulf of Mexico, on the other hand, sometimes responds more readily to the diurnal wave, and at Pensacola, Florida, the diurnal tide is much more pronounced than the semidiurnal tide. At Galveston the tide is semidiurnal around times when the Moon is on the Equator, but becomes diurnal where the Moon's declination South or North of the Equator is around maximum. Tides at Key West are a mixture. Sometimes, at Key West, the highs and lows differ only by a few tenths of a foot. See Fig. 4-5 for typical tides on the West coast of the USA. Note in particular the tide change at Anchorage, and at Seattle, depending upon the Moon's position in its monthly path around the Earth.

Tide Tables. All of the foregoing description of the tides in general must show the mariner the necessity of consulting *Tide Tables* whenever they exist for waters which he might want to visit. Hence, a few facts should be known about *Tide Tables* and the terms used.

Range. The range of the tide is the difference in depth between high and low water at the place. It is apt to vary from day to day because of many factors, all depending for the most part on the Moon, but now it is time to mention the other body which contributes to the tide-raising forces on the Earth. This body is the Sun. The tide-producing forces of the Sun are, on the average, 40 percent of those of the Moon, and are less in importance, but still significant.

Spring Tides. The Sun contributes to cause an unusually large range at spring tide, near the times of New and Full Moon.

Phases of the Moon. The Moon has no light of its own, and so it shines only by reflected sunlight as it revolves around the Earth Eastward in about 29 1/2 days (a mariner may remember the period as being about one month, for practical purposes). The inner circle shows the Moon at all times half illuminated by the Sun's rays, which come in from the right of the picture in Fig. 4-6. The people on the Earth cannot see all around the Moon. At position A people cannot see the Moon at all (except for some reflection from the Earth onto the dark side of the Moon) and the phase of the Moon is said to be *New*. At position C people on the Earth can see half of the illuminated half, or a quarter of the whole Moon. The Moon is said to be at *1st Quarter*. At E the people on the Earth can see all of the illuminated surface, and the Moon is said to be *Full*. At position G again the Earth people see one quarter of the Moon, and this is called the *3rd or last Quarter*. Intermediate positions of the Moon picture the crescent and gibbous phases, which are not too important for the mariner except to give him an idea of the more significant phases New and Full, closely related to the tides and tide theory. At New and Full positions, for instance, the Moon and the Sun will be pulling *together* in the same direction of either the Sun or the Moon, and so a higher tide will be initiated at either New or Full Moon. Spring tides occur then.

Neap Tides. The low tides will begin at times of the Moon's positions at C and G, when the Moon and the Sun will be pulling at right angles to each other, causing the lowest tides of the month—*neap* tides. Using this knowledge of the Moon's phases, you can even make some predictions concerning the tides, but first it is best to investigate the use of the *Tide Tables*.

Examples

TIDE TABLES, TABLE 2. It is often easier, and certainly more fun to learn through an example than it is to pursue pure theory. Hence, let us assume that you are interested in tides at Stonington, Fisher's Island Sound, on your 116-SC Tr Chart. Date is October 27, 1977.

If you pick up the *Tide Tables* (1977), East Coast of North and South America (See Appendix III for other regions), you will first turn to the index at the back and search for Fisher's Island Sound or

TYPICAL TIDE CURVES FOR UNITED STATES PORTS

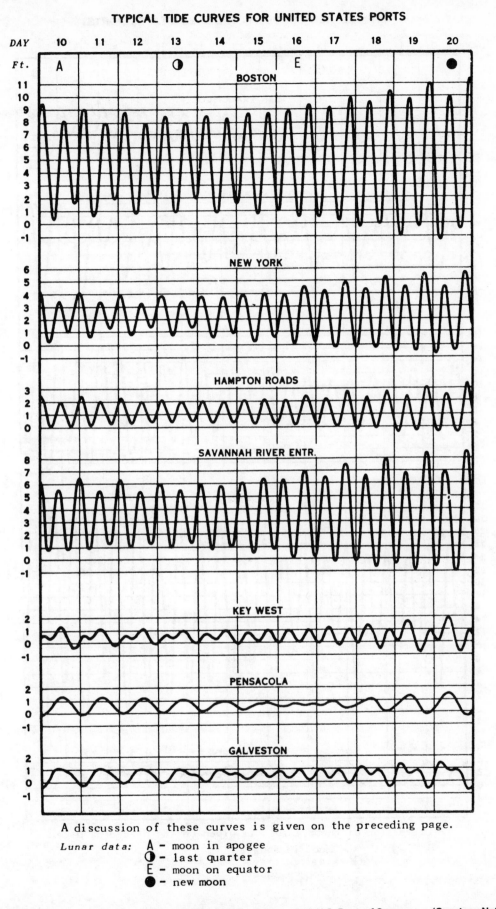

A discussion of these curves is given on the preceding page.

Lunar data: A – moon in apogee
◑ – last quarter
E – moon on equator
● – new moon

Fig. 4-4. Typical tide curves of East coast of USA, from *Tide Tables*, **1977, U.S. Dept. of Commerce. (Courtesy National Ocean Survey, NOAA.)**

TYPICAL TIDE CURVES FOR UNITED STATES PORTS

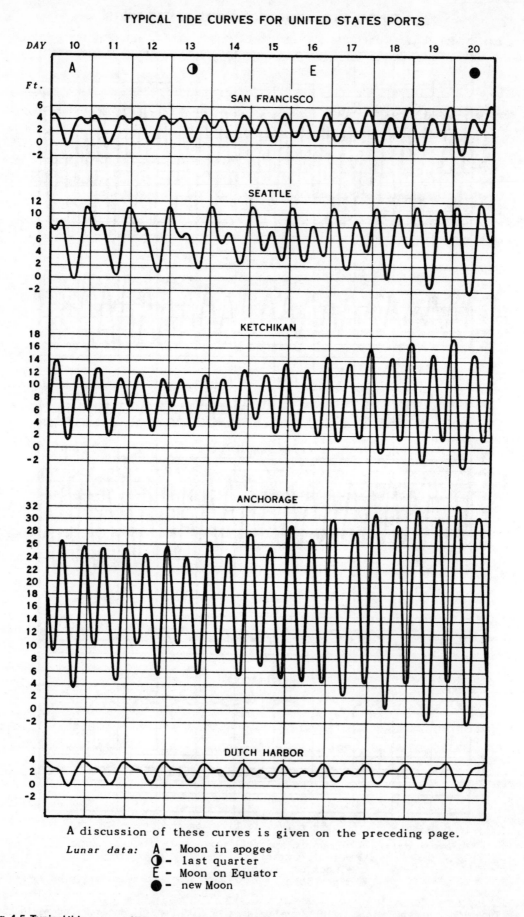

A discussion of these curves is given on the preceding page.

Lunar data: A – Moon in apogee
☽ – last quarter
E – Moon on Equator
● – new Moon

Fig. 4-5. Typical tide curves of West coast of USA, from *Tide Tables,* **1977, U.S. Dept. of Commerce. (Courtesy National Ocean Survey, NOAA.)**

Stonington, Conn., (See Index to Reference Stations, Table 4-1). In this case both names are in the index, with the number 1187 following. The number 1187 is your key number. You find it next in Table 2 of *Tide Tables*, p. 212, left margin. This Table 2 (Table 4-2 in this text) has the title *Tidal Differences and Other Constants*. First of all, it gives the Latitude and Longitude of Stonington, in case you had some trouble in finding Stonington on the chart, or in case you were uncertain of its identity. Second, you will note from the title at the top of the page that Table 2 gives time differences and height differences. In our example, for instance, you note that the reference station is "New London p. 44" (in boldface print in midst of "Differences" column), but before you leave this table, you want to list the differences. In other words, write in a column:

Stonington

$-0^h 33^m$ High Water Difference in Time
$-0^h 41^m$ Low Water Difference in Time
$+0.1$ feet High Water Difference in Height
0.0 feet Low Water Difference in Height

Note: The last three figures in the row for Stonington (in Table 4-2) are given to show the general situation. The mean range, for instance, is 2.7 feet, the spring range is 3.2 feet and the mean tide Level is 1.3 feet. The units are given always at the *top* of the page. Look there if you forget what they are. *For specific heights and times, however, you do not need the last three columns.*

TABLE 4-1
Index to Reference Stations
(from *Tide Tables*)

	NO.		NO.
STONE HARBOR, N. J.	1741	THREEMILE HARBOR ENTRANCE, N. Y.	1399
STONE ISLAND, MAINE	657	THROGS NECK, N. Y.	1263
STONINGTON, CONN.	1187	THUNDERBOLT, GA.	2727
STONINGTON, MAINE	743	TICORALAK ISLAND, LABRADOR	167
STONO RIVER, S. C.	2617 - 2621	TIDNISH HEAD, NEW BRUNSWICK	415
STONY BROOK, N. Y.	1355	TIERRA DEL FUEGO	3841 - 3847
STRAIT OF BELLE ISLE	181 - 185	TIGNISH, PRINCE EDWARD ISLAND	417
STRATFORD, CONN.	1231	TIMBALIER ISLAND, LA.	3247
STRATFORD SHOAL, N. Y.	1357	TIVERTON, NOVA SCOTIA	555
STRAWBERRY HILL, MASS.	985	TIVERTON, R. I.	1149
STUPART BAY	137	TIVOLI, N.Y.	1555
STURGEON ISLAND, MAINE	835	TODD CREEK, GA.	2809
STURGEON POINT, VA.	2403	TODDVILLE, S. C.	2537
SUCCONNESSET POINT, MASS.	1037	TOLCHESTER BEACH, MD.	2079
SUFFOLK, VA.	2373	TOM NEVERS HEAD, MASS.	1041
SULLIVAN, MAINE	705	TOMS RIVER (town), N. J.	1661
SULLIVANS ISLAND, S. C.	2569	TOOGOODOO CREEK, S. C.	2629
SUMMERHOUSE POINT, S. C.	2661	TORRESDALE, PA.	1885
SUMMERSIDE HARBOUR, PRINCE EDWARD I-	437	TOTTENVILLE, N. Y.	1599
SUMMIT BRIDGE, DEL.	1837	TOWN POINT, VA.	2369
SUNBURY, GA.	2749	TOWN POINT NECK, MD.	2087
SUNNYBANK, VA.	2259	TOWNSEND INLET, N. J.	1735
SUNNY ISLES, BISCAYNE CREEK, FLA.	2917	TRACADIE, NEW BRUNSWICK	403
SURINAM	3593 - 3597	TRAFTON ISLAND, MAINE	673
SURINAME RIVIER ENTRANCE * (164)	3595	TRAVIS POINT, VA.	2171
SUSQUEHANNA RIVER, MD.	2095, 2097	TRED AVON RIVER, MD.	2037, 2039
SUWANNEE RIVER, FLA.	3121	TRENTON, N. J.	1895
SWAIN CHANNEL, N. J.	1751	TREPASSEY HARBOUR, NEWFOUNDLAND	223
SWAN CREEK, MD.	2077	TRINIDAD	3577 - 3587
SWAN ISLANDS, WEST INDIES	3326	TRINITY BAY, TEX.	3283
SWEET HALL LANDING, VA.	2337	TROIS RIVIERES, QUEBEC	371
SWIM POINT, NOVA SCOTIA	547	TROPICAL HOMESITES LANDING, FLA.	3062
		TROUP CREEK, GA.	2785

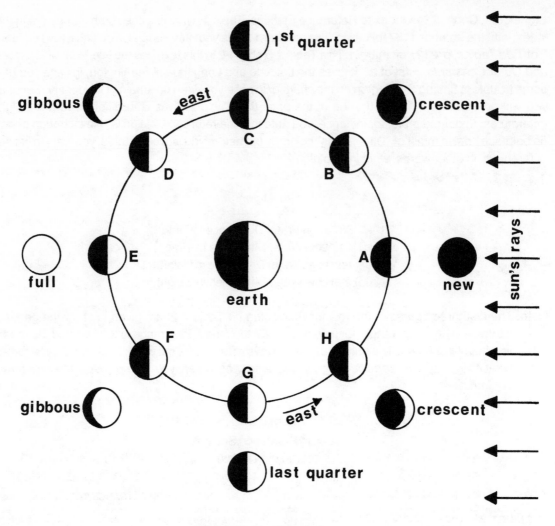

Fig. 4-6. Phases of the Moon.

TIDE TABLES, TABLE 1. Turn, next to the "Reference Station: New London, p. 44". This reference station is one of 48 reference stations (in Table 1 of *Tide Tables*) which present data for every day of the current year of the *Tables*. Times and heights at other stations are based upon these stations according to time and height differences given in Table 2. To return to your particular station, Stonington, you will find that you really want p. 47 (Table 4-3 in this text) because of your date October 27. If you inspect the tide figures for October 27 at New London, and if you write them in columns, you will have:

Form for Finding Tides

(1) New London		(2) Repeated from Above		(3) Answer for Stonington	
Time	Ht.	Time Diff.	Ht. Diff.	Time	Ht.
03^h09^m	0.1 ft.	-0^h41^m	0.0 ft.	2^h28^m	0.1 ft.
09 10	3.1	−0 33	+0.1	8 37	3.2
15 46	−0.1	−0 41	0.0	15 05	−0.1
21 38	2.4	−0 33	+0.1	21 05	2.5

TABLE 4-2
Tidal Differences and Other Constants
(from *Tide Tables*)

No.	PLACE	POSITION		DIFFERENCES				RANGES		Mean Tide Level
		Lat.	Long.	Time		Height		Mean	Spring	
				High water	Low water	High water	Low water			
		° ′	° ′	h. m.	h. m.	feet	feet	feet	feet	feet
	RHODE ISLAND and MASSACHUSETTS **Narragansett Bay — Continued** *Time meridian, 75°W.*	N.	W.	on NEWPORT, p.40						
1159	Fall River, Massachusetts------------	41 44	71 08	+0 31	+0 34	+0.9	0.0	4.4	5.5	2.2
1161	Taunton, Taunton River, Mass--------	41 53	71 06	+1 09	+2 26	-0.7	0.0	2.8	3.5	1.4
1163	Bristol-----------------------------	41 40	71 16	+0 10	0 00	+0.6	0.0	4.1	5.1	2.0
1165	Warren------------------------------	41 44	71 17	+0 21	+0 04	+1.1	0.0	4.6	5.7	2.3
1167	Nayatt Point------------------------	41 43	71 20	+0 12	+0 03	+1.1	0.0	4.6	5.7	2.3
1169	Providence--------------------------	41 48	71 24	+0 14	+0 05	+1.1	0.0	4.6	5.7	2.3
1171	Pawtucket, Seekonk River------------	41 52	71 23	+0 21	+0 14	+1.1	0.0	4.6	5.8	2.3
1173	East Greenwich---------------------	41 40	71 27	+0 16	+0 08	+0.5	0.0	4.0	5.0	2.0
1175	Wickford----------------------------	41 34	71 27	+0 12	+0 07	+0.3	0.0	3.8	4.7	1.9
1177	Narragansett Pier-------------------	41 25	71 27	-0 08	+0 16	-0.3	0.0	3.2	4.0	1.6
	RHODE ISLAND, Outer Coast									
1179	Point Judith Harbor of Refuge-------	41 22	71 29	-0 07	+0 22	-0.4	0.0	3.1	3.9	1.5
1181	Block Island (Great Salt Pond)------	41 11	71 35	+0 05	+0 12	-0.9	0.0	2.6	3.2	1.3
1183	Block Island (Old Harbor)-----------	41 10	71 33	-0 14	+0 17	-0.6	0.0	2.9	3.6	1.4
1185	Watch Hill Point--------------------	41 18	71 52	+0 44	+1 21	-0.9	0.0	2.6	3.2	1.3
				on NEW LONDON, p.44						
1186	Westerly, Pawcatuck River-----------	41 23	71 50	-0 27	+0 02	+0.1	0.0	2.7	3.2	1.3
	CONNECTICUT, Long Island Sound									
1187	Stonington, Fishers Island Sound----	41 20	71 54	-0 33	-0 41	+0.1	0.0	2.7	3.2	1.3
1189	Noank, Mystic River entrance--------	41 19	71 59	-0 23	-0 08	-0.3	0.0	2.3	2.7	1.2
1191	West Harbor, Fishers Island, N. Y---	41 16	72 00	-0 01	-0 06	-0.1	0.0	2.5	3.0	1.2
1192	Silver Eel Pond, Fishers I., N. Y---	41 15	72 02	-0 17	-0 04	-0.3	0.0	2.3	2.7	1.1
	Thames River									
1193	NEW LONDON, State Pier----------	41 22	72 06	Daily predictions				2.6	3.1	1.3
1195	Smith Cove entrance-------------	41 24	72 06	-0 01	+0 10	-0.1	0.0	2.5	3.0	1.2
1197	Norwich-------------------------	41 31	72 05	+0 09	+0 20	+0.4	0.0	3.0	3.6	1.5
1199	Millstone Point---------------------	41 18	72 10	+0 08	+0 01	+0.1	0.0	2.7	3.2	1.3
	Connecticut River									
1200	Saybrook Jetty------------------	41 16	72 21	+1 10	+0 45	+0.9	0.0	3.5	4.2	1.7
1201	Saybrook Point------------------	41 17	72 21	+1 10	+0 53	+0.6	0.0	3.2	3.8	1.6
1202	Lyme, highway bridge------------	41 19	72 21	+1 24	+1 10	+0.5	0.0	3.1	3.7	1.5
1203	Essex---------------------------	41 21	72 23	+1 38	+1 38	+0.4	0.0	3.0	3.6	1.5
1204	Hadlyme†------------------------	41 25	72 26	+2 18	+2 23	+0.1	0.0	2.7	3.2	1.3
1205	East Haddam--------------------	41 27	72 28	+2 41	+2 53	+0.3	0.0	2.9	3.5	1.4
1206	Haddam†-------------------------	41 29	72 30	+2 47	+3 08	-0.1	0.0	2.5	3.0	1.2
1207	Higganum Creek-----------------	41 30	72 33	+2 54	+3 25	0.0	0.0	2.6	3.1	1.3
1209	Portland†-----------------------	41 34	72 38	+3 50	+4 28	-0.4	0.0	2.2	2.6	1.1
1211	Rocky Hill†---------------------	41 39	72 38	+4 43	+5 44	-0.6	0.0	2.0	2.4	1.0
1213	Hartford†-----------------------	41 46	72 40	+5 29	+6 52	-0.7	0.0	1.9	2.3	1.0
				on BRIDGEPORT, p.48						
1214	Westbrook, Duck Island Roads--------	41 16	72 28	-0 23	-0 34	-2.6	0.0	4.1	4.7	2.0
1215	Duck Island-------------------------	41 15	72 29	-0 25	-0 37	-2.2	0.0	4.5	5.2	2.2
1217	Madison-----------------------------	41 16	72 36	-0 20	-0 32	-1.8	0.0	4.9	5.6	2.4
1219	Falkner Island----------------------	41 13	72 39	-0 13	-0 27	-1.3	0.0	5.4	6.2	2.7
1220	Sachem Head-------------------------	41 15	72 42	-0 10	-0 17	-1.3	0.0	5.4	6.2	2.7
1221	Money Island------------------------	41 15	72 45	-0 11	-0 25	-1.1	0.0	5.6	6.4	2.8
1223	Branford Harbor---------------------	41 16	72 49	-0 07	-0 20	-0.8	0.0	5.9	6.8	2.9
1225	New Haven Harbor entrance-----------	41 14	72 55	-0 08	-0 16	-0.5	0.0	6.2	7.1	3.1
1227	New Haven (city dock)---------------	41 18	72 55	+0 02	-0 03	-0.7	0.0	6.0	6.9	3.0
1229	Milford Harbor----------------------	41 13	73 03	-0 07	-0 12	-0.1	0.0	6.6	7.6	3.3
1231	Stratford, Housatonic River---------	41 11	73 07	+0 27	+0 59	-1.2	0.0	5.5	6.3	2.7
1233	Shelton, Housatonic River-----------	41 19	73 05	+1 36	+2 42	-1.7	0.0	5.0	5.8	2.5

†Tidal information applies only during low river stages.

TABLE 4-3
Times and Heights of High and Low Waters
New London, CT, 1977
(from *Tide Tables*)

OCTOBER

DAY	TIME h.m.	HT. ft.	DAY	TIME h.m.	HT. ft.
1 SA	0548	0.3	16 SU	0534	0.0
	1141	2.8		1129	3.4
	1828	0.2		1823	-0.3
2 SU	0011	2.3	17 M	0008	2.6
	0637	0.5		0632	0.1
	1226	2.7		1226	3.3
	1919	0.3		1922	-0.2
3 M	0101	2.2	18 TU	0111	2.5
	0731	0.6		0733	0.2
	1316	2.6		1330	3.1
	2012	0.4		2022	-0.1
4 TU	0156	2.1	19 W	0217	2.5
	0825	0.7		0840	0.3
	1410	2.5		1439	2.9
	2108	0.5		2124	0.0
5 W	0257	2.1	20 TH	0327	2.5
	0923	0.7		0948	0.3
	1509	2.4		1551	2.7
	2201	0.5		2224	0.0
6 TH	0354	2.1	21 F	0434	2.6
	1020	0.7		1052	0.2
	1606	2.4		1657	2.7
	2252	0.4		2321	0.1
7 F	0448	2.3	22 SA	0533	2.7
	1111	0.6		1151	0.1
	1700	2.5		1759	2.6
	2338	0.3			
8 SA	0535	2.4	23 SU	0012	0.0
	1201	0.4		0625	2.8
	1749	2.6		1245	0.0
				1852	2.6
9 SU	0022	0.2	24 M	0100	0.0
	0616	2.6		0712	3.0
	1246	0.2		1334	-0.1
	1834	2.7		1939	2.6
10 M	0106	0.1	25 TU	0144	0.0
	0657	2.9		0753	3.0
	1331	0.0		1421	-0.1
	1916	2.8		2020	2.5
11 TU	0145	0.0	26 W	0227	0.0
	0739	3.1		0832	3.1
	1415	-0.2		1503	-0.2
	2001	2.9		2058	2.5
12 W	0227	-0.1	27 TH	0309	0.1
	0820	3.3		0910	3.1
	1500	-0.3		1546	-0.1
	2045	2.9		2138	2.4
13 TH	0309	-0.2	28 F	0349	0.2
	0902	3.5		0948	3.0
	1546	-0.4		1628	-0.1
	2132	2.9		2216	2.4
14 F	0353	-0.2	29 SA	0433	0.3
	0948	3.6		1025	2.9
	1635	-0.5		1712	0.0
	2219	2.9		2256	2.3
15 SA	0440	-0.1	30 SU	0517	0.4
	1037	3.5		1104	2.8
	1727	-0.4		1758	0.1
	2312	2.8		2339	2.2
			31 M	0605	0.5
				1146	2.7
				1845	0.2

NOVEMBER

DAY	TIME h.m.	HT. ft.	DAY	TIME h.m.	HT. ft.
1 TU	0029	2.2	16 W	0055	2.6
	0656	0.6		0717	0.1
	1232	2.5		1314	2.9
	1935	0.3		1959	-0.2
2 W	0117	2.1	17 TH	0201	2.5
	0749	0.7		0823	0.1
	1322	2.4		1421	2.7
	2028	0.3		2100	-0.1
3 TH	0217	2.1	18 F	0309	2.5
	0847	0.7		0929	0.1
	1418	2.3		1532	2.5
	2120	0.4		2158	0.0
4 F	0313	2.2	19 SA	0414	2.6
	0944	0.7		1034	0.1
	1517	2.3		1638	2.4
	2210	0.3		2253	0.0
5 SA	0405	2.3	20 SU	0514	2.7
	1038	0.5		1133	0.0
	1615	2.3		1740	2.3
	2257	0.2		2346	0.0
6 SU	0455	2.5	21 M	0604	2.8
	1129	0.3		1228	0.0
	1709	2.4		1833	2.2
	2343	0.1			
7 M	0540	2.7	22 TU	0033	0.0
	1218	0.1		0651	2.9
	1759	2.5		1315	-0.1
				1918	2.2
8 TU	0027	0.0	23 W	0118	0.0
	0622	3.0		0731	2.9
	1305	-0.1		1400	-0.2
	1847	2.6		2000	2.2
9 W	0110	-0.1	24 TH	0200	0.1
	0707	3.3		0809	2.9
	1351	-0.4		1442	-0.2
	1936	2.7		2037	2.2
10 TH	0155	-0.2	25 F	0242	0.1
	0752	3.5		0845	2.9
	1438	-0.5		1523	-0.2
	2023	2.8		2114	2.2
11 F	0241	-0.3	26 SA	0324	0.1
	0838	3.6		0921	2.9
	1526	-0.7		1603	-0.2
	2112	2.8		2151	2.2
12 SA	0329	-0.3	27 SU	0405	0.2
	0927	3.7		0957	2.8
	1616	-0.7		1645	-0.1
	2203	2.8		2232	2.2
13 SU	0419	-0.3	28 M	0449	0.3
	1018	3.6		1035	2.7
	1709	-0.6		1728	-0.1
	2256	2.7		2312	2.2
14 M	0515	-0.2	29 TU	0534	0.4
	1112	3.4		1115	2.6
	1803	-0.5		1813	0.0
	2354	2.6		2357	2.1
15 TU	0613	-0.1	30 W	0624	0.5
	1211	3.2		1156	2.5
	1900	-0.4		1901	0.1

DECEMBER

DAY	TIME h.m.	HT. ft.	DAY	TIME h.m.	HT. ft.
1 TH	0045	2.1	16 F	0139	2.5
	0717	0.5		0802	-0.1
	1240	2.4		1357	2.4
	1949	0.1		2030	-0.3
2 F	0135	2.1	17 SA	0241	2.5
	0811	0.5		0907	0.0
	1332	2.2		1503	2.2
	2039	0.2		2126	-0.1
3 SA	0227	2.2	18 SU	0343	2.5
	0907	0.5		1010	0.0
	1431	2.2		1611	2.0
	2128	0.2		2221	-0.1
4 SU	0320	2.3	19 M	0445	2.6
	1005	0.4		1111	0.0
	1529	2.1		1711	1.9
	2216	0.1		2316	0.0
5 M	0412	2.5	20 TU	0539	2.6
	1058	0.2		1204	-0.1
	1629	2.1		1807	1.9
	2303	0.0			
6 TU	0503	2.7	21 W	0005	0.0
	1150	-0.1		0625	2.6
	1725	2.2		1252	-0.1
	2353	-0.1		1854	1.9
7 W	0550	3.0	22 TH	0051	0.0
	1239	-0.3		0707	2.7
	1818	2.3		1336	-0.2
				1936	1.9
8 TH	0039	-0.2	23 F	0135	0.0
	0639	3.2		0745	2.7
	1328	-0.5		1419	-0.2
	1912	2.4		2014	2.0
9 F	0129	-0.3	24 SA	0217	0.0
	0730	3.4		0821	2.7
	1417	-0.7		1459	-0.3
	2003	2.5		2051	2.0
10 SA	0218	-0.4	25 SU	0300	0.0
	0819	3.5		0856	2.7
	1507	-0.8		1539	-0.3
	2054	2.6		2129	2.1
11 SU	0309	-0.5	26 M	0342	0.0
	0910	3.5		0932	2.7
	1557	-0.9		1619	-0.3
	2147	2.7		2207	2.1
12 M	0403	-0.5	27 TU	0424	0.1
	1002	3.5		1010	2.6
	1649	-0.8		1701	-0.3
	2241	2.7		2246	2.1
13 TU	0459	-0.4	28 W	0509	0.1
	1057	3.3		1046	2.5
	1741	-0.7		1743	-0.2
	2337	2.6		2327	2.1
14 W	0557	-0.3	29 TH	0555	0.2
	1153	3.0		1126	2.4
	1837	-0.6		1826	-0.2
15 TH	0036	2.6	30 F	0011	2.2
	0658	-0.2		0643	0.2
	1253	2.7		1209	2.3
	1933	-0.4		1909	-0.1
			31 SA	0053	2.2
				0737	0.3
				1256	2.2
				1956	0.0

TIME MERIDIAN 75° W.   0000 IS MIDNIGHT.   1200 IS NOON.
HEIGHTS ARE RECKONED FROM THE DATUM OF SOUNDINGS ON CHARTS OF THE LOCALITY WHICH IS MEAN LOW WATER.

Ht. stands for the height of the tide at the time given, and it is understood, as confirmed in a footnote at the bottom of the page in *Tide Tables* that all heights here are reckoned from datum of soundings of locality, which is *Mean Low Water Here and in the Majority of Cases*. The minus sign before the height at 1546 indicates a height of 0.1 *below* mean low water. Your answer, in column (3), was obtained by applying the time and height differences at Stonington (2) to the times and heights at New London (1).

If you want the tides for the whole day, you can use the form in columns (1), (2) and (3). List in (1) the time and height values for the reference station (New London in this case). In (2) write the time and height differences, and in (3) apply the difference figures in each case to obtain the tides at your desired place (Stonington in this example).

A form is now presented, with blank spaces, ready to receive figures of your own in another example which you may want to use in a future cruise you may plan to take.

Table for Finding Times and Heights of Tides
(blank form)

Reference Station		Differences		Desired Figures	
Time	Ht.	Time	Ht.	Time	Ht.
h m	ft.	h m	ft.	h m	ft.

A few other factors (also stated in *Tide Tables*) should be remembered in addition to those given. Changes in winds and barometric conditions cause variations in sea level from day to day. In general, with onshore winds or a low barometer, the heights of both the high and low waters will be higher than predicted, while the opposite is true with offshore winds or a high barometer. This is very pronounced along the Gulf Coast. When the North wind blows in Texas, it may seem, along the Northern Gulf Coast, as though most of the water had run out of the Gulf of Mexico!

A further cause for variation in the ranges of a semidiurnal tide is the varying distance of the Moon from Earth. When closest to the Earth, the Moon is said to be *at perigee*, and when farthest from the Earth, it is *at apogee*. These variations are, of course, included in daily predictions given in the *Tide Tables*, but it is well to have some understanding of the reasons. In addition, occasionally there are destructive tidal waves which cannot be predicted. No one would have predicted that people would drown in front of the railroad station in Providence during the 1938 New England hurricane. The tides at river entrances also create numerous special problems. Discharge by rivers cannot be predicted, and so a mariner should never put too much trust in tide predictions at the entrance to a powerful river. In general, since the basic figures at reference stations are mean or average figures, precision in tide figures is not the precision obtained in sextant-sight measures, and although *Tide Tables* figures are given to tenths of a foot, an error of 1/2 foot or more might easily occur. The mariner must always consider the possibility of some error in the *Tide Tables* figures given.

To continue with the tide example, suppose that at the same place, Stonington, on October 27, you wanted the height of the tide at one special time -07^h40^m. The easiest way to find the answer follows:

TIDE TABLES, TABLE 3. A third table (Table 3, p. 247) in *Tide Tables* (Table 4-4 in this text) really gives you the directions for interpolating between times for which you already have figures. First, your

TABLE 4-4
Height of Tide At Any Time—For Interpolation
(from *Tide Tables*)

Time from the nearest high water or low water

Duration of rise or fall, see footnote

h. m.	h. m.	h. m.	h. m.	h. m.	h. m.	h. m.	h. m.	h. m.	h. m.	h. m.	h. m.	h. m.	h. m.	h. m.	h. m.
4 00	0 08	0 16	0 24	0 32	0 40	0 48	0 56	1 04	1 12	1 20	1 28	1 36	1 44	1 52	2 00
4 20	0 09	0 17	0 26	0 35	0 43	0 52	1 01	1 09	1 18	1 27	1 35	1 44	1 53	2 01	2 10
4 40	0 09	0 19	0 28	0 37	0 47	0 56	1 05	1 15	1 24	1 33	1 43	1 52	2 01	2 11	2 20
5 00	0 10	0 20	0 30	0 40	0 50	1 00	1 10	1 20	1 30	1 40	1 50	2 00	2 10	2 20	2 30
5 20	0 11	0 21	0 32	0 43	0 53	1 04	1 15	1 25	1 36	1 47	1 57	2 08	2 19	2 29	2 40
5 40	0 11	0 23	0 34	0 45	0 57	1 08	1 19	1 31	1 42	1 53	2 05	2 16	2 27	2 39	2 50
6 00	0 12	0 24	0 36	0 48	1 00	1 12	1 24	1 36	1 48	2 00	2 12	2 24	2 36	2 48	3 00
6 20	0 13	0 25	0 38	0 51	1 03	1 16	1 29	1 41	1 54	2 07	2 19	2 32	2 45	2 57	3 10
6 40	0 13	0 27	0 40	0 53	1 07	1 20	1 33	1 47	2 00	2 13	2 27	2 40	2 53	3 07	3 20
7 00	0 14	0 28	0 42	0 56	1 10	1 24	1 38	1 52	2 06	2 20	2 34	2 48	3 02	3 16	3 30
7 20	0 15	0 29	0 44	0 59	1 13	1 28	1 43	1 57	2 12	2 27	2 41	2 56	3 11	3 25	3 40
7 40	0 15	0 31	0 46	1 01	1 17	1 32	1 47	2 03	2 18	2 33	2 49	3 04	3 19	3 35	3 50
8 00	0 16	0 32	0 48	1 04	1 20	1 36	1 52	2 08	2 24	2 40	2 56	3 12	3 28	3 44	4 00
8 20	0 17	0 33	0 50	1 07	1 23	1 40	1 57	2 13	2 30	2 47	3 03	3 20	3 37	3 53	4 10
8 40	0 17	0 35	0 52	1 09	1 27	1 44	2 01	2 19	2 36	2 53	3 11	3 28	3 45	4 03	4 20
9 00	0 18	0 36	0 54	1 12	1 30	1 48	2 06	2 24	2 42	3 00	3 18	3 36	3 54	4 12	4 30
9 20	0 19	0 37	0 56	1 15	1 33	1 52	2 11	2 29	2 48	3 07	3 25	3 44	4 03	4 21	4 40
9 40	0 19	0 39	0 58	1 17	1 37	1 56	2 15	2 35	2 54	3 13	3 33	3 52	4 11	4 31	4 50
10 00	0 20	0 40	1 00	1 20	1 40	2 00	2 20	2 40	3 00	3 20	3 40	4 00	4 20	4 40	5 00
10 20	0 21	0 41	1 02	1 23	1 43	2 04	2 25	2 45	3 06	3 27	3 47	4 08	4 29	4 49	5 10
10 40	0 21	0 43	1 04	1 25	1 47	2 08	2 29	2 51	3 12	3 33	3 55	4 16	4 37	4 59	5 20

Correction to height

Range of tide, see footnote

Ft.	Ft.	Ft.	Ft.	Ft.	Ft.	Ft.	Ft.	Ft.	Ft.	Ft.	Ft.	Ft.	Ft.	Ft.	Ft.
0.5	0.0	0.0	0.0	0.0	0.0	0.0	0.1	0.1	0.1	0.1	0.1	0.2	0.2	0.2	0.2
1.0	0.0	0.0	0.0	0.0	0.1	0.1	0.1	0.2	0.2	0.2	0.3	0.3	0.4	0.4	0.5
1.5	0.0	0.0	0.0	0.1	0.1	0.1	0.2	0.2	0.3	0.4	0.4	0.5	0.6	0.7	0.8
2.0	0.0	0.0	0.0	0.1	0.1	0.2	0.3	0.3	0.4	0.5	0.6	0.7	0.8	0.9	1.0
2.5	0.0	0.0	0.1	0.1	0.2	0.2	0.3	0.4	0.5	0.6	0.7	0.9	1.0	1.1	1.2
3.0	0.0	0.0	0.1	0.1	0.2	0.3	0.4	0.5	0.6	0.8	0.9	1.0	1.2	1.3	1.5
3.5	0.0	0.0	0.1	0.2	0.2	0.3	0.4	0.6	0.7	0.9	1.0	1.2	1.4	1.6	1.8
4.0	0.0	0.0	0.1	0.2	0.3	0.4	0.5	0.7	0.8	1.0	1.2	1.4	1.6	1.8	2.0
4.5	0.0	0.0	0.1	0.2	0.3	0.4	0.6	0.7	0.9	1.1	1.3	1.6	1.8	2.0	2.2
5.0	0.0	0.1	0.1	0.2	0.3	0.5	0.6	0.8	1.0	1.2	1.5	1.7	2.0	2.2	2.5
5.5	0.0	0.1	0.1	0.2	0.4	0.5	0.7	0.9	1.1	1.4	1.6	1.9	2.2	2.5	2.8
6.0	0.0	0.1	0.1	0.3	0.4	0.6	0.8	1.0	1.2	1.5	1.8	2.1	2.4	2.7	3.0
6.5	0.0	0.1	0.2	0.3	0.4	0.6	0.8	1.1	1.3	1.6	1.9	2.2	2.6	2.9	3.2
7.0	0.0	0.1	0.2	0.3	0.5	0.7	0.9	1.2	1.4	1.8	2.1	2.4	2.8	3.1	3.5
7.5	0.0	0.1	0.2	0.3	0.5	0.7	1.0	1.2	1.5	1.9	2.2	2.6	3.0	3.4	3.8
8.0	0.0	0.1	0.2	0.3	0.5	0.8	1.0	1.3	1.6	2.0	2.4	2.8	3.2	3.6	4.0
8.5	0.0	0.1	0.2	0.4	0.6	0.8	1.1	1.4	1.8	2.1	2.5	2.9	3.4	3.8	4.2
9.0	0.0	0.1	0.2	0.4	0.6	0.9	1.2	1.5	1.9	2.2	2.7	3.1	3.6	4.0	4.5
9.5	0.0	0.1	0.2	0.4	0.6	0.9	1.2	1.6	2.0	2.4	2.8	3.3	3.8	4.3	4.8
10.0	0.0	0.1	0.2	0.4	0.7	1.0	1.3	1.7	2.1	2.5	3.0	3.5	4.0	4.5	5.0
10.5	0.0	0.1	0.3	0.5	0.7	1.0	1.3	1.7	2.2	2.6	3.1	3.6	4.2	4.7	5.2
11.0	0.0	0.1	0.3	0.5	0.7	1.1	1.4	1.8	2.3	2.8	3.3	3.8	4.4	4.9	5.5
11.5	0.0	0.1	0.3	0.5	0.8	1.1	1.5	1.9	2.4	2.9	3.4	4.0	4.6	5.1	5.8
12.0	0.0	0.1	0.3	0.5	0.8	1.1	1.5	2.0	2.5	3.0	3.6	4.1	4.8	5.4	6.0
12.5	0.0	0.1	0.3	0.5	0.8	1.2	1.6	2.1	2.6	3.1	3.7	4.3	5.0	5.6	6.2
13.0	0.0	0.1	0.3	0.6	0.9	1.2	1.7	2.2	2.7	3.2	3.9	4.5	5.1	5.8	6.5
13.5	0.0	0.1	0.3	0.6	0.9	1.3	1.7	2.2	2.8	3.4	4.0	4.7	5.3	6.0	6.8
14.0	0.0	0.2	0.3	0.6	0.9	1.3	1.8	2.3	2.9	3.5	4.2	4.8	5.5	6.3	7.0
14.5	0.0	0.2	0.4	0.6	1.0	1.4	1.9	2.4	3.0	3.6	4.3	5.0	5.7	6.5	7.2
15.0	0.0	0.2	0.4	0.6	1.0	1.4	1.9	2.5	3.1	3.8	4.4	5.2	5.9	6.7	7.5
15.5	0.0	0.2	0.4	0.7	1.0	1.5	2.0	2.6	3.2	3.9	4.6	5.4	6.1	6.9	7.8
16.0	0.0	0.2	0.4	0.7	1.1	1.5	2.1	2.6	3.3	4.0	4.7	5.5	6.3	7.2	8.0
16.5	0.0	0.2	0.4	0.7	1.1	1.6	2.1	2.7	3.4	4.1	4.9	5.7	6.5	7.4	8.2
17.0	0.0	0.2	0.4	0.7	1.1	1.6	2.2	2.8	3.5	4.2	5.0	5.9	6.7	7.6	8.5
17.5	0.0	0.2	0.4	0.8	1.2	1.7	2.2	2.9	3.6	4.4	5.2	6.0	6.9	7.8	8.8
18.0	0.0	0.2	0.4	0.8	1.2	1.7	2.3	3.0	3.7	4.5	5.3	6.2	7.1	8.1	9.0
18.5	0.1	0.2	0.5	0.8	1.2	1.8	2.4	3.1	3.8	4.6	5.5	6.4	7.3	8.3	9.2
19.0	0.1	0.2	0.5	0.8	1.3	1.8	2.4	3.1	3.9	4.8	5.6	6.6	7.5	8.5	9.5
19.5	0.1	0.2	0.5	0.8	1.3	1.9	2.5	3.2	4.0	4.9	5.8	6.7	7.7	8.7	9.8
20.0	0.1	0.2	0.5	0.9	1.3	1.9	2.6	3.3	4.1	5.0	5.9	6.9	7.9	9.0	10.0

Obtain from the predictions the high water and low water, one of which is before and the other after the time for which the height is required. The difference between the times of occurrence of these tides is the duration of rise or fall, and the difference between their heights is the range of tide for the above table. Find the difference between the nearest high or low water and the time for which the height is required.

Enter the table with the duration of rise or fall, printed in heavy-faced type, which most nearly agrees with the actual value, and on that horizontal line find the time from the nearest high or low water which agrees most nearly with the corresponding actual difference. The correction sought is in the column directly below, on the line with the range of tide.

When the nearest tide is high water, subtract the correction.

When the nearest tide is low water, add the correction.

desired time 07^h40^m lies between 2^h28^m and 8^h37^m and duration of rise = 6^h09^m. As indicated in the table, you want, secondly, the time from the nearest high water or low water. In this case you want the difference between 8^h37^m and 7^h40^m, which is 0^h57^m. The water is rising, since 07^h40^m comes during a rise of the water (8^h37^m is at high tide). Hence, you enter the row nearest 06^h09^m (the 06^h00^m row) and move to the right in this row until you come to the time nearest 0^h57^m. This will be the time 1^h00^m. Hold your finger (or your eye) on 1^h00^m and move down (with finger or eye) until you come to the figures nearest the range in value. You will remember that the range is the difference between the heights of water at 2^h28^m and 8^h37^m, or the difference between 0.1 and 3.2. The range here is 3.1 feet, but you should note one point for future cases. If the low water had been negative in sign (*below* mean low water), you would have *added* the above two heights instead of subtracting as you did before. To return to the present case, your finger (or eye) will stop at the "correction" 0.2 on the row with 3.0 for range. Since a high occurs at 8^h37^m, the height will be lower at 07^h40^m, and so the correction of 0.2 ft. will be subtracted from 3.2 ft. and your answer is 3.2-0.2 or 3.0 feet.

If you do not like to use Table 3 of *Tide Tables* and interpolate for the height of the tide at any time, you might prefer to draw a tide curve for the day and just read the height of the tide at your desired time.

Tide Curve and One-Quarter, One-Tenth Rule. You can easily draw the curve by using the One-Quarter, One-Tenth Rule and construct this tide curve for Stonington, since you already have most of the figures copied from the *Tide Tables*, Tables 2 and 3. You need, in addition, a sheet of graph paper to help in plotting. Use a scale similar to the one in Fig. 4-7 where one large square equals three hours. Plot the times of high and low tide horizontally, against the corresponding heights vertically. The first point, in the Stonington tide curve, for example, is obtained by finding 2^h28^m on the horizontal line, and going above this point to the height of 0.1 feet. (Remember you have already found these figures from *Tide Tables,* as shown in our Form for Finding Tides.) These significant points, at the two lows and the two highs for the day, are designated by small open circles in Fig. 4-7. The next step is to draw straight lines between any two consecutive points, as shown. They will always be between a high and a low, or between a low and a high for a normal curve. Quarter these lines by plotting the midpoints of the lines and then by bisecting the halves. You can do this quickly with dividers by making the divisions first by eye, and then checking with the dividers, and adjusting the points a little if necessary.

The first line in Fig. 4-7 has been quartered into the four segments, PP_1, P_1P_2, P_2P_3, and P_3P_4. The One-Quarter, One-Tenth Rule tells you to take *one-tenth* of the range. The range in this case for the Stonington curve, was 3.1 feet between the first low and high. One-tenth of 3.1 is 0.3 (never carry tide figures further than to tenths). At P_1, on a vertical line there (which you draw) lay off 0.3 feet *down*, and lay off the same 0.3 feet at the point P_3 except that this segment should go *up* on the vertical line (*up* around highs and *down* around lows). This part of your tide curve goes exactly through P, P_2, and P_4, but you also draw it through the *ends* of the vertical lines constructed, as seen in Fig. 4-7. This process is repeated between the high at P_4 and the next low, as well as between the last high and low of the day. A tide curve for the day is quite useful in case you are staying near the same position for most of the day, or in case you are returning to the same region later in the day.

Predicting Tides. Occasionally you might want to predict tides yourself in case you had lost your *Tide Tables* or forgotten to bring them. You can do this fairly well if you know the times of the phases of the Moon. These are often given on calendars or almost surely in almanacs, even in the daily newspapers for the day. If the Moon is New, for instance, it will cross the upper branch of your meridian around noon or around 12^h00^m standard time, which people carry on their watches as a rule. Since the Moon is as nearly overhead as it can be for the day, it will initiate a *high tide*, and the more exact time will depend upon the *high water interval*, as it is called.

High Water Interval. By definition, the *high water interval is the time between the passage of the*

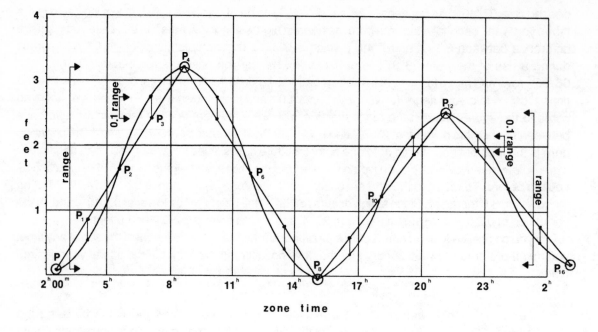

Fig. 4-7. Tide curve for Stonington, Oct. 27, 1977.

Moon across the meridian and the actual time of the next high tide. This interval has the following values for a few places:

High Water Intervals
(approximate)

Halifax	7^h37^m	New London	9^h26^m
Portland	11 10	New York	8 15
Boston	11 17	Savannah	7 56
Newport	7 45	Charleston	7 25

You could have fun finding these figures for yourself at any place if you had the time to do some measuring of the water's height to ascertain when it was highest. The time since the Moon's passage across your meridian would give you the high water interval.

Suppose the Moon crossed the meridian at Stonington at 23^h45^m, which you might have observed. If you knew that the high water interval was 8^h50^m, the time of the next high tide would be 8^h35^m the next day. Even without any previous knowledge of the Moon's phases, if you can see the Moon, you yourself can tell whether it is New or Full. If it is New, it crosses your upper meridian around noon or 12^h00^m, because it is then in line with the Sun, which crosses around that time. (Do not worry about minutes in this rough prediction.) If you know the high water interval, you would just add this value to 12^h to find a rough prediction of the time of the next high tide. For a normal tide, then, in 6^h13^m you would have a low tide, and in another 6^h13^m you would have another high tide. In still another 6^h13^m you would have the last low tide of the day. The next day, the Moon would rise about 50^m later, or it would be behind, by about 50^m, in the same tidal events for that day. In this way, you can predict ahead to some extent, for a rough idea of when to expect high and low tides, if only you know the high water interval, which you can measure and obtain yourself, or which you should ascertain before your departure on a cruise if there is any chance of your needing this information.

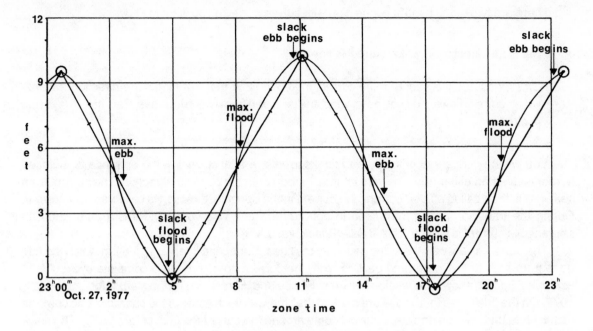

Fig. 4-8. Tides and currents in Boston Harbor, Oct. 27, 1977.

CAPT. LEWIS AND A HIGH TIDE. As a final word on predicting the tides, if the Moon should be Full, it is opposite the Sun (look again at Fig. 4-6), and hence, when it crosses the upper meridian in this situation, it will be approximately midnight. You can then figure from midnight (24^h00^m) instead of from Noon (12^h00^m). Just before the turn of the century, according to G. R. Newell in *SOS North Pacific*, young Capt. Lewis certainly used his knowledge of tides to extricate himself and his steamboat VICTORIAN, when the latter was thoroughly impaled on a jagged pinnacle peak off the sheer mountain coast of Northern British Columbia. Much against Capt. Lewis' better judgment he had followed an older captain close to the shore in order to fill the steamer's tanks with water from the waterfalls which abound in that region. The older captain had been successful in obtaining the water, but as the tide was ebbing, Capt. Lewis found himself in a predicament. The pinnacle peak pierced the VICTORIAN with the hull slipping down until the rock protruded five feet above the level of the lower deck of the steamer. (At low tide in that location the water can fall by 20 feet or more.) While Capt. Lewis was waiting for help to come, he used some timbers to build a cofferdam around the rock embedded in the hull. He had his *Tide Tables* with him, and saw from them that an unusually high tide was due. He plugged up the holes he had made at low tide in order to get all the water out. The next predicted high tide saved his VICTORIAN and the lives of Capt. Lewis and the crew who had remained with him.

This true story may sound like ancient history to present-day mariners, but the fact remains that even today, in the age of supertankers and the most advanced electronics, similar disasters occur again and again, as history tends to repeat itself.

CURRENTS

Tidal. Closely related to the tides, tidal currents in fact follow the tides, and so they too result indirectly from the pull of the Moon and the Sun on the Earth. They are perhaps even more important to the mariner than the tides, because if a mariner ignores the currents, sooner or later he will find himself far from his desired destination. He cannot afford to ignore the currents.

There are two terms used in connection with currents, which you want to know:

(1) *Set* is the direction in which current is flowing.

(2) *Drift* measures the speed of the current in knots. Note that Set marks the direction *towards* which current flows, and not, as for wind, the direction from which it comes. Sets are always *true* in direction.

You will be concerned primarily with tidal currents. A tidal current at the entrance to a closed harbor is directed either from seaward into the harbor, or in the opposite direction. The current from seaward is then called a *flood* current; the current in the opposite direction is called an *ebb* current. During the transition period from flood to ebb current, and vice versa, there is a time when no appreciable current is setting. This is called *slack water*.

The currents vary with the same period as the tides. During the interval 12^h25^m in which the tide goes from high to low water and back to high, the current goes through a complete cycle. As an example, Fig. 4-8 shows the relation between the tide and currents in Boston Harbor for October 27, 1977. On the tide curve for the day are marked the times at which some of the characteristic currents occur. Note that low tide and slack current come around the same time (just before 0500). The slack current is more realistically called *slack; flood begins.* The flood continues, increasing in velocity until the time of maximum velocity at 0812. After maximum flood, the current is still flooding, but slowing down in velocity until the *slack; ebb begins*, around the time of high water, at 1109. An ebb is now in process, which increases in velocity until maximum ebb at 1500. The ebb current then decreases in velocity until the next *slack; flood begins* at 1718, and so on.

For both tides and currents, variety is caused by many factors, such as winds, the nature of the bottom where the tide is occurring, the nature of the land surrounding the tidal basin and proximity of rivers. If the tidal basin is *large* and the entrance is *narrow*, the tidal variation will be very much less than that in the open ocean. For New York Harbor, for instance (narrow entrance, large basin), the turning of the current occurs about an hour later, relative to the tide curve, than for Boston Harbor (wide entrance, small basin). In exposed points on shore, the relation between tides and currents follows generally the same pattern as for Boston Harbor.

Before you deal with the current and find your heading in order to make good a certain course, you will want to know the *set* and *drift* of the current if this is possible. In addition to *Tide Tables*, *Tidal Current Tables* are published each year for many positions along the coasts of the USA. They come from the U.S. Department of Commerce, National Oceanic and Atmospheric Administration, National Ocean Survey. They are similar in style to *Tide Tables*.

There are three tables in one volume. The first gives the set and drift of the current for each day of the year at the reference stations. The second table (Table 2) gives Time Differences and Velocity Ratios. As with the tides, you will need time differences again between the current events at the reference station and the desired place, and also you need the set and drift of the current at the desired place as compared with the set and drift at the reference station.

Let us study the currents at the same place, where you investigated the tides, Stonington, Fishers Island Sound, on the same day, October 27, 1977.

Pick up the *Tidal Current Tables, Atlantic Coast of North America*. This time, if you look in the index first, you will not find Stonington, but you will see Fishers Island Sound, with numbers 1605-1650, given in the index at the end. Again you will not find the name Stonington, but the Latitude and Longitude of Edwards Pt.—Sandy Pt. (between), 41°20'N, 71°54'W, agree with the position given in *Tide Tables* for tide at this point, and so if we are on the East side of Stonington Pt., all is well. It will help to arrange the information from the *Tidal Current Tables* in a simple array, just as you did with the tides—(See Table 2, Current Differences and Other Constants in *Tidal Current Tables*—Table 4-5 in this text):

TABLE 4-5
Current Differences and Other Constants
(from *Tidal Current Tables*)

No.	PLACE	POSITION		TIME DIF-FERENCES		VELOCITY RATIOS		MAXIMUM CURRENTS			
								Flood		Ebb	
		Lat.	Long.	Slack water	Maxi-mum current	Maxi-mum flood	Maxi-mum ebb	Direc-tion (true)	Aver-age veloc-ity	Direc-tion (true)	Aver-age veloc-ity
		° ′	° ′	h. m.	h. m.			deg.	knots	deg.	knots
	GARDINERS BAY, etc.—Continued	N.	W.		on THE RACE, p.34						
	Time meridian, 75°W.										
1587	Jennings Point, 0.2 mile NNW. of	41 04	72 22	+0 25	+0 05	0.6	0.4	290	1.6	055	1.5
1590	Cedar Point, 0.2 mile west of	41 02	72 16	0 00	-0 30	0.6	0.5	195	1.8	005	1.6
1592	North Haven Peninsula, north of	41 02	72 19	+0 15	-0 30	0.8	0.6	230	2.4	035	2.1
1593	Paradise Point, 0.4 mile east of	41 03	72 23	+0 25	+0 05	0.5	0.4	145	1.5	345	1.5
1595	Little Peconic Bay entrance	41 02	72 23	+0 35	+0 10	0.6	0.4	240	1.6	015	1.5
1600	Robins Island, 0.5 mile south of	40 57	72 27	+0 35	+0 10	0.6	0.2	245	1.7	065	0.6
	FISHERS ISLAND SOUND										
1605	Edwards Pt.-Sandy Pt. (between)	41 20	71 54	-2 30	(¹)	0.4	(¹)	035	1.1	235	-----
1610	Napatree Point, 0.7 mile SW. of	41 18	71 54	-0 55	-1 10	0.6	0.6	285	1.7	115	2.2
1620	Little Narragansett Bay entrance	41 20	71 53	-2 00	-2 15	0.4	0.3	090	1.3	270	1.3
1625	Avondale, Pawcatuck River	41 20	71 51	-2 05	(²)	0.2	(²)	060	0.6	255	-----
1630	Ram Island Reef, south of	41 18	71 58	-0 45	-0 50	0.4	0.4	255	1.3	090	1.6
1635	Noank	41 19	71 59	(³)	(³)	0.2	(³)	340	0.5	-----	-----
1640	Mystic, Highway Bridge, Mystic River	41 21	71 58	-2 05	(⁴)	0.2	(⁴)	040	0.5	230	-----
1645	Clay Point, 1.3 miles NNE. of	41 18	71 58	-0 40	-1 00	0.5	0.5	265	1.4	035	1.9
1650	North Hill Pt., 1.1 miles NNW. of	41 18	72 02	(⁵)	(⁵)	0.5	0.4	260	1.5	080	1.2
	LONG ISLAND SOUND										
	The Race										
1655	Race Point, 0.4 mile SW. of	41 15	72 03	-0 35	-0 40	0.9	1.0	290	2.6	135	3.5
1660	THE RACE, near Valiant Rock	41 14	72 04	Daily predictions				295	2.9	100	3.5
1665	0.5 mile NE. of Little Gull Island	41 13	72 06	-0 20	-0 20	1.0	0.7	000	3.3	105	3.1
1670	Little Gull I., 1.1 mi. ENE. of	41 13	72 05	-0 05	-0 30	1.4	1.3	300	4.0	130	4.7
1675	Great Gull Island, 0.7 mile WSW. of	41 12	72 08	-0 40	(⁶)	0.9	0.9	300	2.6	135	3.2
1680	Plum Gut	41 10	72 13	-1 10	-1 50	1.2	1.2	325	3.5	125	4.3
1685	Eastern Point, 1.5 miles south of	41 18	72 05	-1 30	-1 50	0.1	0.1	250	0.4	055	0.4
1690	New London Harbor entrance	41 19	72 05	-1 45	-1 35	0.1	0.1	350	0.1	210	0.2
	Thames River										
1695	Winthrop Point	41 22	72 05	-1 05	(⁷)	0.1	(⁷)	010	0.4	185	-----
1700	Off Smith Cove	41 24	72 05	-1 25	(⁸)	0.2	(⁸)	020	0.7	200	-----
1705	Off Stoddard Hill	41 28	72 04	-1 00	(⁹)	0.2	(⁹)	330	0.7	165	-----
1710	Lower Coal Dock	41 31	72 05	*Current too weak and variable to be predicted.*							

¹A double ebb occurs at this station (see note ᵃ). Time differences: first ebb, -3ʰ 40ᵐ; minimum ebb, -1ʰ 30ᵐ; second ebb, -0ʰ 05ᵐ; maximum flood, -3ʰ 15ᵐ. Velocity ratio for first ebb is 0.3; minimum ebb, 0.1; second ebb, 0.2.

²A double ebb occurs at this station (see note ᵃ). Time differences: first ebb, -3ʰ 40ᵐ; minimum ebb, -1ʰ 10ᵐ; second ebb, +0ʰ 05ᵐ; maximum flood, -2ʰ 40ᵐ. Velocity ratio for first ebb is 0.2; second ebb, 0.1. Minimum ebb is extremely weak, possibly flooding for a short period.

³Flood begins, -1ʰ 35ᵐ; ebb begins, -4ʰ 10ᵐ. A double ebb occurs at this station (see note ᵃ). Time differences: first ebb, -4ʰ 30ᵐ; minimum ebb, -1ʰ 25ᵐ; second ebb, +0ʰ 20ᵐ; maximum flood, -3ʰ 15ᵐ Velocity ratio for first ebb is 0.1; second ebb, 0.1. Minimum ebb is extremely weak, possibly flooding for a short period.

⁴A double ebb occurs at this station (see note ᵃ). Time differences: first ebb, -3ʰ 40ᵐ; minimum ebb, -1ʰ 40ᵐ; second ebb, -0ʰ 20ᵐ; maximum flood, -2ʰ 50ᵐ. Velocity ratio for first ebb is 0.1; second ebb, 0.1. Minimum ebb is weak.

⁵Flood begins, -1ʰ 05ᵐ; maximum flood, -0ʰ 25ᵐ; ebb begins, -0ʰ 20ᵐ; maximum ebb, -1ʰ 35ᵐ.

⁶Maximum flood, -0ʰ 35ᵐ; maximum ebb, -1ʰ 40ᵐ.

⁷A double ebb occurs at this station (see note ᵃ). Time differences: first ebb, -2ʰ 35ᵐ; minimum ebb, -1ʰ 10ᵐ; second ebb, +0ʰ 05ᵐ; maximum flood, -2ʰ 00ᵐ. Velocity ratio for first ebb is 0.1; second ebb, 0.1. Minimum ebb is weak.

⁸A double ebb occurs at this station (see note ᵃ). Time differences: first ebb, -1ʰ 55ᵐ; minimum ebb, -1ʰ 30ᵐ; second ebb, +0ʰ 15ᵐ; maximum flood, -2ʰ 20ᵐ. Velocity ratio for first ebb is 0.2; minimum ebb, 0.1; second ebb, 0.2.

⁹A double ebb occurs at this station (see note ᵃ). Time differences: first ebb, -2ʰ 30ᵐ; minimum ebb, -1ʰ 10ᵐ; second ebb, +0ʰ 25ᵐ; maximum flood, -2ʰ 25ᵐ. Velocity ratio for first ebb is 0.1; second ebb, 0.2. Minimum ebb is weak.

ᵃA double ebb occurs at this station. A similar slackening occurs during the ebb period as is described for the flood period in "footnote ᵃ, page 140". Differences and ratios given for first, minimum, and second ebbs should be applied to the time and velocity of maximum ebb at the reference station. Other values should be applied to the corresponding phases at the reference station.

TABLE 4-6
The Race, Long Island Sound, 1977
F - Flood, Dir. 295°True—E - Ebb, Dir. 100°True
(from *Tidal Current Tables*)

SEPTEMBER

DAY	SLACK WATER TIME H.M.	MAXIMUM CURRENT TIME H.M.	VEL. KNOTS	DAY	SLACK WATER TIME H.M.	MAXIMUM CURRENT TIME H.M.	VEL. KNOTS
1 TH	0122	0445	3.6E	16 F	0052	0408	3.8E
	0754	1038	3.2F		0713	1010	3.7F
	1344	1710	3.6E		1313	1635	4.1E
	2026	2301	2.8F		1948	2238	3.5F
2 F	0206	0528	3.2F	17 SA	0141	0459	3.7E
	0838	1120	2.8F		0801	1058	3.6F
	1428	1757	3.3E		1403	1727	4.0E
	2116	2347	2.5F		2042	2331	3.4F
3 SA	0253	0619	2.8E	18 SU	0235	0552	3.5E
	0926	1205	2.5F		0856	1153	3.4F
	1514	1847	3.0E		1458	1828	3.8E
	2209				2142		
4 SU		0038	2.2F	19 M		0027	3.1F
	0343	0710	2.5E		0334	0657	3.3E
	1018	1254	2.2F		0959	1252	3.2F
	1604	1942	2.7E		1600	1932	3.7E
	2305				2249		
5 M		0132	1.9F	20 TU		0130	3.0F
	0437	0806	2.3E		0438	0804	3.2E
	1116	1349	2.0F		1108	1355	3.1F
	1659	2037	2.6E		1705	2038	3.7E
					2357		
6 TU	0004	0229	1.9F	21 W		0237	2.9F
	0535	0903	2.2F		0545	0911	3.3E
	1215	1449	2.0F		1220	1506	3.1F
	1755	2133	2.7E		1813	2143	3.7E
7 W	0100	0332	1.9F	22 TH	0103	0349	3.0F
	0634	1000	2.3E		0651	1012	3.5E
	1313	1549	2.0F		1327	1617	3.2F
	1851	2226	2.8E		1918	2244	3.9E
8 TH	0152	0428	2.1F	23 F	0203	0457	3.3F
	0728	1053	2.5E		0753	1112	3.8E
	1405	1644	2.2F		1428	1722	3.4F
	1944	2315	3.0E		2019	2339	4.1E
9 F	0239	0518	2.3F	24 SA	0258	0554	3.5F
	0818	1142	2.8E		0850	1207	4.1E
	1452	1731	2.5F		1524	1820	3.6F
	2033				2114		
10 SA		0002	3.2E	25 SU		0032	4.2E
	0321	0601	2.6F		0349	0645	3.6F
	0902	1224	3.1E		0941	1258	4.2E
	1535	1814	2.8F		1615	1911	3.6F
	2118				2205		
11 SU		0045	3.5E	26 M		0120	4.2E
	0400	0640	2.9F		0436	0730	3.7F
	0943	1309	3.4E		1027	1345	4.3E
	1615	1856	3.1F		1702	1954	3.6F
	2201				2250		
12 M	0127	3.7E		27 TU		0207	4.1E
	0437	0718	3.2F		0520	0812	3.6F
	1023	1347	3.7E		1110	1430	4.2E
	1654	1937	3.3F		1747	2035	3.5F
	2243				2333		
13 TU	0208	3.8E		28 W		0250	3.9E
	0512	0759	3.5F		0601	0848	3.5F
	1103	1428	3.9E		1150	1512	4.0E
	1734	2019	3.5F		1830	2113	3.2F
	2324						
14 W	0246	3.9E		29 TH	0014	0333	3.6E
	0549	0840	3.7F		0642	0926	3.2F
	1144	1507	4.1E		1230	1553	3.8E
	1815	2102	3.6F		1912	2149	3.0F
15 TH	0007	0327	3.9E	30 F	0054	0416	3.3E
	0629	0923	3.7F		0721	1002	3.0F
	1227	1550	4.1E		1309	1636	3.5E
	1900	2149	3.6F		1954	2229	2.7F

OCTOBER

DAY	SLACK WATER TIME H.M.	MAXIMUM CURRENT TIME H.M.	VEL. KNOTS	DAY	SLACK WATER TIME H.M.	MAXIMUM CURRENT TIME H.M.	VEL. KNOTS
1 SA	0135	0459	2.9E	16 SU	0126	0442	3.9E
	0802	1045	2.7F		0744	1039	3.8F
	1349	1722	3.2E		1345	1712	4.3E
	2039	2311	2.4F		2026	2311	3.6F
2 SU	0218	0543	2.6E	17 M	0221	0540	3.7E
	0846	1126	2.4F		0843	1134	3.6F
	1432	1808	2.9E		1442	1812	4.1E
	2127	2358	2.2F		2127		
3 M	0305	0634	2.3E	18 TU		0012	3.4F
	0936	1215	2.1F		0321	0644	3.5E
	1520	1900	2.6E		0949	1234	3.3F
	2219				1544	1916	3.8E
					2232		
4 TU		0047	2.0F	19 W		0115	3.2F
	0357	0729	2.2E		0425	0749	3.4E
	1033	1308	1.9F		1059	1343	3.1F
	1613	1955	2.5E		1650	2021	3.7E
	2316				2339		
5 W		0142	1.9F	20 TH		0224	3.1F
	0454	0826	2.2E		0531	0855	3.5E
	1134	1404	1.9F		1210	1457	3.0F
	1710	2052	2.5E		1758	2124	3.7E
6 TH	0012	0241	1.9F	21 F	0043	0339	3.1F
	0551	0923	2.3E		0636	0956	3.6E
	1233	1505	2.0F		1316	1611	3.1F
	1808	2147	2.6E		1904	2226	3.7E
7 F	0105	0339	2.1F	22 SA	0143	0444	3.3F
	0646	1015	2.6E		0737	1055	3.8E
	1328	1601	2.2F		1416	1714	3.2F
	1904	2238	2.9E		2004	2319	3.8E
8 SA	0154	0431	2.4F	23 SU	0238	0539	3.4F
	0736	1103	2.9E		0831	1148	4.0E
	1417	1652	2.6F		1510	1809	3.3F
	1957	2326	3.1E		2059		
9 SU	0238	0515	2.7F	24 M		0010	3.8E
	0822	1151	3.3E		0328	0629	3.5F
	1501	1739	2.8F		0920	1238	4.1E
	2045				1600	1858	3.4F
					2148		
10 M		0011	3.4E	25 TU		0059	3.8E
	0318	0601	3.1F		0414	0710	3.4F
	0907	1233	3.7E		1004	1323	4.1E
	1544	1824	3.2F		1645	1940	3.3F
	2131				2232		
11 TU		0056	3.7E	26 W		0142	3.7E
	0358	0643	3.5F		0456	0749	3.3F
	0949	1316	4.0E		1045	1406	4.1E
	1626	1909	3.5F		1728	2017	3.2F
	2215				2312		
12 W	0136	3.9E		27 TH		0225	3.5E
	0438	0728	3.8F		0536	0822	3.2F
	1032	1357	4.3E		1123	1448	3.9E
	1708	1956	3.8F		1808	2050	3.0F
	2300				2351		
13 TH	0219	4.0E		28 F		0307	3.3E
	0519	0812	4.0F		0614	0857	3.0F
	1117	1440	4.5E		1159	1528	3.7E
	1753	2039	3.9F		1847	2125	2.8F
	2346						
14 F	0303	4.1E		29 SA	0029	0347	3.0E
	0603	0859	4.0F		0652	0931	2.8F
	1203	1528	4.6E		1236	1608	3.4E
	1840	2128	3.9F		1926	2201	2.6F
15 SA	0034	0351	4.0E	30 SU	0108	0429	2.8E
	0651	0948	4.0F		0730	1010	2.6F
	1252	1617	4.5E		1314	1651	3.1E
	1931	2219	3.8F		2006	2242	2.5F
				31 M	0149	0511	2.5E
					0812	1053	2.3F
					1355	1733	2.9E
					2048	2323	2.3F

TIME MERIDIAN 75° W. 0000 IS MIDNIGHT. 1200 IS NOON.

Stonington   Reference Station: The Race, p. 38,   Current Tables

$-2^h 30^m$ = Time Difference for Slacks

For the time difference for maxima you are referred to one of the numerous footnotes in these tables—to Note 1 on the same page, 142, of *Tidal Current Tables* (Table 4-5 of text):

Velocity Ratio at Max, Flood = 0.4

Velocity Ratio at Max, Ebb is given in Note 1

Flood Direction = 035°   Ebb Direction = 235°

(Average velocity given there is for general information)

According to the Note 1, "A double ebb occurs at this station (see Note [a]). Time differences: first ebb, $-3^h 40^m$, minimum ebb, $-1^h 30^m$; second ebb, $-0^h 05^m$; maximum flood, $-3^h 15^m$. Velocity ratio for first ebb is 0.3; minimum ebb, 0.1; second ebb, 0.2", and the Note [a] states, "A double ebb occurs at this station. A similar slackening occurs during the ebb period as is described for the flood period in 'footnote [a], page 140.' Differences and ratios given for first, minimum, and second ebbs should be applied to the corresponding phases at the reference station."

As with *Tide Tables,* you should now turn to Table 4-6 in this text. (Table I of *Tidal Current Tables* gives page 34 for The Race.) Of course, page 34 starts at the beginning of the year, and you are interested in October 27, 1977, and so you turn to page 38 of *Tidal Current Tables,* which gives the basic figures you want for your day. It seems easiest to the author to write down these current figures in order of time (for every time you want currents for the day), as follows:

Form for Currents for October 27, 1977

(*E* stands for Ebb and *F* for Flood)

(*H* stands for Hours and *M* for Minutes)

The Race
Long Island

Time	Maximum Current
H M	knots
0225	3.5 E
0536	Slack
0822	3.2 F
1123	Slack
1448	3.9 E
1808	Slack
2050	3.0 F
2351	Slack

The above figures will be repeated, so that you can fill in the corresponding times and maximum velocities for the desired place, near Stonington Pt.

Time Differences from Table I of *Tidal Current Tables*
for October 27, 1977

The Race

Long Island Sound		Stonington	
Time	Current	Time Differences	
H M	knots		
0225	3.5	-3^h40^m	(1st E), -1^h30^m (Min. E), -0^h05^m (2nd E)
0536	Slack	-2 30	
0822	3.2	-3 15	Max F
1123	Slack	-2 30	
1448	3.9	-3 40	(1st E), -1^h30^m (Min. E), -0^h05^m (2nd E)
1808	Slack	-2 30	
2050	3.0	-3 15	Max F
2351	Slack	-2 30	

Flood Dir. 035°;   Ebb Dir. 235°

The time difference for the slacks is easy, -2^h30^m for each. Write it down for each slack, as above. At 0225 there is a maximum current at The Race. It is an ebb, and Note 1 tells you that the time difference for the first ebb is -3^h40^m. Hence, you can fill in the first row in the third column as shown. Reread notes in the *Tidal Current Tables,* and you will find that it is not as confusing as your first glance at all the notes may lead you to think. In fact, there is one extra note which you should read once, but which really tells you what you have probably decided by yourself. This note applies to floods when you have a double flood, but the same idea holds for a double ebb, and so you will read it at least once. The note states:

"A double flood occurs at this station; the ebb is regular. After flood begins the velocity increases to a maximum (called 'first flood'); it then decreases, reaching a minimum (called 'minimum flood') near the middle of the flood period and at some places may actually run in an ebb direction for a short period at this time; it then again floods with a stronger velocity (called 'second flood') after which it decreases to the slack before ebb. Differences and ratios given for first, minimum, and second floods should be applied to the time and velocity of maximum flood at the reference station. Other values should be applied to the corresponding phases at the reference station." Another note on the same page explains about double ebbs, as follows: "A similar slackening occurs during the ebb period as is described for the flood period in the above note. Differences and ratios given for the first, minimum, and second ebbs should be applied to the time and velocity of maximum ebb at the reference station. Other values should be applied to the corresponding phases at the reference station."

You now have sufficient information to apply both time differences and *velocity ratios*. Velocity ratios are always given for currents instead of height differences as for tides, though even for the tides, sometimes, ratios are presented instead of differences here. The *Tide Tables* always have a footnote to that effect, and so if you are conscious of footnotes and read them, you will obtain the right answers, especially as regards tide and currents.

When a ratio is given, you multiply the drift of the current (or the height of the tide) at the reference station by the ratio given. If, then, you apply both *time differences* and *velocity ratios* to the figures for the day at the reference station, you will have the pertinent Current Data for Stonington, as follows:

Current Data Table for Stonington, October 27, 1977

The Race		Desired Place: Stonington			
Time	Max. Currents (knots) & Slacks	Time h m	Drift knots		Drift Adopted
0225	3.5 E	2245	1.05 (3.5 x .3)	1st Ebb	1.0
		0055	0.35 (3.5 x .1)	Min. Ebb	0.4
		0220	0.70 (3.5 x .2)	2nd Ebb	0.7
0536	Slack; F begins	0306	Slack; F begins		
0822	3.2 F	0507	1.28 (3.2 x .4)	Max. F	1.3
1123	Slack; E begins	0853			
1448	3.9 E	1108	1.17 (3.9 x .3)	1st Ebb	1.2
		1318	0.39 (3.9 x .1)	Min. Ebb	0.4
		1443	0.78 (3.9 x .2)	2nd Ebb	0.8
1808	Slack; F begins	1538	Slack; F begins		
2050	3.0 F	1735	1.20 (3.0 x .4)	Max. F	1.2
2351	Slack; E begins	2121			
	Flooding	1830	1.2 (1.2 x 1.0)	Set 035°	1.2
For Chapter 5:	Flooding	0830	0.13 (1.3 x .1)	Set 035°	0.1

Usually you do not want to know the exact figures for currents during a whole day at one place, and that makes the problem somewhat more simple. Suppose, for instance, you want the set and drift of the current for the time of departure on a cruise from Stonington. *Suppose the desired time is 1830 EST,* the time used here in *Tidal Current Tables*—Eastern Standard Time.

The third table of *Tidal Current Tables* (Table 4-7 of this text) will help you interpolate between the values which you have already found. It consists of two parts, Table A and Table B. Most of the time you would use A as now, since B is for special places, such as Cape Cod Canal, Hell Gate, etc., always noted in *Tidal Current Tables* when you need this information. The directions for use of Table A are easy to follow. First, you need to know the "Interval between slack and desired time," one of the arguments needed for entering Table A. In your case, this interval is between 2121 (nearest slack to your desired time) and 1830 (the desired time). The interval is 2^h51^m. In the ninth row of Table A you will find 3^h00^m (the nearest value to your interval).

You need one other value, so that you will be able to enter Table A with another argument, which you read at the top of the table, "Interval between slack and maximum current." In your present example, you want the interval between 1735 and 2121 (See preceding *Current Data Table for Stonington*). Note that these two times precede and follow your desired time, which should always be the case. This last arithmetic, if you subtract the smaller value from the larger, is 3^h46^m. To return to your interpolation Table A, on the row which you already entered with 3^h00^m, run your eye along the horizontal line until you come to a figure near 3^h46^m. This figure, or time, is 3^h40^m, and so you stop here and read the "f" factor (1.0) by which you multiply your maximum velocity (1.2) to obtain 1.2 for your answer (results should be obtained only to one decimal place). The four main directions which

TABLE 4-7
Velocity of Current At Any Time
(from *Tidal Current Tables*)

TABLE A

Interval between slack and desired time (h. m.)	Interval between slack and maximum current													
	h. m. 1 20	h. m. 1 40	h. m. 2 00	h. m. 2 20	h. m. 2 40	h. m. 3 00	h. m. 3 20	h. m. 3 40	h. m. 4 00	h. m. 4 20	h. m. 4 40	h. m. 5 00	h. m. 5 20	h. m. 5 40
	f.	*f.*	*f.*	*f.*	*f.*	*f.*	*f.*	*f.*	*f.*	*f.*	*f.*	*f.*	*f.*	*f.*
0 20	0.4	0.3	0.3	0.2	0.2	0.2	0.2	0.1	0.1	0.1	0.1	0.1	0.1	0.1
0 40	0.7	0.6	0.5	0.4	0.4	0.3	0.3	0.3	0.3	0.2	0.2	0.2	0.2	0.2
1 00	0.9	0.8	0.7	0.6	0.6	0.5	0.5	0.4	0.4	0.4	0.3	0.3	0.3	0.3
1 20	1.0	1.0	0.9	0.8	0.7	0.6	0.6	0.5	0.5	0.5	0.4	0.4	0.4	0.4
1 40	------	1.0	1.0	0.9	0.8	0.8	0.7	0.7	0.6	0.6	0.5	0.5	0.5	0.4
2 00	------	------	1.0	1.0	0.9	0.9	0.8	0.8	0.7	0.7	0.6	0.6	0.6	0.5
2 20	------	------	------	1.0	1.0	0.9	0.9	0.8	0.8	0.7	0.7	0.7	0.6	0.6
2 40	------	------	------	------	1.0	1.0	1.0	0.9	0.9	0.8	0.8	0.7	0.7	0.7
3 00	------	------	------	------	------	1.0	1.0	1.0	0.9	0.9	0.8	0.8	0.8	0.7
3 20	------	------	------	------	------	------	1.0	1.0	1.0	0.9	0.9	0.9	0.8	0.8
3 40	------	------	------	------	------	------	------	1.0	1.0	1.0	0.9	0.9	0.9	0.9
4 00	------	------	------	------	------	------	------	------	1.0	1.0	1.0	1.0	0.9	0.9
4 20	------	------	------	------	------	------	------	------	------	1.0	1.0	1.0	1.0	0.9
4 40	------	------	------	------	------	------	------	------	------	------	1.0	1.0	1.0	1.0
5 00	------	------	------	------	------	------	------	------	------	------	------	1.0	1.0	1.0
5 20	------	------	------	------	------	------	------	------	------	------	------	------	1.0	1.0
5 40	------	------	------	------	------	------	------	------	------	------	------	------	------	1.0

TABLE B

Interval between slack and desired time (h. m.)	Interval between slack and maximum current													
	h. m. 1 20	h. m. 1 40	h. m. 2 00	h. m. 2 20	h. m. 2 40	h. m. 3 00	h. m. 3 20	h. m. 3 40	h. m. 4 00	h. m. 4 20	h. m. 4 40	h. m. 5 00	h. m. 5 20	h. m. 5 40
	f.	*f.*	*f.*	*f.*	*f.*	*f.*	*f.*	*f.*	*f.*	*f.*	*f.*	*f.*	*f.*	*f.*
0 20	0.5	0.4	0.4	0.3	0.3	0.3	0.3	0.3	0.2	0.2	0.2	0.2	0.2	0.2
0 40	0.8	0.7	0.6	0.5	0.5	0.5	0.4	0.4	0.4	0.4	0.3	0.3	0.3	0.3
1 00	0.9	0.8	0.8	0.7	0.7	0.6	0.6	0.5	0.5	0.5	0.4	0.4	0.4	0.4
1 20	1.0	1.0	0.9	0.8	0.8	0.7	0.7	0.6	0.6	0.6	0.5	0.5	0.5	0.5
1 40	------	1.0	1.0	0.9	0.9	0.8	0.8	0.7	0.7	0.7	0.6	0.6	0.6	0.6
2 00	------	------	1.0	1.0	0.9	0.9	0.9	0.8	0.8	0.7	0.7	0.7	0.7	0.6
2 20	------	------	------	1.0	1.0	0.9	0.9	0.8	0.8	0.8	0.7	0.7	0.7	0.7
2 40	------	------	------	------	1.0	1.0	1.0	0.9	0.9	0.9	0.8	0.8	0.8	0.7
3 00	------	------	------	------	------	1.0	1.0	1.0	0.9	0.9	0.9	0.9	0.8	0.8
3 20	------	------	------	------	------	------	1.0	1.0	1.0	0.9	0.9	0.9	0.9	0.8
3 40	------	------	------	------	------	------	------	1.0	1.0	1.0	1.0	0.9	0.9	0.9
4 00	------	------	------	------	------	------	------	------	1.0	1.0	1.0	1.0	0.9	0.9
4 20	------	------	------	------	------	------	------	------	------	1.0	1.0	1.0	1.0	0.9
4 40	------	------	------	------	------	------	------	------	------	------	1.0	1.0	1.0	1.0
5 00	------	------	------	------	------	------	------	------	------	------	------	1.0	1.0	1.0
5 20	------	------	------	------	------	------	------	------	------	------	------	------	1.0	1.0
5 40	------	------	------	------	------	------	------	------	------	------	------	------	------	1.0

Use table A for all places except those listed below for table B.
Use table B for Cape Cod Canal, Hell Gate, Chesapeake and Delaware Canal and all stations in table 2 which are referred to them.

1. From predictions find the time of slack water and the time and velocity of maximum current (flood or ebb), one of which is immediately before and the other after the time for which the velocity is desired.
2. Find the interval of time between the above slack and maximum current, and enter the top of table A or B with the interval which most nearly agrees with this value.
3. Find the interval of time between the above slack and the time desired, and enter the side of table A or B with the interval which most nearly agrees with this value.
4. Find, in the table, the factor corresponding to the above two intervals, and multiply the maximum velocity by this factor. The result will be the approximate velocity at the time desired.

you need to know in using this interpolation table are given as the four last directions in *Tidal Current Tables* #3 (See Table 4-7), so that you can always refer to them here if you wish. There is only one last figure which you want to set down for future reference. You know that the current at Stonington is between maximum flood (at 1735) and the slack (at 2121). Hence, the current is still flooding at your desired time, 1830. The Table 2 (Table 4-2) data which you wrote down for Stonington gave the flood direction for Stonington as 035°. Hence, as soon as you know that it is flooding there, you know this direction. Note that the ebb direction is also given in the same table, so that if you need the ebb direction at any time, you look for it there. The current figures for 1830 appear near the bottom line of the foregoing Current Data Table for Stonington.

At this time you should be able to find the set and drift of the current at many points off the East coast of North America or at other places for which *Tidal Current Tables* have been published (See Appendix III). Once you know the set and drift of current, you can tell how to head your vessel so as to make good a fixed course when you have to contend with a certain current which may be favorable and help you along your course with accelerated velocity or which may hold you back and even prevent any progress at all, sometimes.

PROBLEMS. Certainly you will be a successful mariner only if you can handle the currents. The *Tide Tables* and *Tidal Current Tables* give you knowledge of current for many regions. Now you must learn how to deal with them. There are, in general, three main types of current problems:

Three Types of Current Problems

---

1. First Type of Current Problem

Current known.

True heading and speed through water known.

What will be the course made good, and the speed made good?

Right away you want to distinguish between the *heading of a vessel through the water* and the *course over the bottom*, or the course made good. In Fig. 4-9 the vessel's point of departure is

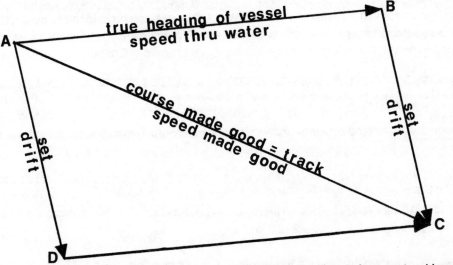

Fig. 4-9. Vector diagram for current problems (Type 1).

supposedly at A. The true heading of the vessel is indicated by the arrow AB. The speed of the vessel *through the water* is such that, in the absence of a current, the vessel would sail to B in the course of an hour. The current is represented by the arrow AD, or by BC. The length of the arrow AD represents the hourly drift of the current and its direction shows the *set* of the current. The current will set the vessel off its intended course. In spite of the fact that the vessel is headed in the direction from A to B, the mariner will find himself at C at the end of an hour's run. The direction from A to C marks the *course made good*, or the "Track" as in air navigation, whereas the length of AC equals the *speed made good*. The lines AB, BC and AC are really vectors, each one representing a direction and the length representing a velocity or speed (distance traveled in *an hour*). It should be clearly understood that the vessel does not proceed along AB, but that the vessel really moves in a sort of crab-like fashion along AC. If you prefer, the term speed on the heading may be used for speed through the water. Similarly, speed over the bottom may be called speed made good. There is one other point to remember. Since the set of the current is always a true direction, with respect to true North, any direction in the vector diagram must represent a *true* direction. In other words, do not mix magnetic directions, either courses or headings, with the set of the current in the same vector diagram.

2. Second Type of Current Problem

Current known.

Desired track known: speed to be made good known.

What will be the heading in order to make good the desired track, and what will be the speed on the heading?

This type arises when you find it necessary to reach a specific point in a certain time interval, which requires a particular speed through the water in order to achieve your objective, as well as a necessary heading, both of which you have to find.

It will help you in drawing the vectors if you use a *maneuvering board* with 360° all marked off separately, and with many concentric circles separated by a division which is divided into ten parts.

If you decide to let one division equal one mile, each smallest division marks a tenth of a mile, or if you let one division equal ten miles, then one small division equals one mile. You yourself can decide on the scale to be adopted, depending upon the figures of the problem, and the maneuvering board saves some time in finding your answer. Otherwise you have to measure angles with a circular protractor and distances with your dividers. The latter are useful however even with a maneuvering board. There is more information about this board in Chapter 5.

Right now you are learning the graphical method of handling the vectors. Later, you will be given a formula which is easy to use (especially with a mini-computer if you are familiar with computers), and you can also purchase plastic devices to give you the answers about your heading and speed made good, but first it is advisable to understand principles, and the graphical method is a great aid in understanding the principles involved here.

We return to the second type of current problem and use of the maneuvering board to aid in the solution. If the known current has a *set of 070°*, and a *drift of 2 knots,* you can draw the vector as seen in Fig. 4-10, labelled BC. You can then draw the desired track BA which has been assumed to be 330° true, with speed on this track of 8 knots.

What heading is necessary, and what is the speed on this heading?

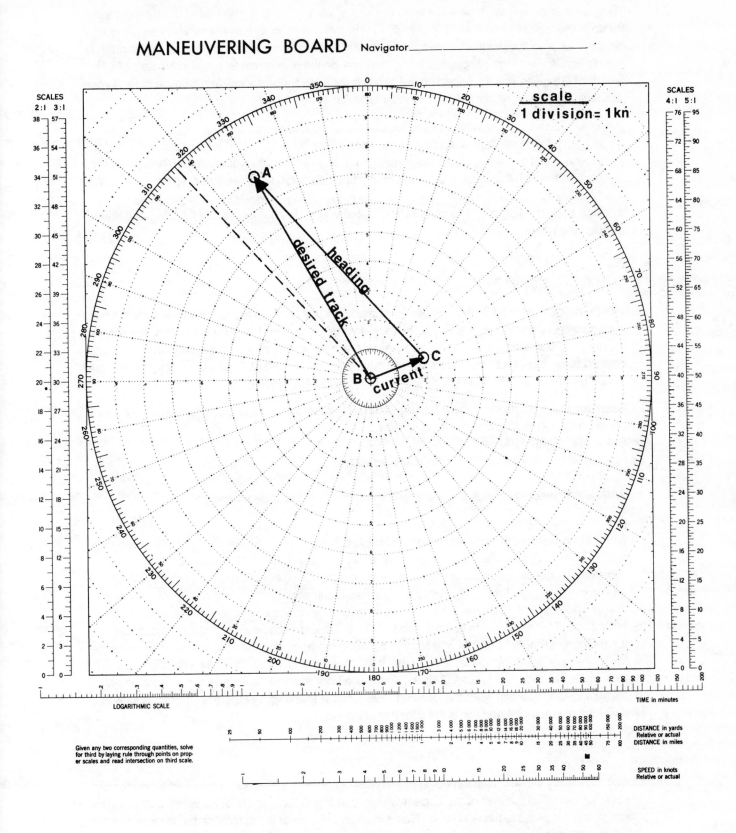

Fig. 4-10. Current vector problem on maneuvering board (Type 2). (Courtesy Defense Mapping Agency Hydrographic/Topographic Center.)

To solve this case, just draw a line from the end of vector BC to A, the end of the BA vector, or through the points C and A. This line gives you the direction to head, and you can bring this direction over to the point B by using your parallel rulers and drawing the dashed line through B parallel to CA. Read the direction of the dashed line, on the outside circle, and find it to be 317°. The *length* of CA gives you the speed on the heading (or through the water), and with the help of your dividers, you measure this length and find it to be 8.6 knots.

When two forces, similar in this case to the current and the speed on the heading, act on a point, it is easier to think of one force as acting alone. Then let the other force act. In this case, if the current acted alone, and carried you from the starting point B to C, then you would think of the other force, your speed through the water of 8.6 knots on the true heading 317°. If that force acted alone now, it would take you from C to A, which you wanted to reach. This was your goal, and you achieved it by drawing a vector diagram of forces which directed you as to your necessary heading and speed through the water.

3. Third Type of Current Problem

The third type of current problem is the most important, as a rule. In the last problem, for instance, what would you have done if your vessel could not make the speed of 8.6 knots? It may have been an impossible situation for you! Hence, we need the third type which assumes a known current and desired track, but which assumes a speed convenient for the vessel. The quantities to find are the heading and the speed made good.

Assume, as an example for the third type of current problem, the same set and drift of the current above in the second type of current problem:
Set = 070°; Drift = 2 knots.
Speed through the water = 5 knots; Track = 175°t.

What is the heading through the water, and what would be the speed made good?

Since the current is the same, the same vector BC can represent it on the maneuvering board (Fig. 4-11). The track can then be plotted from B, in the direction of 175°, but no length can be determined right away, because you do not yet know the speed over the bottom, or track. What you do know is the speed through the water. This speed is 5 knots. Hence, with the scale of 1 division = .5 knot you will want 10 divisions between your divider tips. Place one tip over the point B, the other tip on the tenth circle running down the page. With this 5 knots between your divider tips, place one tip at C, and swing an arc (still with 5 knots between the tips), and the other tip will now cross the track line near the eighth circle, at A, so that now BA will equal 4.1 knots, while a line drawn from C to A gives the required heading. Again, if you use your parallel rulers and construct a line at B parallel to CA, you can read the heading (198°), while the length of the track vector is only 8.2 divisions or 4.1 knots, and this is the speed made good.

Notice, as clearly shown in the foregoing three types of current problems that the heading vector can always be laid off at the end of the current vector, and if you have some established order in your steps, you are less apt to make an error. Some mariners like to set the current off backwards, but the foregoing procedure seems easiest and less apt to cause error. If you always think of the practical side of the problem when you have achieved an answer, you will be checking what you have done in a very practical way. Big blunders are to be avoided!

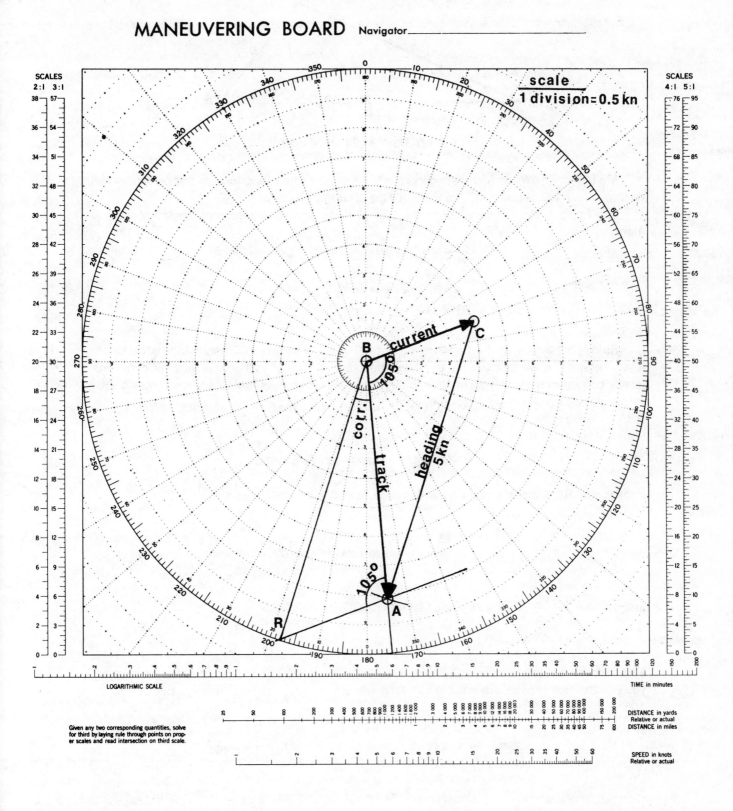

Fig. 4-11. Current problem on maneuvering board (Type 3). (Courtesy Defense Mapping Agency Hydrographic/Topographic Center.)

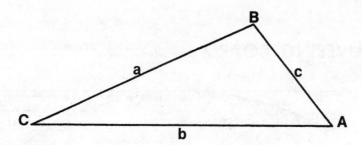

Fig. 4-12. Figure for the Law of Sines.

Mariners with mini-computers might prefer to handle the current with formula and computer, and so the formula will be given next, for the third type of current problem.

The basic formula depends upon the Law of Sines applied to sides and angles of a plane triangle.

The Law of Sines, as applied to any triangle ABC states (Fig. 4-12) that—

$$\frac{\sin B}{b} = \frac{\sin A}{a} = \frac{\sin C}{c}$$

Study your plotting on the maneuvering board (Fig. 4-11) and draw BR parallel and equal to CA. If you know the angle between the track and the heading, you can in this case *add* this correction (corr.) to the track to obtain your heading through the water. And so you want to find the corr. angle (B) in triangle ARB. (RA is equal and parallel to current vector.) Using the Law of Sines and the angle B = RBA = desired corr.

$$A = RAB = 175° \text{ (Track)} - 70° \text{ (Set)} = 105°$$

and the side RA = drift of current = 2 in this case. Hence you have

$$\frac{\sin B}{\text{drift}} = \frac{\sin 105°}{\text{speed through water (5)}}$$

and $\sin B = \dfrac{\sin 105° \times 2}{5}$ or $\sin B = .386$ and $B = 22.7°$.

Your desired heading = track + Corr. angle = 175° + 23° = 198°. To find BA or speed made good, you use the Law of Sines again in the same triangle. BA = speed made good; angle BRA = 180° − 105° − 22.7° = 52.3°. Hence,

$$\frac{BA}{\sin 52.3°} = \frac{\text{drift}}{\sin 22.7°} \text{ or } BA = \frac{\sin 52.3° \times \text{drift}}{\sin 22.7°} = 4.1 \text{ knots.}$$

Although this use of the mini-computer gives a quick and easy answer to the mariner who is familiar with trigonometry, it is full of danger for the mariner who is *not* familiar with it, and the author is a strong advocate of the graphical method on a maneuvering board. Sometimes the correction angle would be *subtracted instead of added*. A plot must be made anyway, unless the mariner can safely do all this in his own head, he will be wise to take a few more minutes or seconds, as the case may be, to obtain an accurate answer as to how to head and steer to cope with current and reach the position desired. Except in races, a mariner has plenty of time for working out answers and, as a rule, speed is not a requisite for the best navigation.

Rotary Tidal Currents. There are some currents offshore, especially for the Atlantic Coast, which are different from the flood and ebb currents already described. For these currents, flood and ebb no longer have any meaning. The drifts of these currents vary with time, and *set in many directions*. Hence, they are called *rotary currents*. The following Table 4-8 gives figures for the direction and set of these currents at different times, from Table 5, of *Tidal Current Tables*. One of the nearest rotary currents to the region of Chart 116-SC Tr is the rotary current at Little Gull 1., 3.7 miles ESE of, Block Island Sound, Lat. 41°11′N.; 72°02′W—South and East of Great Gull Island, which is *on* the chart.

If you had such a current where you were planning to cruise, the *Tidal Current Tables* will inform you when you consult its pages for Table 2. It will say "See Table 5" in the volume for the Atlantic Coast of North America.

TABLE 4-8
Rotary Tidal Currents
(from *Tidal Current Tables*)

Hours after Max. Flood at The Race

Time	Direction (true) Degrees	Velocity
0	271	0.8
1	284	0.5
2	320	0.2
3	68	0.2
4	77	0.7
5	95	1.1
6	118	1.6
7	128	1.2
8	150	0.6
9	171	0.2
10	221	0.4
11	228	0.7

In addition to the above tables for currents, there are about a dozen *tidal current charts* published for various sounds and harbors, such as Block Island and Eastern Long Island Sound, Narragansett Bay to Nantucket Sound, Puget Sound and San Francisco Bay. They depict, by means of arrows and figures, the direction and velocity of the tidal current for each hour of the tidal cycle. The charts may be used for any year. They present a comprehensive view of the tidal current movement in waterways as a whole and also supply a means for readily determining for any time the direction and velocity of the current at various localities throughout the water areas covered. Most of them require the annual *Tidal Current Tables*. The New York and Narrangansett Bay tidal current charts are to be used with the annual *Tide Tables*. In addition, tidal current diagrams for Boston Harbor are a series of 12 monthly diagrams to be used with the charts to give the user a convenient method to determine current flow on a particular day. Directions for use of the charts and diagrams are given in their respective publications, and will not be repeated here. Note that Spring velocities, printed on the charts, must be modified. No matter whether the set and drift of the current are found from figures in tables or from charts and diagrams, the figures for set and drift can be treated, as already explained in this chapter, in vector diagrams.

World-Wide Currents. Tidal currents account for only a part of the known ocean currents. There is an extensive system of world-wide currents. These currents are not caused by the variable attraction of the Moon, but originate because of conditions in the oceans themselves and in the Earth's atmosphere. One cause for existence of large-scale currents is difference in temperature between oceans. The higher temperature of the water in the equatorical region leads to a lower density there than in the polar regions. Variations in the salt content of the oceans lead also to variations in density, the water being densest where there is most salt.

The atmosphere affects ocean currents in two ways. The presence of a permanent center of low pressure, such as the one over Iceland, will tend to set up ocean currents that move very much as regular atmospheric cyclones do. Circulation will also occur around the semi-permanent centers of high pressure.

The most powerful cause for existence of world-wide currents is found in prevailing winds, blowing over wide-open oceans. The relation between a prevailing wind and the resulting current is, however, not simple. The depth of the ocean has considerable influence, but generally, because of the effect of the Earth's rotation, the set of a wind-driven current will differ by about 45° from that of the wind. In the Northern hemisphere the current will set in a direction about 45° to the right of the wind, whereas in the Southern hemisphere it will be deflected 45° to the left. The relation between surface currents (chief concern of the mariner) and frequently opposed, deep-seated currents is complex.

Finally, in dealing with tides and currents, there is a word of caution to offer. Find the figures, which are the best average figures available, but use them with caution, and *do not become over-confident!*

PROBLEM SET 4

Tide Problems

To find answers to these problems, you will need to consult Tables 4-2, 3 and 4 in this chapter (extracts from *Tide Tables, 1977, East Coast of North and South America, Tables 1, 2 and 3).*

1) List time difference and height differences for tide at West Harbor, Fishers Island, N.Y. (Lat. 41°16′N; Long. 72°00′W).

2) List times and heights for tide at New London on October 2, 1977 (label your figures). Then list tidal events, with corresponding times and heights, at West Harbor, Fishers Island, for the same day, October 2, 1977.

3) Plot a tide curve for the day, October 2, 1977 (using one-quarter, one-tenth rule) at (a) New London; (b) West Harbor in 1 above.

TABLE 4-9
Current Differences and Other Constants
to Cover Data for Bartlett Reef and for Black Point
(from *Tidal Current Tables*)

No.	PLACE	POSITION		TIME DIF-FERENCES		VELOCITY RATIOS		MAXIMUM CURRENTS			
								Flood		Ebb	
		Lat.	Long.	Slack water	Maximum current	Maximum flood	Maximum ebb	Direction (true)	Average velocity	Direction (true)	Average velocity
		° ′	° ′	h. m.	h. m.			deg.	knots	deg.	knots
	LONG ISLAND SOUND—Continued	N.	W.	on THE RACE, p.34							
	Time meridian, 75°W.										
1715	Goshen Point, 1.9 miles SSE. of-------	41 16	72 06	-1 05	-1 25	0.4	0.5	285	1.2	060	1.6
1720	Little Gull Island, 0.8 mile NNW. of--	41 13	72 07	(¹)	-1 00	0.7	0.8	260	1.9	045	2.9
1725	Bartlett Reef, 0.2 mile south of------	41 16	72 08	-1 30	-1 10	0.3	0.3	255	1.4	090	1.3
1730	Twotree Island Channel----------------	41 18	72 08	-0 55	-1 35	0.4	0.4	265	1.2	100	1.6
1735	Niantic (Railroad Bridge)-------------	41 20	72 11	-0 55	-0 50	0.6	0.2	350	1.6	180	0.8
1740	Black Point, 0.8 mile south of-------	41 17	72 12	-1 25	-1 40	0.5	0.4	265	1.4	080	1.3
1745	Black Point-Plum Island (between)-----	41 14	72 12	+0 25	+0 15	0.7	0.7	235	2.1	075	2.4
1750	Plum Island, 0.8 mile NNW. of---------	41 12	72 12	(²)	-0 30	0.6	0.7	245	1.7	065	2.4
1753	Hatchett Point, 1.1 miles WSW. of-----	41 16	72 17	(³)	(³)	0.4	0.3	240	1.3	045	1.2
	Connecticut River										
1755	Lynde Point, channel east of-------	41 16	72 20	+0 30	+0 40	0.3	0.2	345	0.9	160	0.7
1757	Saybrook Point, 0.2 mile NE. of----	41 17	72 21	+0 40	+0 40	0.5	0.4	355	1.5	160	1.5
1760	Railroad drawbridge----------------	41 19	72 21	+0 50	+1 00	0.5	0.5	000	1.6	180	2.1
1765	Eustasia Island, 0.6 mile ESE. of--	41 23	72 24	+1 40	+1 30	0.4	0.4	290	1.1	070	1.4
1767	Eddy Rock Shoal, west of-----------	41 27	72 28	+1 50	+1 50	0.3	0.2	350	0.8	155	0.6
1769	Higganum Creek, 0.5 mile ESE. of---	41 30	72 33	+2 50	+2 55	0.3	0.3	270	0.8	080	1.0
1770	Wilcox Island Park, east of-------	41 34	72 39	(⁴)	+3 35	0.3	0.3	355	0.9	160	1.0
1773	Rocky Hill-------------------------	41 40	72 38	(⁵)	+3 35	0.2	0.2	335	0.6	135	0.8
1775	Hartford Jetty---------------------	41 45	72 39	(⁶)	+4 35	(⁶)	0.2	290	0.1	095	0.7
1777	Saybrook Breakwater, 1.5 miles SE. of-	41 14	72 19	-1 10	-1 35	0.7	0.6	260	1.9	070	2.0
1780	Mulford Point, 3.1 miles NW. of--------	41 12	72 19	-0 05	(⁷)	0.7	0.6	270	1.9	065	2.3
1783	Orient Point, 1.0 mile WNW. of--------	41 10	72 15	-0 50	(⁸)	(⁸)	0.9	250	----	055	3.1
1785	Terry Point, 1 mile north of----------	41 10	72 19	-0 05	-0 10	0.8	0.7	255	2.7	070	3.2
1787	Cornfield Point, 3 miles south of-----	41 13	72 22	-0 30	-0 20	0.6	0.4	255	2.0	095	1.7
1790	Cornfield Point, 1 mile south of------	41 15	72 23	-1 25	-1 50	0.5	0.4	270	1.6	100	1.8
1793	Kelsey Point, 2.1 miles SE. of--------	41 14	72 28	-0 45	-1 00	0.5	0.5	260	1.5	070	1.8
1795	Six Mile Reef, 1.5 miles north of-----	41 13	72 29	-0 20	-0 25	0.3	0.4	290	1.0	095	1.3
1797	Six Mile Reef, 2 miles east of--------	41 11	72 27	-0 20	-0 25	0.6	0.6	235	1.6	040	2.1
1799	Horton Point, 1.4 miles NNW. of-------	41 06	72 27	0 00	-0 05	0.5	0.6	260	1.4	040	2.0
1800	Kelsey Point, 1 mile south of--------	41 14	72 30	-1 15	-1 25	0.6	0.3	250	2.0	120	1.5
1805	Sachem Head, 1.0 mile SSE. of--------	41 14	72 42	-0 35	-0 50	0.4	0.3	255	1.1	065	1.0
1810	Sachem Head, 6.2 miles south of-------	41 09	72 42	+0 10	+0 10	0.2	0.3	260	0.6	065	0.9
1812	Roanoke Point, 5.6 miles north of-----	41 04	72 43	-0 10	-0 15	0.2	0.3	255	0.7	050	0.9
1814	Roanoke Point, 2.3 miles NNW. of------	41 01	72 43	(⁹)	-0 25	0.3	0.2	270	0.9	070	0.7
1815	Sachem Head, 1 mile south of---------	41 14	72 43	-0 40	-0 15	0.3	0.3	280	0.9	085	1.2
1820	New Haven Harbor entrance¹⁰ -----------	41 14	72 55	-0 55	-1 25	0.4	0.2	320	1.4	150	0.9
1822	City Point, 1.3 miles NE. of---------	41 18	72 54	+0 20	+0 20	0.1	0.1	015	0.3	215	0.4
1823	Oyster River Pt., 1.3 miles SSE. of---	41 13	72 58	(¹¹)	-0 30	0.1	0.1	255	0.3	060	0.3
1825	Pond Point, 4.2 miles SSE. of--------	41 09	72 58	-0 10	-0 05	0.2	0.2	265	0.6	065	0.6
1826	Stratford Shoal, 6.0 miles east of----	41 05	72 58	-0 05	-0 05	0.2	0.2	265	0.6	060	0.6
1827	Sound Beach, 2.2 miles north of-------	41 00	72 58	-0 10	-0 15	0.3	0.3	270	0.9	075	0.9
1828	Charles Island, 0.8 mile SSE. of------	41 11	73 03	-0 40	-0 45	0.1	0.1	250	0.4	070	0.4

¹Flood begins, +0ʰ 15ᵐ; ebb begins, -2ʰ 30ᵐ.
²Flood begins, +0ʰ 05ᵐ; ebb begins, -1ʰ 15ᵐ.
³Flood begins, -2ʰ 35ᵐ; maximum flood, -1ʰ 10ᵐ; ebb begins, -0ʰ 50ᵐ; maximum ebb, -2ʰ 35ᵐ.
⁴Flood begins, +4ʰ 05ᵐ; ebb begins, +3ʰ 05ᵐ.
⁵Flood begins, +4ʰ 40ᵐ; ebb begins, +3ʰ 20ᵐ.
⁶Flood begins, +5ʰ 45ᵐ; ebb begins, +3ʰ 20ᵐ; maximum flood current is weak and variable.
⁷Maximum flood, -1ʰ 05ᵐ; maximum ebb, -0ʰ 25ᵐ.
⁸A double flood occurs at this station (see note 6 on page 139). Time differences: first flood, -2ʰ 00ᵐ; minimum flood, -1ʰ 00ᵐ; second flood, -0ʰ 10ᵐ; maximum ebb, -1ʰ 15ᵐ. Velocity ratios: first flood, 0.5; minimum flood, 0.3; second flood, 0.7.
⁹Flood begins, -1ʰ 20ᵐ; ebb begins, -0ʰ 10ᵐ.
¹⁰Inside breakwaters, in channel, the current is only 0.4 knot.
¹¹Slacks are indefinite.

4) What is height of tide at 1100 on October 2, 1977, at New London, using Table 4-4?

5) Does your answer in 4 agree with an answer from tide curve which you drew? _____ If different, what is difference? _____

6) What is height of tide at 11:00, October 2, 1977, at West Harbor, Fishers Island, N.Y., using Table 3?

Current Problems
See Tables 4-5, 6 and 7 (Abstracts from *Tidal Current Tables*, nos. 1, 2 and 3).

1) What are time differences and velocity ratios at Great Gull Island, 0.7 miles WSW of, and what is reference station?

2) Write, in order of time, with labels, the times and corresponding current velocities of current events of day, September 10, 1977, at The Race, Long Island Sound (on Chart 116-SC Tr). (See Table 4-6)

3) Write, in order of time, with labels, corresponding current events of day at Great Gull Island 0.7 miles WSW of, for September 10, 1977.

4) What is set and drift of current on September 10, 1977, at Great Gull Island, 0.7 miles WSW of, at 0955 (on Chart 116-SC Tr)?

5) What is set and drift of current on October 14, 1977, at The Race (Lat. 41°14′N; Long. 72°04′W) at 15^h20^m?

6) What is set and drift of current at Black Point, 0.8 miles South of, at 13^h50^m on September 26, 1977? (See Table 4-9)

7) At Black Point and position given in Problem 6 on same date, with current obtained at 1350, assume track of 180°, speed through the water 6 knots. What is heading to make good the desired track, and what is speed made good? (See Table 4-9 for data.)

8) With same conditions as Problem 7, except that now you would like to compute speed through water necessary to reach a point 4 miles due South in 30^m, and you would also like to know necessary heading. What is heading?

Chapter 5

Piloting Techniques

At this point, if the art of plotting courses on charts was very precise, if the compass had no errors, if tide and current figures were constantly very accurate and weather always predictable and not variable, the mariner might feel prepared, almost, for launching a real cruise. As matters stand, however, there may be changes and variations in all these factors. They are apt to be more complex; figures which are *average* may not be true for every day, and the result of all this complexity is that the mariner must also know more about *piloting* in coastwise navigation, for *piloting is the art of guiding a vessel safely through coastal waters.* It uses all of the knowledge contained in previous chapters, but in addition, some special techniques listed here under the heading of piloting. Further progress comes with persistent practice and study. As a student, under favorable wind and weather conditions you will have an opportunity to perfect your piloting techniques. If you make good use of chances in fair weather, you will find your efforts repaid tenfold when wind and weather conspire to make the task a difficult one. You will know how to cope with fogs, and at night you will be able to proceed without endangering your vessel. Piloting not only checks your position on many occasions, but often provides new data.

It might help if a list was made right away of all techniques which you should know under piloting.

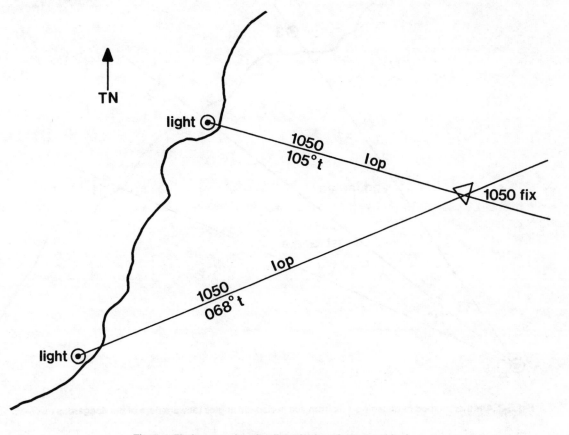

Fig. 5-1. Fix from two bearing lines (only point on *each* lop).

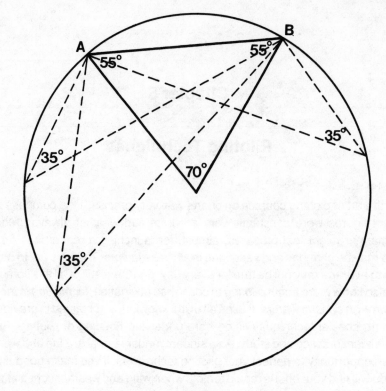

Fig. 5-2. Circle of position from measure of horizontal angle between A and B. Latter here = 35°. Then 55° angles (90° – 35°) are laid off at two points, A and B. Intersection of last two lines drawn gives the center of your circle of position. You could be anywhere on the long arc of the circle through A and B.

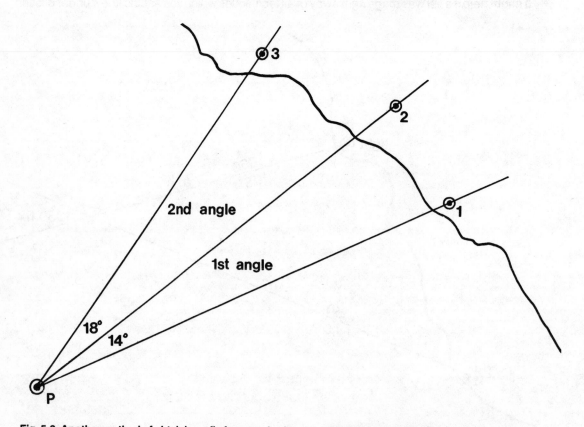

Fig. 5-3. Another method of obtaining a fix from two horizontal angles (beware here of the dangerous *revolver*).

CLASSIFICATION LIST OF PILOTING TECHNIQUES

A: Best Methods

Page Number   Figures

91, 94, 103   1. Fix by cross bearing (deviation must be known)   5-1
103   2. Intersection of two ranges (independent of deviation) . . . .
102, 106-109   3. Fix by 3-point method (horizontal angles) (independent
                      of deviation) 5-2, 5-3
104   4. Intersection of range and bearing (depends upon deviation) . . . .
95, 101, 110-112   5. Fix by bearing and distance (deviation must be known)   5-4
                   6. Combination of above . . . .

B: Next Best Methods (all dependent on a run)

105   1. Running fix by plotting and advancing lop (deviation must be known .   5-5
104   2. Doubling of angle on the bow   5-6
                      Special:
104   a) Bow and beam bearings (45° - 90°)   5-7
104   b) 7/10ths rule: (22 1/2° - 45°)   5-8
104   c) 7/8ths rule: (30° - 60°) . . . .
104   3. Run equals distance abeam . . . .
                      Special:
                      a) (26 1/2° - 45°) . . . .
                      b) (63 1/2°-116 1/2°) . . . .
104   4. Table 7 of *Pub. 9,* (Bowditch) . . . .

C: Special Methods

                   1. Danger bearings and angles . . . .
105   a) Danger bearings   5-9
105   b) Horizontal danger angle   5-10
106   c) Vertical danger angle   5-11
103, 104   d) Ranges . . . .
                   2. Check speed and position by noting times at which navigation
                      marks are being passed abeam . . . .
102, 103   3. Fix by line of soundings . . . .
                   4. Use of sound signals (See Chapter 7) . . . .
                   5. Radio Navigation (See Chapter 7) . . . .
                      a) Fix by bearings on two or three radio direction finder stations . . . . .
112   6. Radar . . . .

Inspection of this list shows that best methods depend upon one of the following:

- Bearing
- Range
- Angle

In Chapter 1 you saw that a *bearing* is a direction (from 0° to 360°) while Chapter 2 explained the difference between true, magnetic and compass directions or bearings.

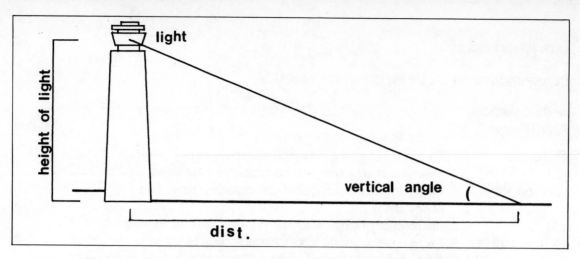

Fig. 5-4. Distance off, from a vertical angle (height is known, vertical angle measured).

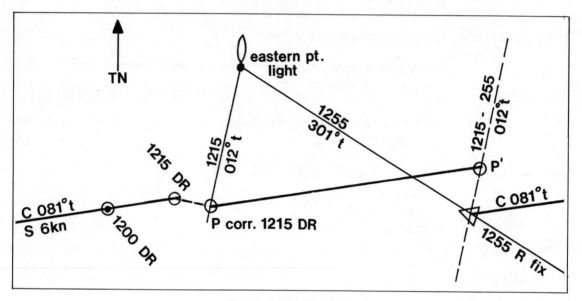

Fig. 5-5. Advancing a lop.

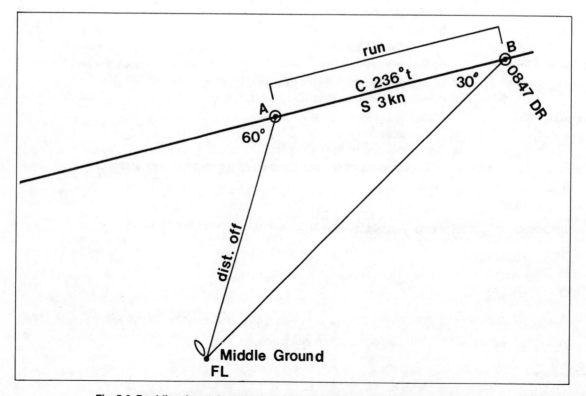

Fig. 5-6. Doubling the angle on the bow (distance off at A = run between bearings).

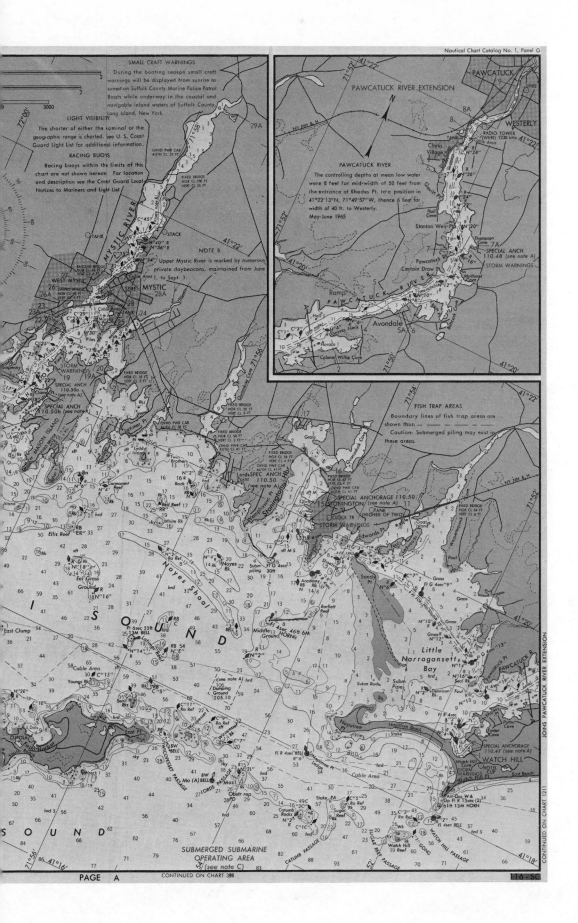

SCALE 1:40,000
NAUTICAL MILES
STATUTE MILES
YARDS

ANCHORAGE AREAS
110.147 (see note A)
NAVAL ANCHORAGE - for barges and small
vessels drawing less than 12 feet.
GENERAL
NOTE A

...ation regulations are published in Chapter 2, Coast
... or subsequent yearly supplements and weekly
... to Mariners. Copies of the regulations may be
...d at the office of the Division Engineer, Corps of
...rs in Waltham, Mass.
...orage Regulations may be obtained at the office of
...mmander, 3rd Coast Guard District in New York.
... to section numbers shown with area designation.

SPECIAL ANCHORAGE
Anchor lights not required on vessels less
than 65 feet long.
NOTE C
... limits of Submerged Submarine Operating
...own by a solid magenta line. As submarines
...merged in these areas, vessels should proceed
... During torpedo practice firing, all vessels
...d to keep well clear of Naval Target Vessels
...ge red flag at the highest masthead.

CAUTION
Temporary changes or defects in aids to
navigation are not indicated on this chart.
See Notice to Mariners.
During some winter months or when en-
dangered by ice, certain aids to navigation
are replaced by other types or removed. For
details see Coast Guard Light List.
Improved channels shown by broken lines
are subject to shoaling, particularly at the
edges.
Mariners are warned to stay clear of the
protective riprap surrounding navigational
light structures shown thus:

JOINS CHART 362

FOR INSTRUCTIONAL PURPOSES ONLY. NOT TO BE USED FOR NAVIGATION.

NIANTIC BAY

SUBMERGED SUBMARINE
OPERATING AREA
(see note C)

Dumping Ground
205.10 (see note A)

BARTLETT REEF
Fl 4sec 35ft 6M
HORN
R "4" BELL

R "2A"
Fl R 4sec
WHISTLE

L O N G   I S L A N D   S O U N

BW "P1"
Mo (A) WHISTLE

SUBMERGED SUBMARINE
OPERATING AREA
(see note C)

Cable Area

Plum Island is U.S. Government
property and is closed to the public.

Plum Island
East Pt

Great Gull Island

Little
Gull Island

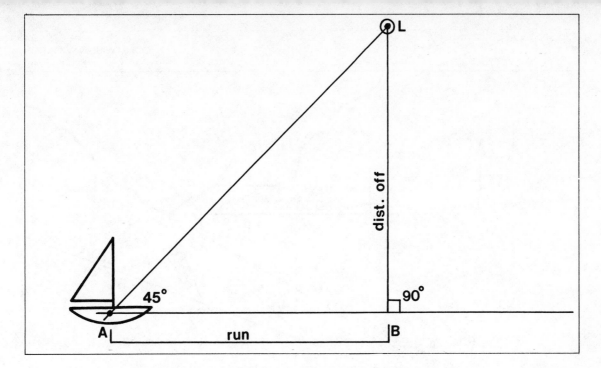

Fig. 5-7. Bow and beam bearings: special case of Fig. 5-6.

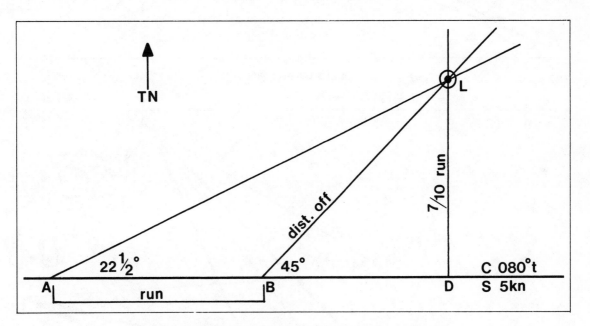

Fig. 5-8. Seven-tenths rule. Distance off when L is abeam = 0.7 x run.

A *range* is the straight line between any two objects, and you are on that range when you are on the same line through the two objects.

An *angle* in navigation is the number of degrees (or degrees and minutes of arc) between any two objects. The angle can be *horizontal* (in or parallel to the plane of your horizon) or *vertical* (at right angles to your horizon).

The different *methods* are labeled or classified as we anticipate the cruise of TUCANA and are indicated in subsequent remarks on piloting techniques.

Line of Position. The term *line of position* (lop) is one of the basic terms in all navigation, including piloting. *A line of position is any line on which a vessel is placed at a given instant.* You should clearly understand this concept, both for coastwise and celestial navigation. The bearing lines of Chapter 1

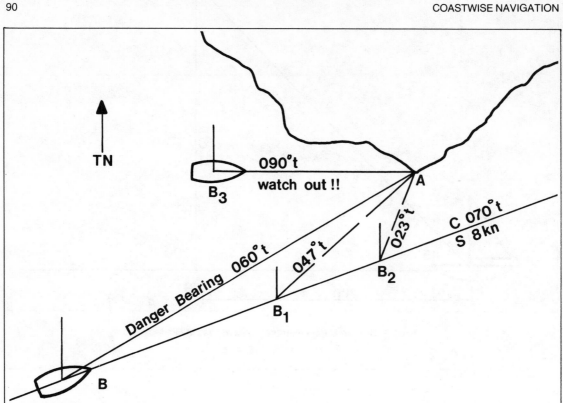

Fig. 5-9. Danger bearing.

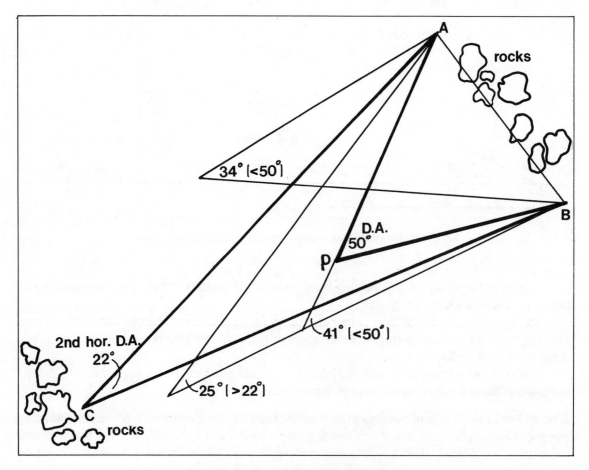

Fig. 5-10. Keeping safe with horizontal angles.

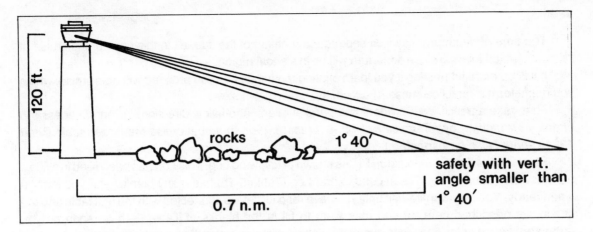

Fig. 5-11. Vertical danger angle (vertical angle not drawn to scale here).

were all lines of position. If a lop is obtained as the result of a single observed bearing of a navigational aid, it will be plotted on your chart as a straight line from the marked position of the navigational aid in the direction of the reciprocal bearing. If it represents the result of an estimate of the distance to a navigational mark, it will appear on the chart as a *circle of position,* with the navigational mark at its center and with a radius equal to the estimated distance.

FIX AND DR

The intersection of two or more simultaneous lops gives the vessel's position on the chart (Fig. 5-1).

You should be very clear about the distinction between a fix and a dead reckoning (DR) position. If the observations underlying a fix are properly made, the vessel's position is certain. Any DR position, while derived by exact calculations, remains, to some extent, guess work. A well determined fix is selected at the starting point (Pt. of Dep.). The vessel is then placed on the desired course and its speed noted. A taffrail log which measures distance (and indirectly the speed through the water) is very useful. At regular intervals the probable position of the vessel is found, either by plotting or by computation. The position found without considering the probable effect of a current is termed the *DR position*. It is the basic reference for positions between fixes. If information about current is available, you should derive a more probable *Estimated Position* (EP) by correcting the DR position for the effect of estimated current. EP then replaces DR in labeling.

In spite of all your efforts, however, uncontrollable errors are apt to enter computations, resulting in errors in successive DRs and EPs. Errors will increase. As soon as you can, check with the aid of a fresh fix, and remember that a good fix is a *fact*, a DR, a *hypothesis*.

Clear and accurate labeling is a necessity in good piloting. If your labeling is properly done, any other mariner can take over and carry on where you left off, and in general, good labeling is good seamanship. Often the accuracy of the fix depends upon the accuracy in plotting. Circle and label the Pt. of Dep., *preceded by the time*, as shown by the 0736 Pt. Dep. off New London in the cruise of VEGA, Chapter 3 (See Chart 116-SC Tr). *Label a bearing line* with the direction underneath the lop and with time (in hours and minutes) *above* the lop.

In deciding upon your legs or courses for a cruise around the region of the chart, your best guides, in addition to your charts, are the following:

- *Coast Pilot* of the Region, which for Chart 116-SC Tr is *U.S. Coast Pilot 2, Atlantic Coast, Cape Cod to Sandy Hook,* for year of cruise.
- *Light List Volume I, Atlantic Coast,* latest available.
- *Tide Table, East Coast of North and South America,* for year of cruise.
- *Tidal Current Tables, Atlantic Coast of North America,* for year of cruise.
- *Time, Speed, Distance Table,* to accelerate plotting.

The time of departure may well depend upon height of the tide, as in this case of the cruise of TUCANA, (which follows) since departure will be in a shoal region.

It will be more interesting if you learn piloting techniques as you proceed with this cruise, which you might term a "practice cruise." Facts of the cruise now follow.

First, take a pencil, your dividers and parallel rulers, and follow directions given. *If necessary, check your plotting by reference to Figs. 5-14 to 16. (For an actual cruise the larger-scale Chart 13214 should also be inspected.)*

Pt. of Dep. is East of Stonington Pt., as shown in following Log. This Log has been filled in with all the answers (Table 5-1a). The second, extra, Log (Table 5-1b) has many blanks—for you to fill in when ready. You may want to wait until you have read all details connected with the first table and the cruise, as described here, or you may want to fill in the blanks of Table 5-1b as soon as you understand each entry. If you can complete the Log with understanding, you know that you are then ready for piloting *on* water.

LOG

Cruise of TUCANA

Pt. Dep. is at Western end of marked channel, East of Stonington Pt.

Lat. 41°19.8′N, Long. 71°54′08″W

Speed through water 2 knots on first leg,
3 knots afterwards, as indicated in Log

Draft of TUCANA = 4 feet

DATE OF DEPARTURE: October 27, 1977   TIME = 0830
(Ascertained as a favorable time by studying times of high and low water)

Before plotting, be quite sure to read the *Coast Pilot* for your region. For your cruise on Chart 116-SC Tr, for instance, you need *U.S. Coast Pilot 2, Atlantic Coast, Cape Cod to Sandy Hook.* More special regions may be found first in the index at the back of the publication. For your cruise of TUCANA, it would be well to read generally, first about tides and currents, etc., in Little Narragansett Bay and Stonington Pt. Besides learning about dangers in the way of shoals and rocks, you will be directed where you may purchase marine supplies, fuel and water. After studying *Coast Pilot*, you might decide on the tracks (courses) given in the first column of Table 5-1a, to be made good. You may choose the six legs given there and then proceed to fill in the rest of the table for your practice cruise. You will now, as you continue this chapter be guided through these details.

As TUCANA takes departure, at the end of the marked channel, the nun buoy number 4 is to port, and soon becomes broad on the port quarter as TUCANA rounds the buoy to make good the first leg of 194°t, the track for 0.55 miles. Buoys often drift in storms, and positions may be off. *Coast Pilot* has already told you that shoal water extends for about 200 yards off Stonington Pt., and the shoal area North of Stonington Pt. is subject to continual changes. "Shoaling" is even marked on the chart. That is why you decide to leave these waters around high tide.

Question 1: (a) What is the time of the morning high tide? (b) What is the height then? (c) What is the depth of the water at Pt. Dep.?

On this short, first leg you can check your plotted course or desired track by noting the relative bearing of the tank almost dead astern, slightly to port. You see that the clock tower, lower in height, is

TABLE 5-1a
Log for the Cruise of TUCANA

Track Desired	True Hdg.	Mag. Hdg.	psc Hdg.	Dist. (n.m.)	Current Set	Drift	Speed thru wat.	Speed made good	Time	Lat. Long. at end of Leg
						kn.		kn.		
1 194° t	195°	209°	216°	0.55	035°	0.1	2.0	1.9	0847	41°19.3'N, 71°54.3'W
2 236° t	236°	250°	256°	0.46	Slack		3.0	3.0	0856	41°19.0'N, 71°54.8'W
3 166° t	166°	180°	194°	0.50	near slack		3.0	3.0	0906	41°18.5'N, 71°54.7'W
4 238° t	221°	235°	240°	0.95	285°	1.1	3.0	3.6	0922	41°18.0'N, 71°55.7'W
5 270° t	273°	287°	290°	4.55	255°	0.8	3.0	3.8	1035	41°18.0'N, 72°01.8'W
6 253° t	253°	267°	276°	4.60	260° 0.1 / 055° 0.3		3.0	2.7 (av)	1217 = ETA	41°16.6'N, 72°07.6'W

Total Dist. = 11.61   (Note: Current at 0906 actually between 1.1 and 1.2 knots)

TABLE 5-1b
Log for the Cruise of TUCANA (to be filled in)

Track Desired	True Hdg.	Mag. Hdg.	psc Hdg.	Dist. (n.m.)	Current Set	Drift	Speed thru wat.	Speed made good	Time	Lat. Long. at end of Leg
						kn.				
1 194° t				0.55	035°	0.1	2.0			
2 236° t				0.46	Slack		3.0			
3 166° t				0.50	near slack		3.0			
4 238° t				0.95	285°	1.2	3.0			
5 270° t				4.55	255°	0.8	3.0			
6 253° t				4.60	260° 0.1 / 055° 0.8		3.0		= ETA	

(Consult Table 5-1a and text for any help needed; for currents, review Chapter 4 first.)

behind, to starboard. Also, almost dead ahead is the Middle Ground flashing light. Remember that structures fixed to land are safer than possibly drifting buoys for bearings and reference points.

Current, Leg 1. You have already investigated the 0830 current and determined the set and drift on this first leg, as shown in your Log, with set 035°, drift 0.1 kn. You now want to know the correct heading (t) in order to make good your desired track of 194°. A very convenient place for the construction of vectors is the compass rose on your 116-SC chart, where both true directions and magnetic directions are shown. (Note the variation for the region at the center of the compass rose on the chart.) Applying the variation, you can enter magnetic courses in your Log.

PILOTING, METHOD C 2.

Note that you will pass the flashing red buoy number 2 close to starboard on leg 1. You predict that you will reach the end of leg 1 at 0847, after you have drawn your vector current diagram on the compass rose, as suggested. (Of course, a maneuvering board, Chapter 6, would have a larger scale, but the compass rose is at hand!) Check the figures for current by reference to abstracts from *Tidal Current Tables*, and use the *speed made good in estimating the time of arrival at ends of legs.* Plot a track of 236°t for second leg.

DOUBLING THE ANGLE ON THE BOW, METHOD B 2.

On leg 2 you decide to double the angle on the bow (Fig. 5-6). Using Middle Ground light at the beginning of leg 2 you measure a relative bearing of 030° to port, and then measure a relative bearing of 060° off the port bow, keeping track of distance run between the two bearings. At the end of this run your distance from the light will be equal to your run. If your run is accurate, this is a good method. It certainly depends upon the run, which may be inaccurate because of current, in spite of your endeavors to keep track of and account for the current continually. Any angle < 90° can be measured easily. If you can only double it, the method is sometimes useful. Also note, on leg 2, that you are crossing the *range* made by Middle Ground light and the Stonington Inner Breakwater flashing green light. (The Middle Ground light is really the Stonington Outer Breakwater flashing W light.) However, this use of a range is not as accurate as using a closed range (See Open and Closed Ranges subhead later on in this chapter).

Current, Leg 2. You have already determined that the current on leg 2 was slack and hence your speed through the water is your speed made good. The time for the DR at end of leg 2 is 0856.

At one point on leg 3, track 166°t, you will be on a range between bell buoy number 3 and Middle Ground light (the "3" indicates that the number 3 will appear on the buoy for identification) and you will be fairly close to the bell buoy.

Question 2: Find set and drift of current at 0856, assuming that the current at Edwards Pt.—Sandy Pt. (between) still holds (#1605 in *Tidal Current Tables*). (See Table 5-1a for answer.)

CROSS BEARINGS, METHOD A 1.

You can check the 0906 DR position at the end of leg 3 by bearing lines. The true bearing of Stonington Outer Breakwater light (Middle Ground light) is 014°. Plot this lop through the light. The true bearing of Latimer Reef light is 255°. Plot this lop through Latimer Reef light. The two lops will intersect to give you a fix at 0906 if both bearings were obtained at this time. If, in reality, your fix, or intersection in this case, of the two lines of position came at a different point, then *this* point would be your 0906 Fix, and you would then plot your 4th leg from this fix. As it is, the 0906 Fix coincides with the 0906 DR, and you label it *0906 Fix*, as shown on Chart 116-SC Tr. Remember that bearings, when taken, would be compass bearings if you used a magnetic compass, and so the compass bearings would have to be corrected to true bearings (or to magnetic bearings), as explained in

Chapter 2. If the compass had deviation different from your deviation table, the bearing lines could be in error, but if the deviation curve still applies, and the lines are accurate, the method is good and easy to use. You may think that a check at the end of leg 3 is entirely unnecessary because you are so close to nun buoy number 2, but remember that positions of buoys may not be too accurate, as stated previously, and the best rule to remember and practice is that *every* method should be checked by another method if possible. *This technique of checking by two different methods when possible is using constant vigilance and ensuring a safe voyage.*

Current, Leg 4. At the beginning of leg 4 you are rather near the point 41°18′N, 71°54′W (Napatree Point, 0.7 mile SW, of) a point given in the *Tidal Current Tables*, at which figures for the current are given (number 1610 in their Table 2—see Table 4-5 in previous chapter) and the reference station is *The Race*. The time differences are:

Velocity Ratios

Slack - 0^h55^m Max Current - 1^h10^m Max F 0.6

Max E 0.6

F Direction 285° Ebb Direction 115°

Your desired time is 0906, as you change course for the desired track 238°t. Referring to *The Race* (Table 4-6) the two time figures and others are:

The Race		Napatree Point	Drift	Answer
0822	3.2 F	0712 (0822 − 1^h10^m)	1.9 (3.2 x .6)	Drift 1.2 knots
1123	Slack	1028 (1123 − 0^h55^m)		F Dir. 285°

Time between slack and desired time = 1^h22^m (1028 - 0906)
Time between slack and max current = 3^h16^m (1028 - 0712)
Table 3 gives you .6 as the f factor (Table 4-7 in this text)
Drift = 1.9 x .6 = 1.1 knots   Set = 285°t   (See Fig. 5-13.)

Assuming this current for leg 4, you enter figures in Log as shown, after you have constructed your vector diagram for the current assumed on this leg 4, to obtain your results.

VERTICAL ANGLES, METHODS A5 AND C 1c.

On leg 4 at the point labeled P on your Chart 116-SC Tr (Fig. 5-14) (.05 n.m. to E of "38" sounding on the chart) you can check your position by measuring the vertical angle of the Stonington Outer Breakwater (Middle Ground light). Get as close to the water line as possible. Suppose you measure a vertical angle of 0°26′ with your sextant. The height of the light is 46 feet above mean high water, explained under the title of the chart. For greatest accuracy and safety, you should consider the height of the water at this time, depending upon the tide. In the blank form (See Chapter 4, *Tide Tables* subhead) which you made for the height of the water at Stonington, you can estimate the

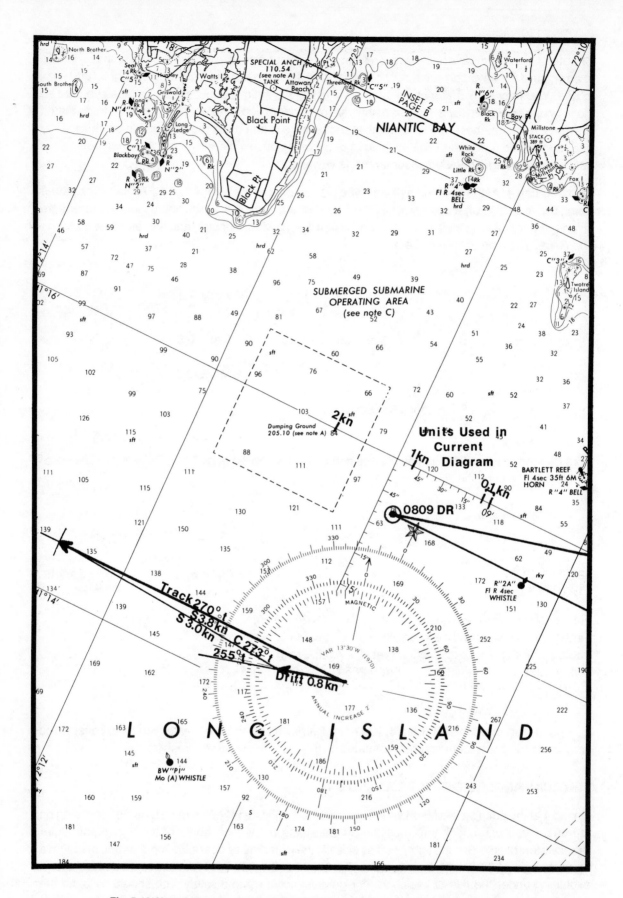

Fig. 5-12. Use of compass rose to determine heading and speed made good on leg 5.

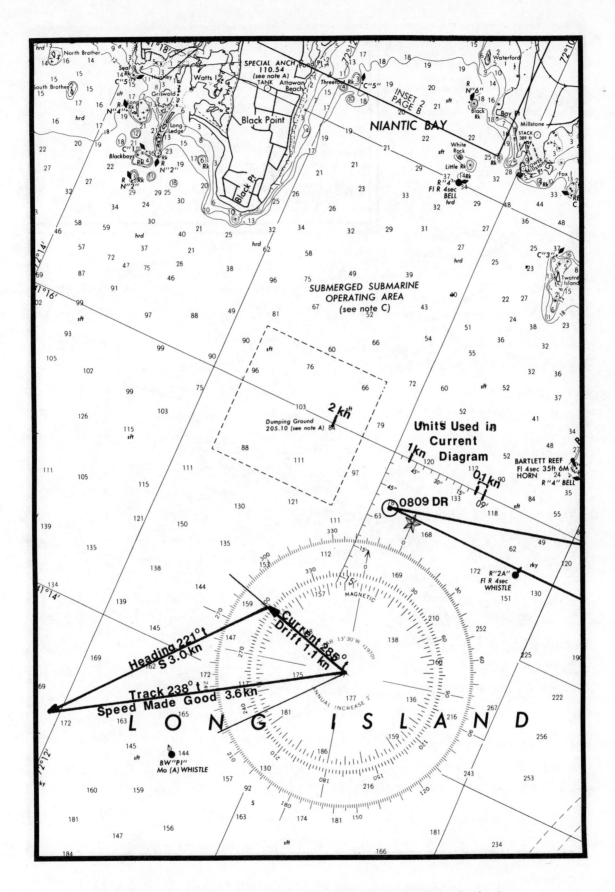

Fig. 5-13. Use of compass rose to determine heading and speed made good on leg 4.

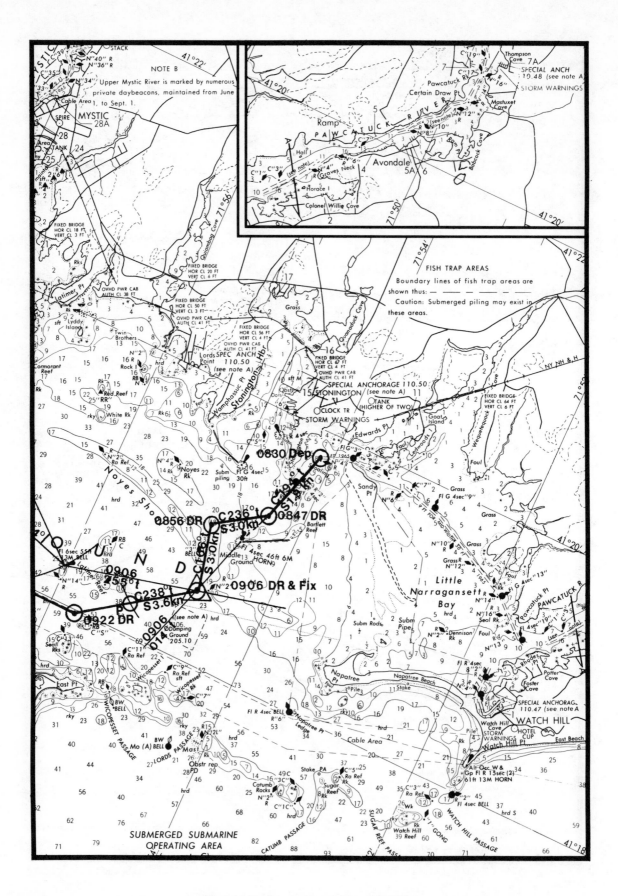

Fig. 5-14. Eastern section of Chart 116-SC Tr.

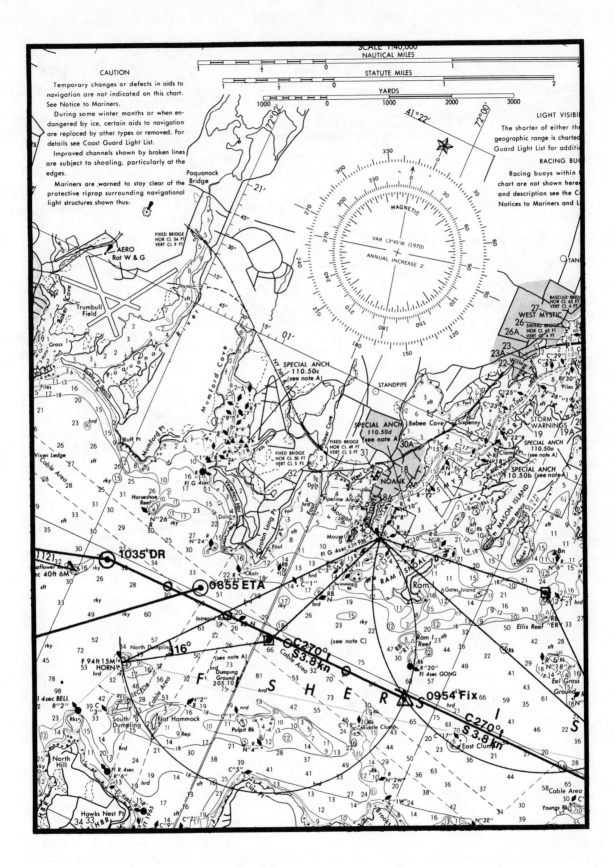

Fig. 5-15. Middle section of Chart 116-SC Tr.

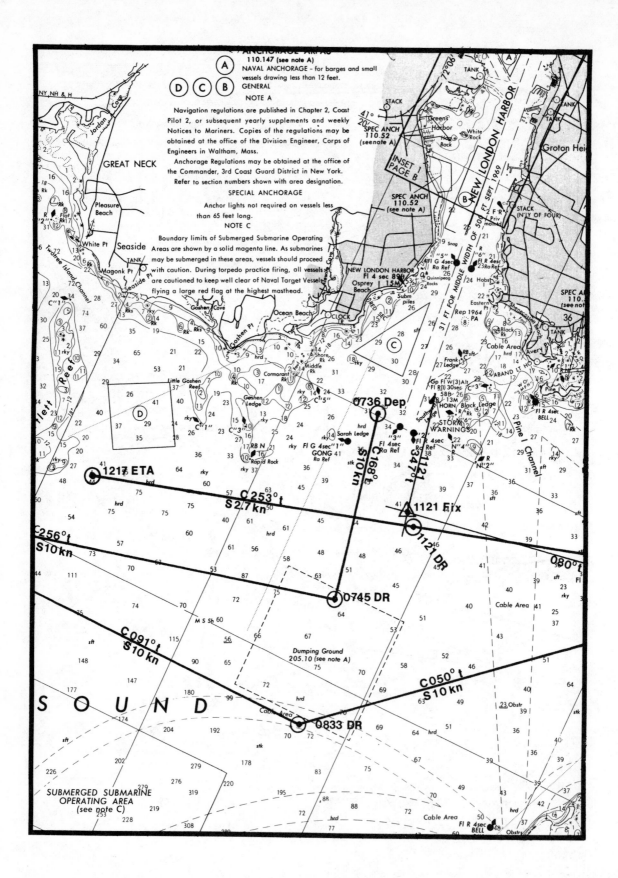

Fig. 5-16. Western section of Chart 116-SC Tr.

height of the water at Stonington at 0916, the DR time at P. This height is about 3.1′, since height of high water is 3.2′. The additional height of the Middle Ground light above the water will be 3.2 - 3.1 or 0.1′. Added to 46 feet, the height of the light is equal to 46.1′ above the water line. Now you can use a convenient table (See Appendix IV, Table 10) which gives your distance off if you know the height of the object and measure the vertical angle which the object (in this case, the light) subtends. The distance off in this case equals about 0.95 miles. Draw an arc with radius equal to this distance, and note that it cuts the track at P, and you can feel reassured at this point (Fig. 5-4).

Note, when you have reached the point P on leg 4, that you are now in the red sector of North Dumpling fixed light. Inspection of the area within this red sector shows many possible dangers, in the way of rocks and reefs, mostly. You need to be more careful in this area, and so proceed with caution. You are nearing the end of leg 4, and when you change to track 270°t, you will soon be out of this red sector.

The measurement of *vertical angles* to obtain the distance off does sound simple and easy, but in practice the angle is usually very small as shown and the measurement somewhat uncertain, as there is apt to be doubt of where the bottom is and the light itself is not too easy to see in daytime. Objects far off, such as mountains, may be below the visible horizon, and corrections for this fact must enter the calculations.

Current, Leg 5. At 0922 the track changes to 270°t (leg 5), for a distance made good of 4.55 miles. If you first investigate the current, you will find the *Tidal Current Tables* give the current for a point near Ram Island Reef buoy "20", which should give us the current for at least half of this leg 5. Proceed to investigate the current, as follows:

This point is #1630 (Table 2, *Tidal Current Tables*), the reference station is *The Race* again (Table 4-5 in this text):

Time Differences	Velocity Ratios
Slack -0^h45^m	Max F 0.4
Max Current -0^h50^m	Max E 0.4

F Direction 255°   Ebb Direction 090°

Your desired time is 0922, as you change course for the desired track 270°t. Referring to The Race (Table 4-6), the two time figures and others are:

The Race		Ram Island Reef	Drift
0822	3.2 F	0732 (0822 − 0^h50^m)	1.3 (3.2 x .4)
1123	Slack	1038 (1123 − 0^h45^m)	

Time between slack and desired time = 1^h16^m
Time between slack and max current = 3^h06^m
Table 3 gives you .6 as the *f* factor (Table 4-7 in text).
Drift = 1.3 x .6 = 0.8 kn   Set = 255°

To obtain your results, assuming this current for leg 5, you enter figures in the Log as shown, after you have constructed your vector diagram for the current assumed. (See Fig. 5-12.)

HORIZONTAL ANGLES, METHOD A 3.

After two miles on leg 5, you want to obtain a good check on your position, as the weather is becoming unfavorable and you expect some fog. You plan, now, to use the technique dependent upon two horizontal angles, (Fig. 5-2), each one giving you the measure of the horizontal angle between two charted objects. In this case you choose, for your three charted objects, North Dumpling fixed light, with a horn, the flashing green Noank light (North of Ram Island shoal), and third, Latimer Reef flashing light. The angles are as follows, measured with sextants:

(1) and (2): Angle between North Dumpling light and Noank light, 074°
(2) and (3): Angle between the second, Noank light and Latimer Reef light, 114°
(The center object is used twice.)

REDUCTION OF HORIZONTAL ANGLES, METHOD A 3.

There are two ways of reducing these measures to obtain a fix. One way depends upon the fact that *one* horizontal angle alone, between two charted objects, gives you a *circle of position.* You can construct this first circle of position on your chart, as follows:

- Draw a line between lights (1) and (2).
- Lay off angle at (1) (towards your position) which is equal to $90° - 74° = 16°$
- Lay off same angle (2) (Fig. 5-2)

The intersection of the two new lines drawn give you the center of your *circle of position* which passes through (1), (2), and also through the point where you are, but you cannot tell yet what this point is. You need the *other* circle for this, as *two* circles of position are necessary to provide a fix. (A small square is drawn on the chart to show the center of this first circle of position.)

Since your second horizontal angle is greater than 90°, you take the difference just the same, between 90° and your measured angle 114°, (or 24°), but in this case you lay the angle off *away* from your position or on the other side of the straight line between (2) and (3). The two circles intersect in two points, one of which is Noank light, the other of which is the 0954 Fix, about 0.2th of a mile South of red buoy number 20, and about half a tenth of a mile South of the 0954 DR. This is an excellent fix, quite independent of deviation of the compass, and independent of a run which may be set off by an unknown current. The two angles may be measured simultaneously if two sextants are available. If you are alone, or with one sextant only, you may measure the first angle, timing it, then the second, and finally the first *again,* with the time taken for each sight. Use the time of the second, and the mean of the first and third angles, and the results will be satisfactory. (See later sections in this Chapter for another method of finding a fix from horizontal angles. Plot the last half of leg 5 from your 0954 Fix.)

LINE OF SOUNDINGS, METHOD C 3.

You now assume, since your 0954 Fix was good, that your computation for the current on this leg was satisfactory, and you expect your time of arrival at the end of leg 5 will be 1035. However, just as you make this decision, the fog suddenly closes in, and you make sure of the last half of leg 5 by using a line of soundings. Every 8.2 minutes you find the depth of the water by using a fathometer (or lead and line if you lacked a fathometer). The first sounding is obtained at 0954.

The line of soundings run as follows, towards the West:

74, 75, 66, 19, 32, 26 in feet

72, 73, 64, 17, 30, 24 are the same figures with two feet subtracted in each case, since you figure that the height of the tide is about two feet at this time (based on the tide at Noank). Write these figures along the edge of a sheet of paper at intervals of 0.52 mile (your distance covered in 8.2

minutes at speed made good of 3.8 knots). Place a sheet in several positions to see which line best fits the line of soundings. As it is, the best fit lies along the plotted course, or approximately along the 41°18′N. Lat. line (See Figs. 5-15, 16).

You should always plan what you will do in case the fog rolls in quickly, and a line of soundings, obtained and plotted in the above fashion is one of the best techniques for this situation. Do not hesitate to use it. Inspect this line on the chart. In the described cruise, the fog now lifts, and you are safely at 1035 position.

Current, Leg 6. On leg 6 there are current figures for three places which can affect your heading and ETA (Estimated Time of Arrival) (See Table 4-5). First there are current figures for North Hill Pt., 1.1 miles NNW of. Second, further along on leg 6 there are figures for Eastern Point, 1.5 miles South of, and finally for Bartlett Reef, 0.2 mile South of (See Table 4-9 to cover Bartlett Reef in this text). It is excellent practice to study each one separately, and estimate the set and drift of the current at the appropriate times when your leg 6 would be close to these regions. Then adopt an approximate average as the heading and speed made good for leg 6, and check your opinion with the figures given in the Log for this cruise. This is a good example of a case when an average figure has to be adopted sometimes for practical reasons. It also emphasizes the point that piloting techniques should be used along the leg as much as possible, to check the estimated position. You have a good chance to study the different possibilities and select the best, according to circumstances. Assume that there is no fog on this leg.

FIX BY CROSS BEARINGS, METHOD A 1.

On leg 6, at 1121, you obtain a fix from simultaneous bearings on New London Ledge light, on Southwest Ledge, and the Seaflower Reef light. (Fig. 5-1.) The first bearing taken over the pelorus is found to be 347°t, and the second is 080°t. (Of course these bearings were probably measured as compass bearings, and then transposed into true bearings.)

Question 3: What are the compass bearings actually obtained first, to give the above true bearings on these two lights?

Plot these two true bearings, to obtain a fix (from cross bearings).

Question 4: What is the Lat. and Long. of the fix obtained?

Answer: This 1121 Fix should be close to your 1121 DR, at 41°17.4′N, 72°04.4′W.

You want this cruise of TUCANA to end at a point .5 to .6 of a mile East of Bartlett Reef light. You figure that the ETA is 1217-1219.

Note that soon after your 1121 Fix, you entered the red sector of New London Harbor light, and you will still be in this sector at 1217. Proceed with caution, and you can pass the rocks and ledges safely! This point marks the end of the practice cruise. There was not sufficient time, and the conditions were not always appropriate on this cruise for trying all the techniques listed and classified near the beginning of this chapter. Hence, the rest of the chapter will be devoted to descriptive and supplementary explanations of those techniques.

RANGE, METHODS A 2 AND A 4.

You are on a range when you are on a straight line between or through two objects, which are more useful when they are charted. If, in addition, you happen to be on *two* ranges plotted on a chart, you have an excellent fix right there, at the intersection of the two lines, or ranges. The compass with its possible errors is not involved. However, on many charts you will find no ranges plotted, and so you cannot count upon them, but welcome them when you find them. In addition, it is often helpful to make a range of your own. You might have two towers or tanks on land; they might even be plotted on the chart, and you might like to cruise for a while on the range which they make.

Open and Closed Ranges. Ranges are called *open* when you see them as two objects. When you see them only as one, the range is called *closed.* Both are then in one direction from you. If you wish, you may measure on your chart (with parallel rulers) the direction of a line drawn through the two charted objects. On some charts, this direction might be stated for you. You might like to cruise in the direction of this range and check (as you cruise) that you are still on the range. Based on this idea, sometimes a range direction is placed on a chart purposely so that you can use it in entering a harbor or in proceeding along a channel.

Range and Bearing, Method A 4. You can always combine techniques when the opportunity arises. For instance, you might like to use one range and one bearing. The intersection would give you a fix. Merely read the Lat. and Long. of the point of intersection from the corresponding scales on your chart.

DOUBLING THE ANGLE ON THE BOW, METHOD B 2.

Among the next best methods of piloting, there are a few which depend upon *doubling the angle on the bow* (Fig. 5-6). The proof of this method now follows for certain cases. Consider the special *bow and beam bearings*, when the first (relative angle off the bow is 45° (See Fig. 5-7 at A). The second relative angle, (at the end of a run) is 90°, at B in the figure. The angle at the light (L) must also equal 45°, since there are 180° in a triangle. Then the triangle ABL is isosceles, and BL (distance off) must equal AB, the run. The relationship holds for any angle, if, at the end of the run, it is doubled (Fig. 5-6). (Note that angles are *relative*.) There are many occasions when this technique is appropriate, but it is also true that if your distance from the light is found to be too small, you are already *there*, and you cannot do much about it.

7/10THS RULE, METHOD B 2b.

The 7/10ths rule has a great advantage. Here the angles are special—22 1/2° for the first and 45° for the second. As before, you know that at the end of the run your distance from the light will equal the run, but *in addition*, (Fig. 5-8), when the light comes *abeam*, your distance from the light will be 7/10ths of the run, and what is more significant, you know this fact *when* you are at B, the end of the run, and when you still have time to change course and head away from the light if the position at D is going to be dangerously close to the light or to any other dangers shown there on the chart. There is time for preventive action on your part!

   If you missed measuring the 22 1/2° angle, you could use the next rule, B 2c, in this list. Here the first angle is 30°, and the angle at the end of the run is 60°. When, however, you reach D, where the light is abeam to your course, your distance from the light would here be 7/8ths of the run. The easiest way of proving these last two rules is with trigonometry, but if you do not enjoy trigonometry, just accept the rules and use them whenever the occasion is appropriate.

Methods B 3 AND B 4. The rules are almost self-explanatory. The run equals the distance off when the light comes abeam. Rule 3 is most helpful among pairs of angles which would give you distance from the light. No mental arithmetic is necessary after the second relative angle is measured. However, if you find it difficult to obtain an exact bearing given in one of the rules, you might enjoy Table 7 in *Bowditch*, where many pairs of angles are presented for your choice. The explanation of Table 7 you may need in order to use these other angles. Note that occasionally a piloting technique comes under two classifications, as with the 7/10ths rule.

ADVANCING A LOP, METHOD B 1.

Use of cross-bearing lines is one of the most popular piloting techniques. Sometimes, however, there is only *one* light or object which you can use. This one light gives you only one lop, but you can advance it along the course to use with another lop obtained from the same light at a later time. Hence, it is important to understand about *advancing a lop*—perhaps the most difficult of all piloting techniques in theory.

For an example, consider that you are skipper of CANOPUS, off Eastern Point light on Cape Ann, on a true course of 081°, with DR positions at 1200 and 1215 as marked (Fig. 5-5). At 1215 you obtain a true bearing of 012° on Eastern Point light. Since the plotted bearing line does not pass through the 1215 DR, drop a perpendicular from the 1215 DR to the 1215 lop. The point P where this perpendicular intersects the lop at this time is your best position at 1215. Note that this point is on the lop at this time, and is also the closest point on the lop to your 1215 DR. Suppose the fog rolled in instantly after you had obtained the one bearing line, and that you cannot see this light again until 1255. You can at least *advance* the 1215 lop along the course just by marking off four miles (distance covered in 40 minutes) from the intersection of the first lop and the course (at P). Think of the first lop as marching along the course for four miles, to reach P′. At P′ draw a line parallel to the first lop (with parallel rulers) to obtain the advanced lop at 1255. The advanced lop is marked with 1215-1255 above the line and with the direction below the line. You are somewhere on this advanced lop, and if you take another bearing of the Eastern Pt. light when the fog lifts at 1255, and the bearing is 301°t, you will plot this second lop through the Eastern Pt. light and obtain a running fix which is labeled with the *time followed by R Fix*. You can mark a small triangle at this intersection point, the symbol used in air navigation. Some navigators use a circle, but the fix should be conspicuous, and a triangle will be used in this text to denote a fix. The accuracy, of course, depends in this case on the accuracy of the run, but as a rule, a running fix is apt to be much more reliable than a DR. The student mariner should try to understand the theory behind advancing a lop, because this is an important technique, not only in coastwise, but also in celestial navigation.

DANGER ANGLES, METHOD C 1b.

There is one other general type of method which you can use in piloting. It is listed under *Danger Bearings and Angles, Special Methods*. The horizontal danger angle, used with a sextant in the measuring of horizontal angles, is most useful in certain circumstances. For example, if you were South of some charted rocks, and wanted to make sure that you remained to the South, you could select two points (A and B) on the chart, on the Southern edge of the rocks. They must be two points which stand out, so that you could measure the horizontal angle which they subtend from your position (P). If this angle was 50°, for example, and you kept measuring the angle subtended by these same two points A and B, as long as the angle measured remained smaller than 50°, you would be further away from the rocks and safe! Watch out, on the other hand, if this horizontal angle suddenly became larger than 50°, which is called a *Danger Angle*. (Fig. 5-10) With this method you could safely pass between two dangerous regions. Your angle could always remain smaller than one danger angle and larger than another. In either case there might be a point, such as a day beacon at C in the figure which you could mark on your chart, and then on the chart measure with a circular protractor the number of degrees in the angle ACB, or the angle subtended at C. This angle in the example here could be your critical danger angle for the second danger to the South in the figure. In order to pass between the two dangers safely, you would make sure that the horizontal angle measured always remained between the two values 22° and 50°.

DANGER BEARING, METHOD C 1a.

If you were approaching some dangerous shoals or sunken rocks, and wanted to make sure that you did not run aground because of an adverse current, you might note that you could observe the

Southern end of a headland at A, and you might decide to take a bearing on A. Your bearing might be 060°t. You could call this bearing the danger bearing, and as you approached the headland on your course of 070°t, you could keep taking bearings of the headland. As long as the true bearings remained smaller than 060°, you would be safe (Fig. 5-9). (Compare the true bearings at B1 and later, at B2.) Of course this method involves taking compass bearings first, and then applying variation and possible deviation to obtain true bearings. You could work with magnetic bearings more quickly than with true bearings, with the same results as long as *every* bearing was magnetic. At some distance from shore, danger bearings are not of much help.

VERTICAL DANGER ANGLE, METHOD C 1c.

Under these special methods a vertical danger angle could be established in case a light, tower or any tall object was in sight. The vertical angle could be measured at the first position B1, after you had established the danger vertical angle by deciding after inspection of your chart that you wanted to remain further than 0.7 miles from the light or tower. If the height of the light was 120 feet, a table (See Appendix IV) would tell you that your vertical angle at this distance is 1°40' (Ho). If you measured the vertical angle frequently and made sure that it remained smaller than 1°40', then you would be further from the light than 0.7 miles. Note that vertical angles are difficult to measure, partly because it is difficult to be sure of the top and the bottom of the object. This method has low priority among all the methods listed (Fig. 5-11).

MEASURING HORIZONTAL ANGLES WITH SEXTANT, METHOD A 3.

More should be said, now, about the third method listed under *Best Methods*—fix by three points, or *Method Using Horizontal Angles*, an excellent technique because it is independent of the compass and its deviations. In the TUCANA cruise you used this method. You can merely follow the instructions given there. The supplementary information is concerned with *measuring* the horizontal angles with a sextant. Sextants were first constructed in 1730 by the Englishman, John Hadley, and by the American, Thomas Godfrey. It was invented just for the purpose of measuring the angle, in degrees and minutes, between any two objects. The mariner who has taken sextant sights need not worry about the following paragraphs. The mariner who has never handled a sextant needs this information. Look at Fig. 5-17 where a section of the sextant is shown. It shows the *window* where the measured angle is read. The position of the arrow (or sometimes just a heavy line on the arc of the sextant) gives you a reading in degrees. The numbers on the arc of the sextant denote degrees, and the smallest unit here is one degree. You can also measure minutes of arc, on the *micrometer drum* of the sextant, where 60 divisions (for 60 minutes of arc) are marked. The reading in Fig. 5-17 is 41°30.3'.

Index Error. In general, whenever you use a sextant, your first act should be to determine the index error of the sextant. (Almost any instrument is apt to have an error and the sextant is no exception, but you can easily find this error yourself.) Here are the rules for finding the index error (I.E.) of your sextant:

1. Set the reading of your sextant approximately at 0°.
2. Hold the sextant in your right hand, *vertically*, with the plane of the arc at right angles to the plane of your horizon, through your feet (Fig. 5-18).
3. Holding your sextant vertically, look in the eyepiece at the distant horizon, and see two horizons in the field of the eyepiece—one in the clear glass, and the other one in the mirror or silvered side of the horizon glass.
4. Focus the eyepiece for clear images.
5. Make the horizon in the silvered part of the horizon glass exactly in line with the horizon in the clear glass, by turning the micrometer drum and looking through the eyepiece continually.
6. Take the reading, which should be only a matter of minutes for the I.E., but note that this I.E. may

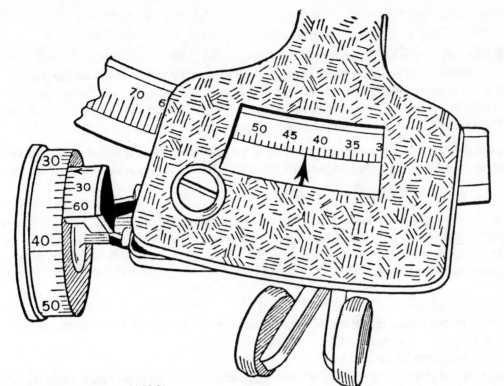

Fig. 5-17. Reading the sextant: 41°30.3′.

Fig. 5-18. Holding the sextant vertically, to obtain the index error from the horizon.

Photo by Eugene Franck

be *on* the arc (with the arrow among numbers which are increasing) or *off* the arc (with the arrow among numbers which are decreasing), see Fig. 5-19 (I.E. here is 4.7′ *off* the arc).

Note: If the reading for I.E. is greater than half a degree (30′), the sextant needs adjusting, and you should take your sextant to an expert, who can manipulate two small screws behind the horizon glass so as to make the I.E. zero. He will turn one of them at a time, in rotation, and watch what is happening every second, with the first setting of 0°0′. These screws are very delicate and can be used so much that they will have no effect at all.

7. As a correction to apply, remember the rule: "If the error is *off* (the arc), it's *on*, or to be added to the Hs (angle first measured on sextant). If the error is *on* (the arc), it's *off,* or to be subtracted from the Hs."

The rules above have been given to cover all measures of sextant angles, *Hs,* but note that with horizontal angles, since you cannot plot *minutes of arc* accurately here, you do not have to worry about an I.E. of minutes. You can merely read the Hs of your angle in terms of degrees and possibly tenths of a degree if you wish.

RULES FOR MEASURING HORIZONTAL ANGLES
1. Hold the sextant in your right hand, with the plane of the arc *parallel* to the plane of your horizon, through your feet. (This position does not have to be exact!)
2. Focus the eyepiece for clear images.
3. Look at the *left* charted object of the two which you are using for your horizontal angle, and *keep*

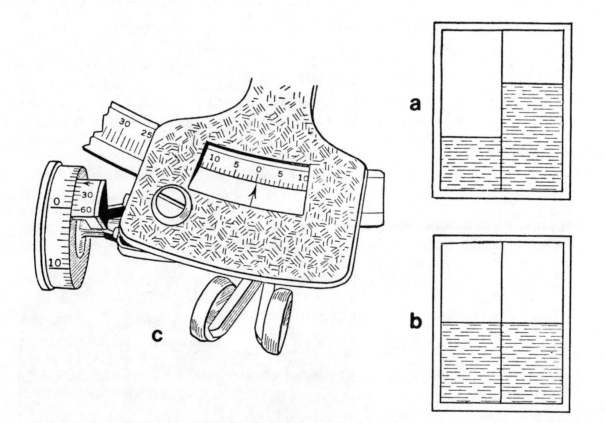

Fig. 5-19. Sextant reading *off* the arc: I.E. = 4.7′ *off* arc (c); horizon seen in clear glass (a) and (b) at left and reflected image of horizon seen in mirror (a) and (b), at right side of horizon glass.

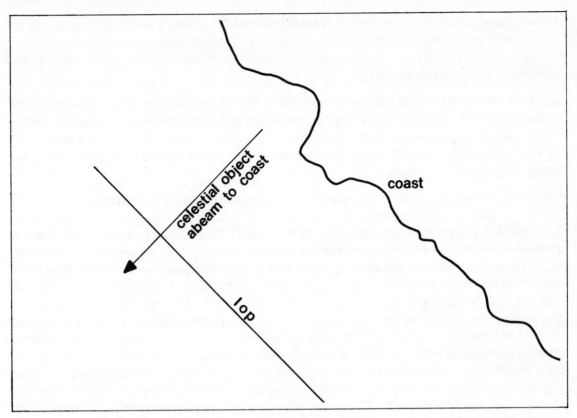

Fig. 5-20. Lop parallel to the coastline can give your distance off.

looking at it in the clear part of the horizon glass (clear part will be *above* the silvered part). While looking at the left object, move the index arm of your sextant *away* from you (with your *left* hand) until you sight in the silvered mirror the right charted object, which you have brought around so that you can view the two objects superimposed, or with one *above* the *other in the same vertical line*. Take the reading at this point and you have a measure of your horizontal angle. If, by chance, you lose your second object, on the right as you were bringing it around, you can retrieve it by tipping your sextant a little, usually *down*. With practice you will not lose your right-hand charted object.

For your second horizontal angle, if you have a third charted object, to the *left* of the left one of the two used in the first horizontal angle, proceed to measure a second horizontal angle between the third object and the left object of the first two. This second horizontal angle gives another circle, and one of the intersections of the two circles of position *is* your fix, as you saw on the TUCANA cruise. The only weakness of this method is the necessity of having three charted objects, but when you have them, this method is recommended, and worth packing a sextant aboard.

REDUCTION OF HORIZONTAL ANGLES; OTHER METHODS

Finally, if you plot the two circles, as you did in the TUCANA cruise, you do not have to worry about the dreaded *revolver* (See Problem Set 5-3). However, another method of finding a fix from two horizontal angles should be mentioned, especially if you do not like to construct circles. With a circular protractor you can lay off the two angles on a thin sheet of paper. Make the sides of the angles long enough so that you can sweep the sheet of paper around on your chart until you obtain a perfect fit, with the lines going right through the charted objects. The point *P* of intersection of the two angles shows your fix. A 3-arm protractor can replace constructing the two angles, *and is a real help if you have room* for it in your navigational equipment. However, if you use this 3-arm method (or the thin piece of paper) watch out for the revolver (doubtful case here) by making sure that the middle of the three objects is closer to you than the other two (Fig. 5-3). Without a sextant, you might achieve a fair measure of these angles over your compass or with a pelorus, but certainly the most accurate angles are always measured with a sextant.

Lop from Celestial Object Abeam to Coast. The sextant can be used for vertical angles also, (as already explained) and in addition you should remember that a lop obtained from celestial objects, with celestial navigation techniques, is also useful in coastwise navigation at any time when you can take the sight, with the celestial object more or less abeam to the coast, so that you have a clear horizon (Fig. 5-20).

Measuring a Vertical Angle. On the TUCANA cruise you used the technique of measuring a vertical angle. The measure of the vertical angle was given to you in this case, but if you measured it yourself, with a sextant, you would need to consider and measure the I.E. because a vertical angle is usually quite small, and the minutes of arc are important. For rules, just follow those given. There is, however, one method which does not require the application of the I.E. You could measure the vertical angle first by placing the *top* of the reflected image against the *bottom* of the clear-glass image and then measure again by placing the *bottom* of the reflected image against the top of the clear-glass image. The mean of these two measures would give you your correct vertical angle, without application of the I.E. (as suggested by Eric C. Hiscock, in his book, see Appendix III). You then have your distance from measured object (Fig. 5-4). If, however, you wish to measure only one vertical angle, measure the first angle (top of reflected image against bottom of clear-glass image), and apply your I.E., which you would have obtained already, probably, and remember the preceding rule number seven for adding or subtracting correctly. (The shade glasses may always be placed out of the way for measurement of horizontal and vertical angles; they are used mostly with the Sun for celestial

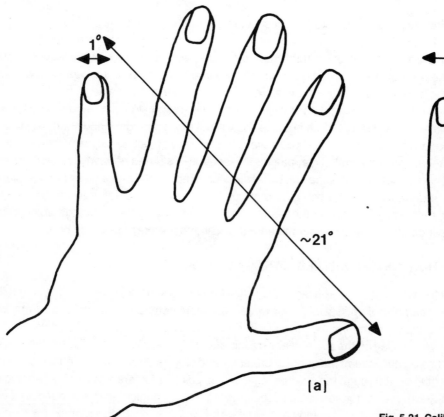

Fig. 5-21. Calibration of your hand.

navigation.) Measurement of vertical angles is most accurate when your eye is on the same level as the foot of the object measured. Your *distance off* depends upon the height of the measured object, which is given on charts as the height above mean high water. At this time then, if the light has its foundations on the bottom, the measured angle should be accurate. At other times, adjustment for height of tide should be considered, as in the TUCANA cruise. Beware of distant objects (especially mountains) which might have their bottoms *below* your horizon. A correction is necessary, but the author advises a different technique, if possible. However, if you use it, remember Appendix IV, Table IV-10.

Speed—Time—Distance Formula. Several of the methods mentioned above depend upon the run between two points. A formula for distance was given in Chapter 3. If you have some kind of a mechanical *log* with you, it can give you the run. There is another formula which is sometimes useful for determining the speed of your vessel. It requires almost any heavy object which will float. This object can be used to measure the speed of your boat. Tie a line to the object and note how long it takes to pay out a given length of line. A good formula to know is the following:

$$\text{Speed (in knots)} = \frac{\text{length (in feet)}}{\text{time (in seconds)}} \times 0.6$$

DISTANCE, METHOD A 5.

Another handy thing to do is to calibrate your hand, so that you know how many degrees you have between the tip of your thumb and the tip of your little finger when your hand is extended in front of you and also stretched out comfortably. You might have an approximate measure of 20-21′ (Fig. 5-21). You could measure your hand more exactly if you used either your star chart (Fig. 5-22) where degrees are shown, or a sextant. You could calibrate your hand against some distant steeples or towers first, (finding two which match your hand). Then measure the number of degrees between the same towers accurately with your sextant, see foregoing pages. You need this measure only to the nearest degree and tenth of a degree! Then you use your hand any time when a sextant is lacking, to obtain a rough measure of the distance off. Extend your hand in similar fashion (same position as in calibrating it) and measure the number of degrees between the top and the bottom of an object (as in

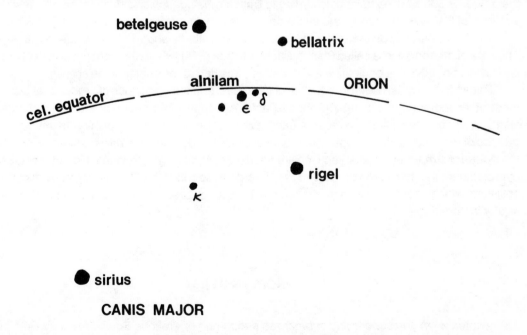

Fig. 5-22. Use of *Orion* to calibrate your hand: 19° between *Betelgeuse* and *Rigel*; 7° between *Betelgeuse* and *Bellatrix* and 3° across the three stars of *Orion's* belt in the middle (use scale of degrees on star chart for other measures).

obtain a rough measure of the distance off. Extend your hand in similar fashion (same position as in calibrating it) and measure the number of degrees between the top and the bottom of an object (as in measuring a vertical angle) or else the length of the object from left to right (as in measuring a horizontal angle). Your formula for estimating the distance off is the old *Rule of Sixty*:

Divide sixty by the measured angle. To find the distance, multiply the known height by the factor just obtained. The answer is the distance off in terms of the same unit used in the height or length. If, for an example, a tower is 100′ in height, and you measured the height as 2°, the formula would be:

$$\frac{60}{2} \times 100 = 3,000 \text{ feet}$$

This formula depends upon the fact that a radian is equal, roughly, to 60°, and so the results will be a little more accurate if you substituted 57.3 for 60 in the formula. Remember that the height, or length, of the distant object has to be known, in *linear measure*, and also, the rule works only if the angle measured does not exceed around 7°. There are times, however, when you might not be able to run below for your sextant. It might be dark, and you might be approaching a strange harbor with a cliff of known height. (Heights are apt to be marked on charts, if the objects can be used in navigation.) You also might be approaching a beach of known length. The more knowledge you have stored away, the more often you can bring forth the most appropriate tools for varied occasions, and with this rule you can consider yourself as having a built-in sextant. You could calibrate, in similar fashion, other measures of 1 finger, 2 fingers, 4 fingers, etc.

RADAR, METHOD C 6.

The name *radar* was derived from the first one or two letters of radio detection and ranging. It provides distances, bearings and consequent fixes. The distance is determined by measuring the time between the transmission and return of an electromagnetic signal which may be reflected back to the receiver by a target. It uses extremely high frequency (3,000 - 30,000 MHz), higher than frequencies of Omega, Decca, Loran A and C, and even higher than Omnirange. A 3 cm radar is in the 3,320 - 9,500 MHz band, and according to Dutton's *Navigation and Piloting*, small transistorized versions of the 3 cm band radar are available for use by yachtsmen in boats as small as 30 feet.

The information is usually presented on a screen called a *scope* of a cathode ray tube (CRT). The type of presentation is called Plan Position Indicator (PPI), where the transmitted beam of energy is shown as a radial line originating at the vessel's position at the center of the screen.

Radar can be most useful in fog, haze or darkness, and during periods of reduced visibility, when most other methods of piloting are not available. Although radar bearings are less accurate than visual bearings, navigation by radar is often more accurate than other piloting techniques during periods of reduced visibility. If you equip your vessel with radar, *be sure that you become familiar wth the operator's manual for your set.* Repairs should be made only by experts. Do not, ever, become overconfident just because you have radar aboard (as seems to be the case in many disasters—in collisions which should never happen). You must use it with great and wise judgment, and remember to *plot* the bearings.

PROBLEM SET 5

Many notes warn you concerning submerged submarine operations South of Niantic Bay, but you decide to proceed with caution and practice piloting techniques on your Chart 116-SC Tr in this region.

Cruise of ALPHECCA

1) The time is 1623 EST, your course is 101°t, speed 3 knots. With the pelorus and an assistant, you obtain a true bearing of 080° on Bartlett Reef light, and a simultaneous true bearing of 346° on Black Point tank, in the Northwest corner of your Chart 116-SC Tr, near Attawan Beach.

Give your Lat._____ and Long._____.

2) Almost immediately after your 1623 Fix in Problem No. 1 you decide to find some distances from Bartlett Reef light, using the *7/10ths Rule.*
At $16^h25^m36^s$ you measure a relative bearing of 22 1/2° to port, using Bartlett Reef light.
You stand by, ready to measure another relative bearing of 45° to port, using the same light. (You have doubled the angle on the bow.)
You note that the time of the second bearing (45°) is $16^h55^m12^s$. Compute your run in miles, and check that the distance from Bartlett Reef light equals the run.

1. What is the run in miles? _____

2. What is the distance of Bartlett Reef light at the time of the bearing of 45° ($16^h55^m12^s$)? __
_____

3. What will be the distance of Bartlett Reef light when the latter is abeam to port?_____
_____

Note that when Bartlett Reef light will be abeam, the R 2A flashing red buoy will be almost abeam at 0.2 miles approximately. This buoy is another check on your position.

3) At 41°16′09″N, 72°13′12″W, on your true course of 101° in number one of this Problem Set, but preceding your 1623 Fix, you thought it would be fun to try the 3-point method, measuring at 16^h04^m the horizontal angles as follows:

	Angle
1. Between Black Point tank (near Attawan Beach) and the stack at Millstone, Eastside of Niantic Bay	33°
2. Between Millstone stack and Bartlett Reef light	40°

When you lay off the angles according to the instructions in this chapter of your text, you find that instead of *two* circles, you have only *one* practically, which passes through *all* three objects which you used for horizontal angles, and also through *many* possible positions for you, all around most of the circle which you may have drawn. Note that the first circle which you drew through two of the objects passes also through the third. In other words, this is a case of what has been called a *revolver.* You might realize this at once because you have only one circle rather than two. However, you can still combine this one circle with a bearing line. You might obtain the latter from Bartlett Reef light. Assume that you do. If the latter was found to be 085°t at 16^h04^m, plot this bearing line, and note that it intersects your circle of position in *two* points. One intersection is the

Bartlett Reef light itself, and you certainly know you are not there! Then you must be at the *other* intersection of the circle and the bearing line. In other words, your 1604 DR is also your 1604 Fix, and you can proceed cheerfully, but still with caution, and prepare to obtain another check as soon as possible, as you did in number one here.

4) In these problems no mention has been made of the corresponding compass and magnetic bearings and readings. This is because at the beginning it often helps to concentrate on one thing at a time. Finally, on the water, all the bits of information have to be combined into a symphonic whole, when any one of the bits must be remembered and applied at the appropriate moment. It would seem suitable now to ask some questions which were assumed or ignored during problem sets, one through three.

Question 1. Use the deviation curve shown in Fig. 2-6 and also in Table 2-4. Variation will be found on your chart. Use these values only to nearest degree as a rule. Your true course in Problem No. 1 of this Problem Set 5 was 101°.
What is the corresponding magnetic course?_____
What is the corresponding compass course?_____
What was the corresponding magnetic bearing of Bartlett Reef light? (Brg. t = 080°) _____
_____
What compass bearing was first obtained for Black Point tank? (at 1623 EST; bearing t = 346°)
_____
What was the corresponding magnetic bearing of Black Point tank? _____
_____

Question 2.
In Problem No. 2 do you have to use deviation?_____
In Problem No. 2 do you have to use variation? _____

Question 3.
In Problem No. 3 and the measurement of horizontal angles, do you have to think about deviation and variation?_____

If you have difficulty with the first questions in this section, review Chapter 2, until you can handle variation and deviation as easily as you can sign your name. This subject is most necessary on the water!

5) If you have not filled in Table 5-1b, the blank Log where you should handle the data for the TUCANA cruise, do it at this time. It also has blanks to fill in for compass and magnetic headings.

6) In the following problems (a.through g. inclusive) use the same deviation curve (Fig. 2-6 or Table 2-4, the Figure being better for interpolation). Read the variation on the Chart 116-SC at the compass roses. Answers to problems are given in Appendix II.

a. On the TUCANA cruise (on true heading of 166° at 0906, end of leg 3) you were told that the true bearing of Stonington Outer Breakwater light (Middle Ground light) was 014°. What is the corresponding magnetic bearing?

*Ans:*_____

b. What is the corresponding compass bearing of this light?

*Ans:*_____

c. On the same true heading of 166° at 0906, the true bearing of Latimer Reef light was 255°. What was the corresponding magnetic bearing of this light?

*Ans:*_____

d. What was the corresponding compass bearing of this light?

*Ans:*_____

e. On a true heading of 253°, the true bearing of New London Ledge light (on Southwest Ledge) was found to be 347°. What was the corresponding magnetic bearing?

*Ans:*_____

f. What was the corresponding compass bearing which you would have found in actual practice?

*Ans:*_____

g. On the same true heading of 253°, the true bearing of Seaflower Reef light was found to be 080° at 1121. What was the corresponding compass bearing first found?

*Ans:*_____

Chapter 6

The Maneuvering Board and Relative Motion Problems

Primarily, up to this point, you have been concerned with the movement of single vessels. Methods for single vessels will not suffice if the vessel happens to be a part of a larger unit. The navigator may be more concerned with the movement of his particular vessel *relative to the other vessels of the unit* rather than with piloting or dead reckoning (DR) navigation. The solution of relative movement problems is a part of the regular routine of the navigator on board a naval vessel during maneuvers with the fleet. The navigator on board a merchant vessel in a convoy is also more concerned with the solving of relative movement problems rather than with celestial and DR navigation.

It should be emphasized, however, that this type of problem can be encountered in more ordinary conditions, with just *two* vessels and there must be at least two involved. You and a friend might be cruising in separate vessels, and you might wish to meet for lunch. If you knew the course and speed of the friend's vessel, and also your present position with respect to the friend, you might like to know what course and speed would be necessary for you to meet this friend within a certain time interval. The maneuvering board (WOBZP 5090) will help you solve this type of problem. Here in this chapter you will find a description of the method and also some typical problems which might arise. (Note that *true* directions are always used here.)

As a mariner, imagine that you are interested in the movement of the vessel M relative to the Guide G. Since the absolute movement is of no concern for this problem, G can be kept conveniently at the center of the maneuvering board. The diagram of relative position, or *relative plot*, will show two positions M_1 and M_2, *as observed from G*, at the beginning and end of the maneuver respectively. In Fig. 6-1, for illustration, the vessel is at M_1 at the beginning of the maneuver and at M_2 at the conclusion. In this case M_1 is located at a distance of 2.5 miles bearing 290′ from G. M_2 is located at a distance of 2.0 miles bearing 200′ (t) from G, while the latter remains at the center of the relative plot. (Note the scale adopted in Fig. 6-1, always written in the upper right-hand corner of the maneuvering board.)

The same sheet of paper (or board) on which the relative plot is reproduced is also used to show course and speed of G and the other vessel. In the vector diagram the arrow *eg* represents speed and course of G, the arrow *gm* speed and course of other vessel relative to G. The arrow *em* completes the triangle and represents the resultant of the first two, or actual speed and course of M. Again you have a vector triangle. If vectors are new to you, relate this triangle to the triangle which you have in dealing with currents. Your heading could be eg through the water and gm could be the current. The resultant is the third side (em) which could be your course over the bottom, or track, and the *lengths* of the vectors represent *speeds*, first on the heading, next of the current, and finally the resulting track-speed made good. (All courses and bearings are true.)

In our illustration, Fig. 6-1, G is on a course of 010′ (t), speed 12.0 knots, whereas the other vessel M is on a course 111′ (t), speed 13.0 knots. The length of gm (19.2 knots) represents the relative speed of the vessel M with respect to G.

Note that there are two different diagrams in Fig. 6-1, yet they are related, as follows: since M_1M_2 and gm both represent the direction of relative movement, you have the rule that *gm must always be parallel to M_1M_2.*

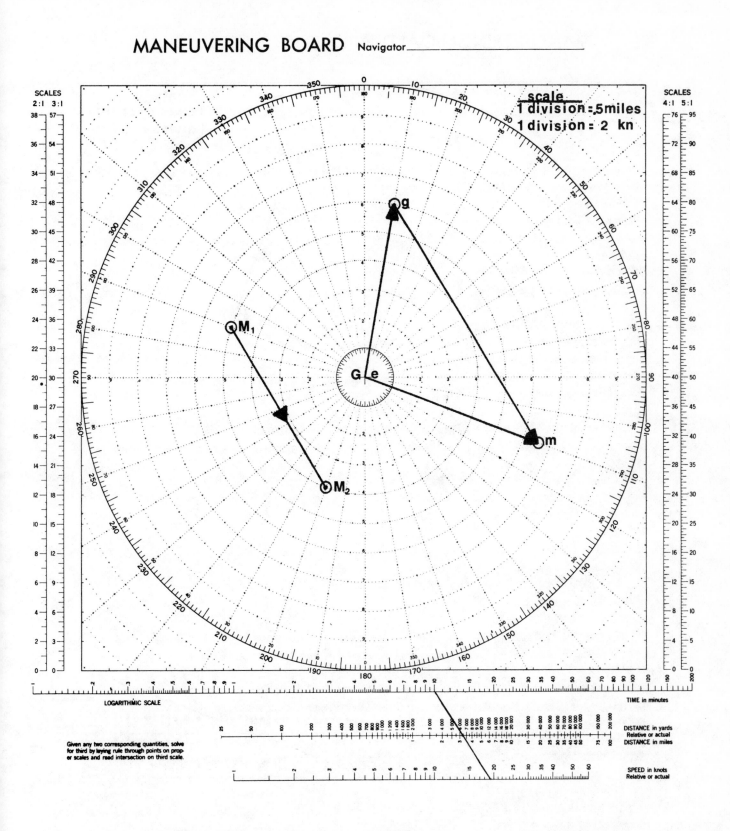

Fig. 6-1. Illustration for explanation of techniques used on a maneuvering board. (Courtesy Defense Mapping Agency Hydrographic/Topographic Center.)

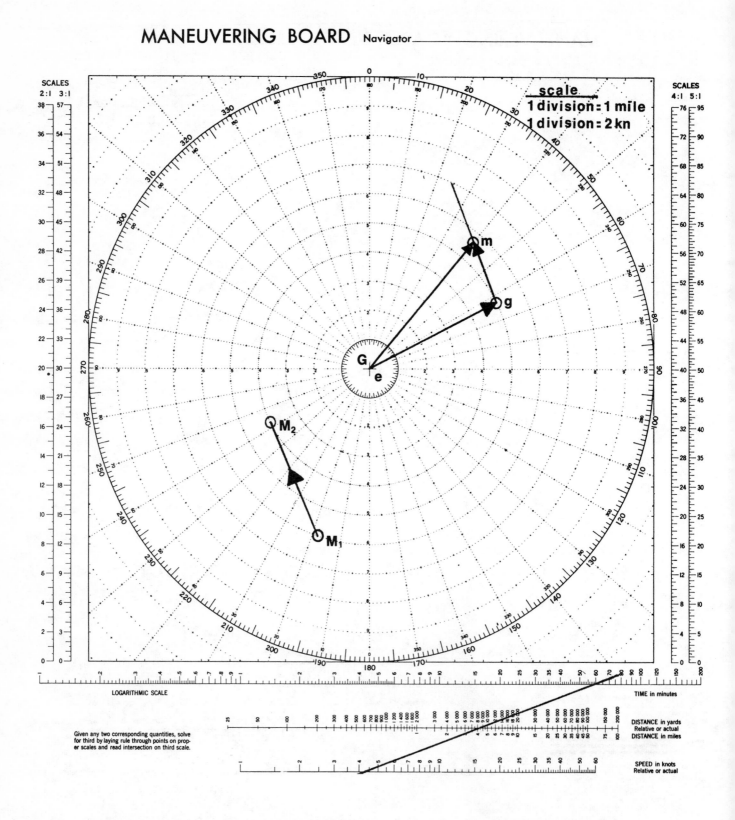

Fig. 6-2. Illustration for solving example one. (Courtesy Defense Mapping Agency Hydrographic/ Topographic Center.)

M_1M_2 is really a relative distance (in nautical miles), and as just explained, gm is a relative speed, in knots. Hence it follows that

$$M_1M_2 = gm \times t$$

where t is the time needed to complete the maneuver in hours. This is the fundamental and important *time* formula in maneuvering board problems. (Of course this is the same formula already explained in Chapter 3.)

You can be quite free in the choice of the scale for each diagram, but for convenience the diagrams should not be too large, and also not too small, because in the latter case the results will not be as accurate. You want the scale as large as possible without running off the board. In addition, the scales do not have to be the same in the relative plot and the vector plot. Whatever your chosen scale, it should be *noted* in the upper right-hand corner of the board, both for the relative and for the vector plots. In Fig. 6-1, the scale for the relative plot is 1 division = 0.5 mile. The scale for the vector plot is 1 division = 2 knots.

The maneuvering board has several added features. Scales (2:1, 3:1, 4:1 and 5:1) are reproduced along the left and right-hand edges of each board, *vertically*. At the bottom of each board there are two nomograms dealing with time, speed and distance. The simplest nomogram uses the three lowest lines of the board (running horizontally) and is called a three-scale nomogram. In this same illustration, Fig. 6-1, the relative distance M_1M_2 measures 3.2 miles. Place a dot at this point (3.2 on the distance-scale) in *miles* (using numerical figures under the line). As noted above, gm was found to be equal to 19.2 knots. Place a dot at the point 19.2 on the speed scale (lowest line of all, running horizontally). Then connect the two dots which you have drawn, and this last line will cut the time scale line, running horizontally, at the desired time, which in this case is *ten minutes. Your own arithmetic will give the most accurate answer to the nearest minute!* Plotting is a good rough check.

If you are a good mariner, who practices "Constant Vigilance," after you have finished any calculations for a maneuvering board problem you will not sit back without checking frequently to make sure that the maneuver can be completed without risk of collision or other disaster.

SUMMARY OF MANEUVERING BOARD PROBLEM

A. *Relative Plot*—capital letters
   1. G represents Guide, with G remaining at center in relative plot.
   2. M_1 represents position of other vessel relative to G at beginning of maneuver.
   3. M_2 represents the position of the other vessel relative to G at the end of the maneuver (with interception M_2 at center).
B. *Vector Diagram*—small letters
   1. e is the origin, at center of board.
   2. eg represents course and speed of G.
   3. em represents course and speed of other vessel M.
   4. gm represents relative speed of vessel M with respect to G.
C. *Relations*
   1. gm is parallel to M_1M_2 and *in same direction.*
   2. $M_1M_2 = gm \times t$ (nomogram is useful in this relation).
   3. Choice of scale should be noted in upper right-hand corner.
   4. It is assumed during one maneuver that course and speed are not changed in the problems presented in this text.

EXAMPLES FOR MANEUVERING BOARD

Example I. G is on a course of 063°t, speed 10 knots. At 0830 another vessel M, 6.0 miles broad on the starboard quarter of the first, wants to take a position four miles dead astern, using a course of 040°t.

Required:
    (a) The speed of vessel M.
    (b) The time necessary for M to complete maneuver.
    (c) Time at end of maneuver.

Solution:
    (Plot M_1 and M_2 as given (Fig. 6-2) M_1M_2 = 4.3 miles, after plotting and measuring.

    eg = 10 knots, as given.
    A line thorough g must be *parallel* to M_1M_2 and in the *same direction* as M_1M_2.

    Intersection of line through g and the 040° direction gives em, since M is on a true course of 040°.

    Measure of gm = 4.3 knots.

    Scales, or arithmetic, now give t = 60^m or 1^h.

Answer:
    (a) = 11.2 kn
    (b) = 1^h
    (c) = 0930

Note: Due to plotting inaccuracies, differences of 1 min., 0.1 kn, or 1° can be expected.

Example II. The yacht CHRISTIANA is heading to windward at 7 knots on a course of 180°t off Campobello Island, N.B., where she expects to rendezvous with some friends in a small auxiliary LADY BLUE. CHRISTIANA sights LADY BLUE 1 mile broad on the port bow. LADY BLUE is not under sail.

    (a) The skipper of CHRISTIANA wants to know the minimum speed at which LADY BLUE would have to motor to meet CHRISTIANA if the latter does not alter course or speed.
    (b) Also, what would be the time for this maneuver, and
    (c) What is the heading for LADY BLUE?

The navigator of LADY BLUE estimates that LADY BLUE can make 5.5 kn for maximum speed,

    (d) If the LADY BLUE navigator prefers to use his maximum speed, with minimum time, how should LADY BLUE head for this meeting, assuming that the course and speed of CHRISTIANA have not changed?
    (e) How long will the last maneuver take?

    _____

(CHRISTIANA = Guide (G)   LADY BLUE = Other Vessel)

Answer:
    (a) = 4.9 kn
    (b) = 12 min.
    (c) = 225°t
    (d) = 251°t
    (e) = 8 min.

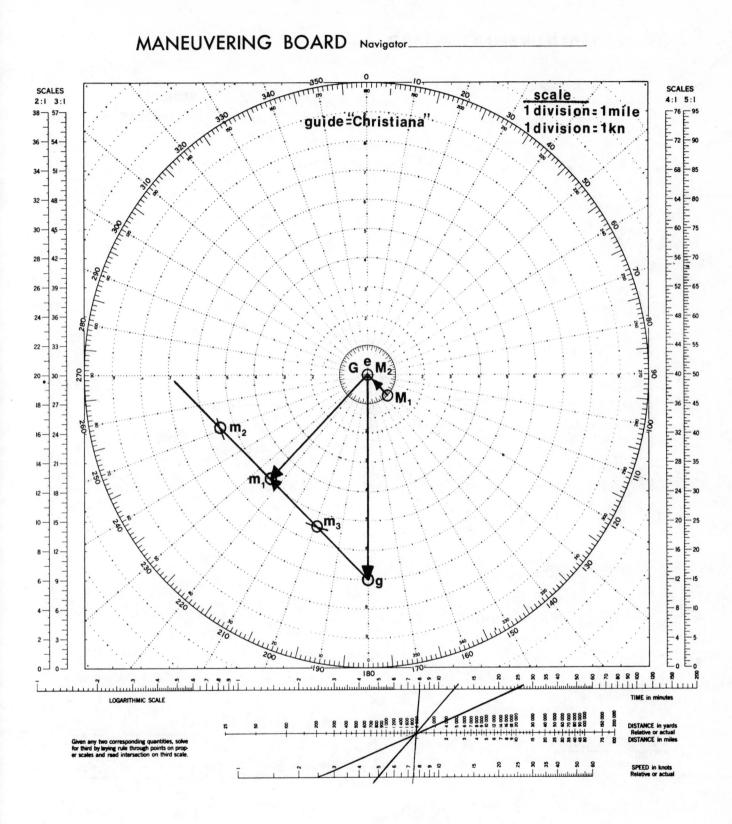

Fig. 6-3. Illustration for solving example two. (Courtesy Defense Mapping Agency Hydrographic/ Topographic Center.)

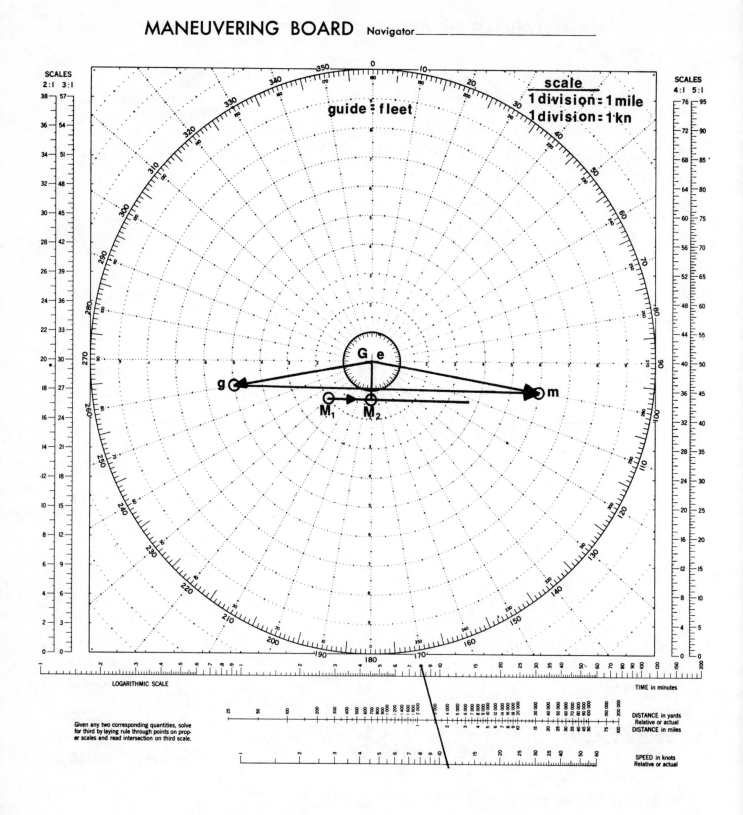

Fig. 6-4. Illustration for solving example three. The central circle of 1 n.m. represents the fishing fleet.
(Courtesy Defense Mapping Agency Hydrographic/Topographic Center.)

Note (in Fig. 6-3) that eg = 180°t at 7 kn. gm is parallel to M_1M_2, and em_1 (for first part of example) must be perpendicular to gm because minimum speed for LADY BLUE is desired. There are two intersections of the 5.5 knot circle with gm. The one which interests the LADY BLUE Captain is the gm (gm_2 in this case) which is longest, representing maximum relative speed, and hence shortest time. Time (t) will then be shortest in the formula:

$$M_1M_2 = gm \times t = 1.0$$

gm_3 would have been possible if the LADY BLUE Captain had not wanted to reach the rendezvous in the least time. If you measure the length of gm_3 (=2.5), you will find that it would have taken 24 minutes, three times as long as the 8 minutes on heading 251°.

Example III. A fleet of fishing vessels has a radius of about a mile, (Fig. 6-4). At 1400, the center of the fleet bears 050°t, distance 2 miles from another vessel, VIGILANCE, which is on a course of 100°t, speed 6 knots. The fishing fleet is proceeding on a course of 260°t, speed 5 knots.

Will VIGILANCE clear the fishing fleet? If so, what will be the minimum distance of approach to the fleet, and at what time will the closest approach take place? Although either vessel may be chosen as G, it is often easier to solve the problem with one rather than the other as G. (In this example, let the fleet be G.)

Solution:

Plot eg and em, since the data for both these vectors are known.

Draw gm, and plot M_1. Remember in this instance that the bearing of the VIGILANCE from the fleet was given. Hence, the desired bearing here is the reciprocal of 050°, or 230°t.

Draw a line through M_1 parallel to gm.

A perpendicular from G to this last line intersects this last line at M_2, since a perpendicular is the shortest line from a point to another line, and you are interested in the *point of closest approach* to the fleet. Measure of M_1M_2 gives 1.5 miles for the relative distance. Measure of gm gives 10.8 for the relative speed. Your formula for time, or use of the nomogram, shows 8 minutes for t. Hence, the closest approach will take place at 1400 + 8 or at 1408 to the nearest minute, at a distance of 0.3 miles.

Example IV. Suppose that you were skipper of a cabin cruiser, (Fig. 6-5), SCOUT, and you wanted to maneuver on a constant relative bearing with respect to another cruiser, SS CANOPUS. Suppose that you wanted to proceed as far as possible on this relative bearing and return to your initial relative position after two hours. What would be your headings *out*, and *in*, and at what time should you change course to return to your starting position, all on the same relative bearing? For a more specific case, consider the following.

At 1820, suppose that your true bearing from CANOPUS is 010° at a distance of 1.0 mile from her. The course and speed of SS CANOPUS are 305°t, at 10.0 knots. You are to proceed as far as possible, maintaining your relative bearing (or t bearing of 010°), with speed 14 knots. You want to return to your initial position with respect to SS CANOPUS *in two hours*.

What are the headings of SCOUT, out and in, and at what time should SCOUT change course to return to the starting position?

Solution:

You can plot M_1 and the direction 010° through M_1, for the course *out* and the course back or *in*, (in the reciprocal direction).

Then plot g on circle 5 in the direction of 305°, using the scale indicated in Fig. 6-5. You now have the vector eg.

Through g plot a line parallel to 010° (the constant true bearing for SCOUT). The latter line intersects the 14 knot circle at m_1 for m_1 -*out*, and also at m_2 for m_2 -*in*. These two points provide the desired em_1 for course$_{out}$ and em_2 for course$_{in}$. (*Ans:* 330° and 230°).

To obtain the time out, you have two equations, after you have measured gm_1 (6.6) and gm_2 (15):

$$6.6 \times t_{out} = 15 \times t_{in} : (\text{Distance}_{out} = \text{Distance}_{in})$$
$$t_{out} + t_{in} = 2 \text{ hrs.} = 120 \text{ minutes}$$

$$\text{Then } 6.6 \times t_{out} = 15 (120 - t_{out})$$
$$21.6 \, t_{out} = 1800$$
$$t_{out} = 83 \text{ minutes, to nearest minute}$$

Answer:

Time to turn back (to reciprocal course) = in 83 minutes or in *1 hour 23 minutes, at 1943.*

As a final remark on the subject of the maneuvering board, the above solutions are not the only solutions possible. They are, however, often neater and more clever than solutions involving absolute rather than relative motion. Further examples follow, in Problem Set 6.

PROBLEM SET 6

There are three blank maneuvering boards here, Figs. 6-6, 6-7 and 6-8; you may use them for solutions of the following:

1) The G is on a course of 163°t, speed 10.0 knots. At 0820 a ship M, 1.0 mile dead astern of G, is ordered to take a position 4 miles broad on the starboard quarter of G, using a course of 220°t.

Reguired: (a) The speed of ship M.
(b) The time necessary for M to reach new position.

(a) _____
(b) _____

Ans: (a) em = 9.2 kn,; (b) t = 22 minutes

2) You are at sea on VEGA, and receive a message from another vessel, ZUBENELGENUBI, that she requires assistance. She gives her position and says that she will remain on course 090°, speed 6 knots. The plot shows her to bear 030°t from your position, distant 200 miles. You, on your ship VEGA, can maintain 20 knots.

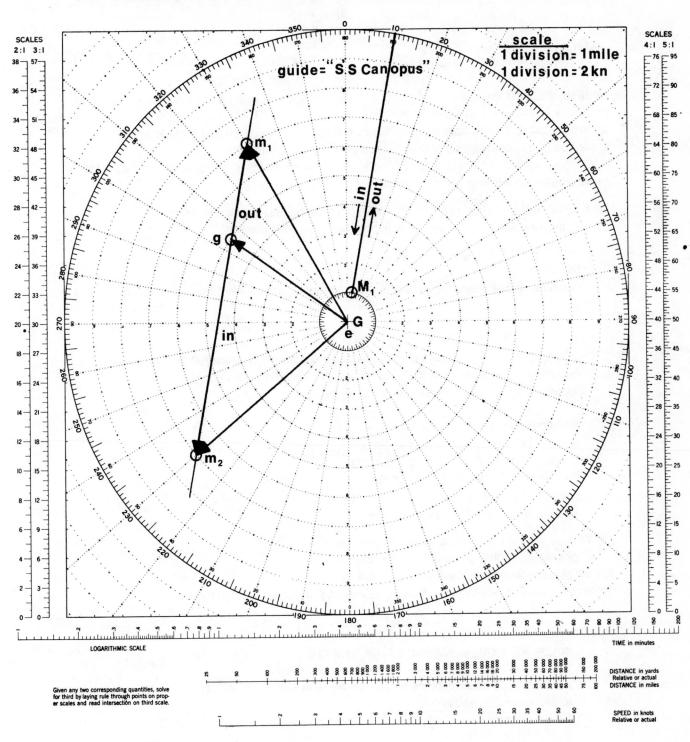

**Fig. 6-5. Illustration for solving example four. (Courtesy Defense Mapping Agency Hydrographic/
Topographic Center.)**

Required: (a) Your course to reach ZUBENELGENUBI in minimum time.
(b) The time it will take to reach the rendezvous.

(a) _____

(b) _____

Ans: (a) eg = 045°t; (b) t = $12^h 12^m$

3) At 0810, WEZEN is on a course of 069°t, averaging 2.5 knots, and heading for Plum Gut. Slack (*flood begins*) occurs at 0940 in the Gut, and the navigator of WEZEN estimates that he is approximately 6.2 miles from the Gut. He also estimates that he should be able to get through before current becomes greater than his speed.

VIXEN, WEZEN's competitor, is sighted North, (bearing 342°t) distance about 5 miles. With a fresh breeze VIXEN is averaging 3.2 knots.

(a) If VIXEN decides to intercept WEZEN, what should be her interception heading (t)?
(b) Will the interception take place before both boats reach Plum Gut?

Ans: (a) em = 111°
(b) Time for the maneuver = $2^h 22^m$. Both boats should make it through the Gut, but just barely!

4) Sometimes you read newspaper reports about collisions between an aircraft carrier and a cruiser. It is interesting to speculate as to the cause; it is partly a maneuvering board problem.
Suppose that we assume a similar problem, for study.

Consider an aircraft carrier K and a cruiser B.
Speed of K is 20 knots, on course 180°t.
B is at station 1000 yards dead ahead of K.
B is ordered to station 3000 yards distant from K, on relative bearing of 160° to port from K, with speed 10 kns.
1820 = Time of beginning of maneuver.

(a) What is the required course (t) of B for this maneuver?
(Consider possibility of more than one solution.)
(b) What is the time when B will arrive on station?
(c) What is the distance between K and B at the point of closest approach?

Ans: There are two possibilities to consider:
1. em_1 = 163°t, gm_1 = 10.8 kns. 1831 = Time of arrival.
2. em_2 = 048°t, gm_2 = 27.6 kns. 1824 = Time of arrival.
3. At closest approach distance between K and B is 300 yards. Which case would you prefer to see executed, and why? _____
If as much time as possible for the maneuver is required, Answer is case 1?

The following problem came from some of the data in Alvin Moscow's *Collision Course*. This problem does not, necessarily, present facts as either actual or as stated in the book. All of these are not known; ANDREA DORIA's Log went down with the ship.

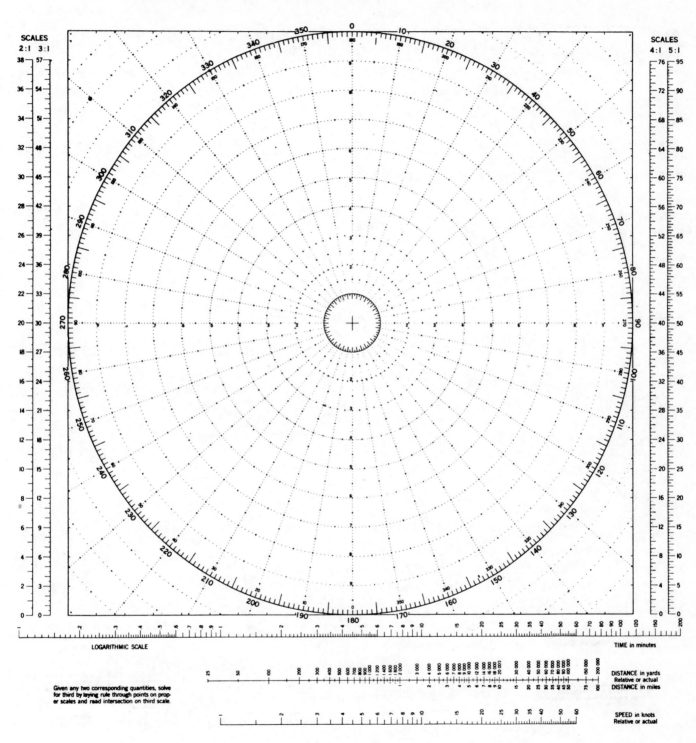

Fig. 6-6. Blank maneuvering board for use with Problem Set. (Courtesy Defense Mapping Agency Hydrographic/ Topographic Center.)

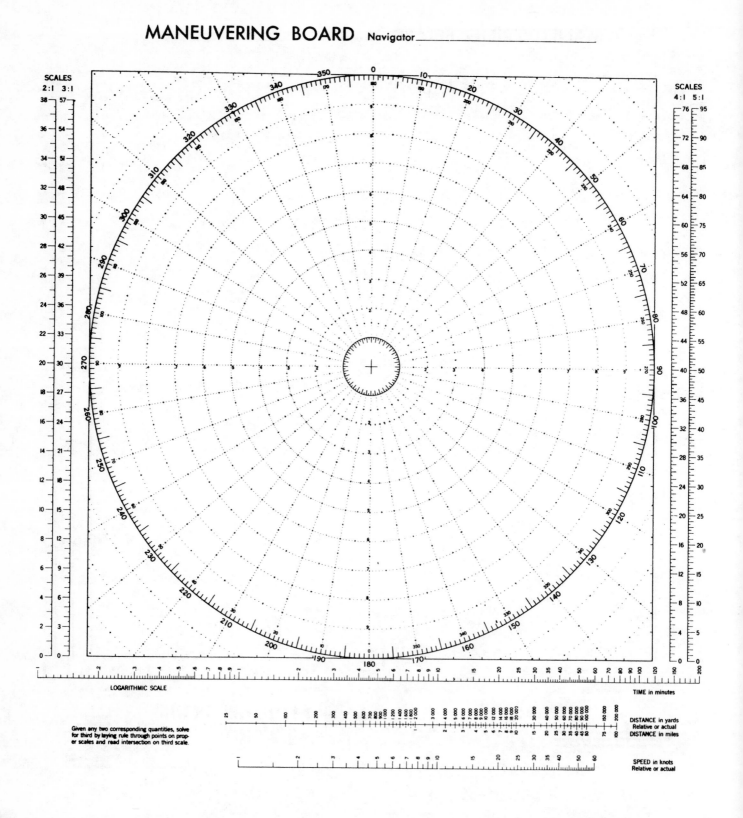

Fig. 6-7. Blank maneuvering board for use with Problem Set. (Courtesy Defense Mapping Agency Hydrographic/
Topographic Center.)

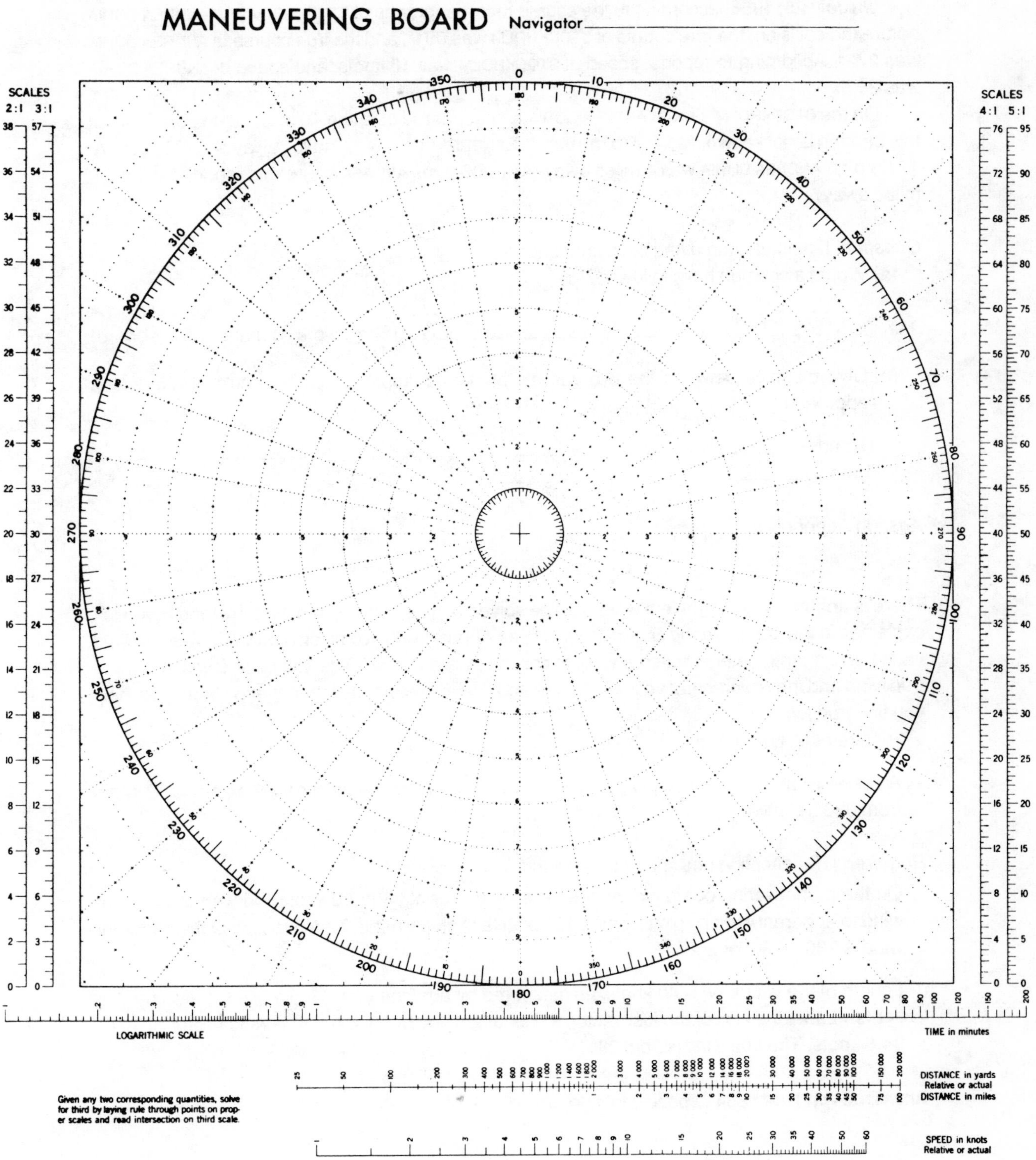

MANEUVERING BOARD Navigator _____

Fig. 6-8. Blank maneuvering board for use with Problem Set. (Courtesy Defense Mapping Agency Hydrographic/Topographic Center.)

5) Evidence of the following disaster is often confusing and contradictory. Use data which seems most consistent.

On July 25, 1956, according to the course recorder graphs of STOCKHOLM and ANDREA DORIA before the collision, the true course of STOCKHOLM was 091°, and the true course of ANDREA DORIA was 272°. According to reports, speed of STOCKHOLM was 18 knots, and speed of ANDREA DORIA was 21.8.

On the STOCKHOLM's radar ANDREA DORIA first appeared at range 10 miles, 2° to port. Time of this bearing is not known. At 11:00 p.m., July 25, ANDREA DORIA was 6 miles away and 4° to port. At 11.03 p.m. ANDREA DORIA was 4 miles away. At 11:06 p.m., ANDREA DORIA was reported to be 1.9 miles away.

Question: If neither course had been changed:
   (a) Would a collision have followed?

Ans: _____(Show work on maneuvering board)

   (b) Give distance between the two vessels at closest approach (CPA) and time at closest approach.

   Distance _____
   Time _____

Ans: (in Appendix II).

6) There is another type of problem which can be solved conveniently on the maneuvering board, as explained in the *Maneuvering Board Manual* (See Appendix III). It concerns only one vessel. Wind vanes and anemometers measure what is called *apparent wind*. The latter is the vector sum of true wind and the reciprocal of vessel's course and speed vector. The maneuvering board can help you find *true wind*.

For example, consider this method:

A vessel is on a true course of 230°, speed 20 knots. Relative wind across the deck is 40 knots from 030° relative.

Required: The direction and speed of true wind.

On the maneuvering board plot er, the vessel's vector of 230°, 20 knots. Convert the relative wind to apparent wind by plotting rw, 030° relative to ship's head. True direction of the apparent wind is 230° + 30° or 260°.

Length of the vector rw is 40 knots, as measured by anemometer. (Scale used, 1 division = 4 knots.) Label the end of the last vector w. Resultant vector ew is the true wind vector of 104°, 24.8 knots. The true wind is *from 284°*.

Ans: True wind from 284°, speed 24.8 knots.

As a final lesson related to relative motion, remember:
You are on a collision or interception course with another vessel (as the distance between the two decreases) if relative bearing of other vessel does not change. Keep a good watch, and act to keep both vessels safe *before* it is too late. (Ships cannot be stopped at once, nor can they reverse direction instantly!)

Chapter 7

Radio Aids to Navigation

PUBLICATION 117 (A or B)

Your best reference for radio navigational aids is the *Pub. 117*, printed yearly. (See Appendix III.) *Pub. 117 A* covers the Atlantic and Mediterranean Area, and *Pub. 117 B* covers the Pacific Coast and Indian Ocean.

As soon as you pick up this publication, you note on the cover:

IMPORTANT
This publication should
be corrected each week
from the
Notice to Mariners

Most mariners remember to consult *NM* regularly for chart corrections as well as for any changes made in the navigational aids, *Light Lists* and *Coast Pilots*. (See Appendix III.) Here are the different chapter titles in *Pub. 117*:
1. Radiobeacons
2. Radio Direction-finder and Radar Stations
3. Radio Time Signals
4. Radio Navigational Warnings
5. Distress, Emergency and Safety Traffic
6. Stations Transmitting Medical Advice
7. Long Range Navigational Aids
8. Miscellaneous Information—International Morse Code—Abbreviations to be Used in Radio Communications—Technical Radio Broadcast Services and Radio Stations WWV and WWVH
9. U.S. Flag Merchant Vessel Locator Filing System (USMER)—Selected Voice Transmissions
10. Interim Emergency Procedures and Communications
    Instructions for U.S. Merchant Ships
11. Allied MERCAST System
12. Alphabetical List of Radio Stations

According to the type and size of your vessel and equipment only certain chapters may interest you. *Pub. 117* points out equipment you may find necessary for your safety and you should glance through all the pages *before* undertaking any cruise.

Radiobeacons. The first chapter is probably of greatest interest since a radio direction finder (RDF) can be carried on a boat, its cost is not too great, relative to navigational equipment in general, and it will be your chief aid most of the time in fog or bad weather, when you cannot see further than the rail of your vessel. Some sections will now be devoted to this navigational aid.

There are three types of radiobeacons:

1. Directional radiobeacons which transmit radio waves in beams along fixed bearings.
2. Rotating radiobeacons by which a beam of radio waves is revolved in azimuth in a manner similar to the beam of light sent out by rotating lights.
3. Circular radiobeacons which send out waves of approximately uniform strength in all directions so that vessels may take radio bearings on them by means of the vessel's RDF. This is the most common type.

With an RDF even in poor weather you can take radio bearings of transmissions from other vessels, aircraft, shore stations, marine radiobeacons and coastal stations of the radio communication network, shown in *Pub. 117*. The designation RBn and a magenta circle mark the location on a chart.

Most RDF's are portable, and you may have to align this instrument yourself, or check one already in position on your boat. If you understand the principles involved, you can handle all types. You may note a lubber's line, as with the magnetic compass, and in case your instrument is quite separate from the compass, it is usually easier to set it up with its lubber's line along the keel of your vessel, or parallel to the lubber's line of the compass. There is probably a 360° circle on the set, which can be rotated. If you place 0° on the lubber's line of the RDF *for every bearing,* you will be measuring *relative bearings*. This method requires *adding* each time, to obtain the corresponding compass bearing. It is much easier to set the RDF to agree with the compass and obtain compass bearings directly. If you understand the principles of Chapter 2, you can arrange the instrument to suit your own tastes, but remember that when it comes to plotting bearing lines on a chart, you want to plot either *true or magnetic bearing lines* through the radiobeacons which you used. You will be substituting radio bearing lines for the visual bearing lines which you studied in previous chapters here. Each line is really a line of position (lop) on which you are situated. Hence, two or three will give you a fix even in poor weather. There are, however, a few more facts to know about the whole procedure.

The mariner must know and identify the radiobeacon or radio station which he is going to use. There are *area* charts at the end of Chapter 1. which, pictorially, show the possible radiobeacons for each area of *Pub. 117*. In each publication chapter, stations are generally arranged in geographical order so the mariner may determine which station in his vicinity renders services most suited to his immediate needs. Radiobeacons and stations are arranged alphabetically by name in the index at the back. Corresponding numbers there give the number you need in order to find the desired beacon in Chapters 1 or 2.

For example, Little Gull Island Light Station is in area D and also in the index, number 1099 (*Pub. 117, 1978*). Its frequency is 306 kHz, and its characteristic is the letter J of the Morse code (.---). Looking up this number in Section I-27 of *Pub. 117* we find the frequency and several details given there. Its characteristic (.---), for instance, is heard for 50 seconds, there is then a long dash for 10 seconds, and silence again for 300 seconds or 5 minutes. The period from beginning to end of this cycle is 360 seconds, or 6 minutes, and then the cycle is repeated. The range is 15 miles.

The most important function of this radio station for you is the fact that during the 50 seconds, while you are hearing the letter J (.---), you can be turning the pointer of your RDF until you have a *null*, the bearing where the signal cannot be heard at all. This is the case if you have a ferrite rod antenna (the usual type today). In more modern RDFs, there is usually a null meter, apt to be more sensitive to your eye than the sound signal to your ear. You can see when you have a null by looking at the needle, and in this position of the pointer you will hear nothing. When the null has been obtained you know, by reading the direction of the pointer against the 360° scale, the direction of the station or beacon. In other words, if you plot this bearing line through your radiobeacon or station, you have a lop on which you are situated. For accuracy, however, since a radio bearing does not have the accuracy of a visual line of position, you have a few other facts to consider. *To take care of the fact that the accuracy is less than with a visual line, you can draw a sector at the radiobeacon,* as shown in Fig. 7-1 for the time 1030. After drawing the first lop through your radiobeacon, draw lines on either side making an angle of at least 2° with the first line. You would make the 2° larger (3-5°) if the arc of the null was larger.

You now have a *sector* in which you are situated according to this one radio bearing, and that is much better than not knowing at all where you are, especially in a fog or bad weather! To fix your position more closely you may have another radiobeacon which you can use to obtain another lop (or sector). Just as the intersection of two lines of position gives you a fix when you take visual bearings, the intersection of the two sectors gives your radio fix. The only difference is that instead of a point-fix you have an *area* for a fix, *common to both sectors* (or to three sectors if you can use three radiobeacons). You probably already expected this, because the radio bearing lines are less accurate, but there are many times in bad weather when this technique will save you and tell you where you are. To be absolutely sure of the safe procedure to follow at this point, you can proceed as if the worst position were possible. This is the technique used by Francis Chichester in crossing Nantucket Shoals in 1960 with the use of RDF—it is a good one, certainly the best one to use with

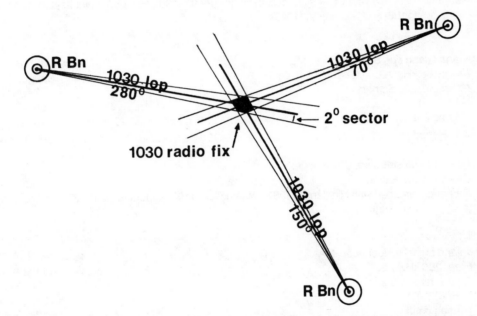

Fig. 7-1. Radio Fix: area common to all sectors is your probable position (from three radiobeacons).

present equipment. Also, you may agree with Chichester in, *The Lonely Sea and the Sky*,—that with accurate information, navigation is simple. Finding the truth from *inaccurate* data is more of an art,—and can be fascinating!

In the present example, using Little Gull Island light in area D to give you one radio bearing line or sector, the other beacon or station to give a lop is Montauk Point Light Station, NY (1098 in *Pub. 117*). This station is off Chart 116-SC Tr, but it is probably the best one to use with Little Gull Island Light Station beacon if you were in that region. The frequency of Montauk Point Light Station was changed in 1977 to 286 kHz so that Montauk is no longer in sequence with Little Gull. However, with appropriate frequencies you can still use these two stations for a fix. Always consult the latest *Pub. 117*, and keep track of changes through *Notice to Mariners*.

Fig. 7-2 lists six radiobeacons with the same frequency (286 kHz, *Pub. 117*, 1978). These are in group sequence (because of same frequency), and as noted in *Pub. 117* the order in the sequence (denoted by Roman numerals) is Highland I (#1087), Nantucket II (#1090), Montauk III (#1098), Ambrose IV (#1106), Great Duck V (#1077), and Manana VI (#1079). It is somewhat of a help to keep the same frequency for several radiobeacons as you sail or maneuver along the coast between Maine and New York.

Fig. 7-2. Six radiobeacons along the East Coast from New York to Maine.

RADIO NAVIGATIONAL AIDS   RADIOBEACONS

1077. Great Duck Island Light Station, ME   44°08′32″N 68°14′47″W
    Freq: 286 kHz, A2.   *Range:* 50 mi.
    Characteristic Signal: Seconds:
       GD (--. -..)   50
       Long dash   10
       Period ....   360 (6 min.)

    Hours of Transmission: Continuous.
    Group Sequence: V
    Remarks: Grouped with Highland I (1087), Nantucket II (1090), Montauk Point III (1098), Ambrose IV (1106) and Manana VI (1079).

1079. Manana Island Fog Signal Station, ME   43°45′48″N 69°19′38″W
    Freq: 286 kHz, A2.   *Range:* 100 mi.
    Characteristic Signal: Seconds:
       MI (-- ..)   50
       Long dash   10
       Period ....   360 (6 min.)

    Hours of Transmission: Continuous.
    Group Sequence: VI
    Remarks: Grouped with Highland I (1087), Nantucket II (1090), Montauk III (1098), Ambrose IV (1106) and Great Duck V (1077).

1087. Highland Light Radiobeacon, MA   42°02′24″N 70°03′40″W
    Freq: 286 kHz, A2.   *Range:* 100 mi.
    Characteristic Signal: Seconds:
       HI (..... ..)   50
       Long dash   10
       Period ....   360 (6 min.)

    Hours of Transmission: Continuous
    Group Sequence: I
    Remarks: Grouped with Nantucket II (1090), Montauk III (1098), Ambrose IV (1106), Great Duck V (1077) and Manana Island VI (1079).

1090. Nantucket Shoals Lightship, MA   40°30′00″N 69°28′00″W
    Freq: 286 kHz, A2.   *Range:* 100 mi.
    Characteristic Signal: Seconds:
       NS (-. ...)   50
       Long dash   10
       Period ....   360 (6 min.)

    Hours of Transmission: Continuous.
    Group Sequence: II
    Remarks: Grouped with Highland I (1087), Montauk III (1098), Ambrose IV (1106), Great Duck V (1077) and Manana Island VI (1079).

Fig. 7-2 (continued)

1098. Montauk Point Light Station, NY   41°04′15″N 71°51′27″W
     Freq: 286 kHz, A2.   *Range:* 20 mi.
     Characteristic Signal: Seconds:
       Y (-. --)   50
       Long dash   10
       Period ....   360 (6 min.)

    Hours of Transmission: Continuous.
    Group Sequence: III
    Remarks: Grouped with Highland I (1087), Nantucket II (1090), Ambrose IV (1106), Great Duck V (1077) and Manana VI (1079).

1106. Ambrose Light Station, NY   40°27′32″N 73°49′52″W
     Freq: 286 kHz, A2.   *Range:* 125 mi.
     Characteristic Signal: Seconds:
       T (-)   50
       Long dash   10
       Period ....   360 (6 min.)

    Hours of Transmission: Continuous.
    Group Sequence: IV
    Remarks: Grouped with Highland I (1087), Nantucket II (1090), Montauk III (1098), Great Duck V (1077) and Manana Island VI (1079).

At some radiobeacon stations, sound signals are *synchronized* with the radiobeacon signals for distance finding. These stations are identified by special notes in *Pub. 117*. Ordinarily the sound signals do not operate during transmission period of the radio signal in clear weather. The methods in use employ, as a rule, distinctive signals to indicate the point of synchronization and use the difference in velocity of the various speeds of signals which travel in air or water as compared with the speed of radio signals, which might be termed *instantaneous* travel, for practical purposes. A short table here will give you an idea of the distance in case at any time you are able to count seconds (or use a stop watch preferably) between the reception of a radio signal and the corresponding sound or submarine signal:

TABLE 7-1

Interval in Seconds	Distance in Nautical Miles from Sound Signal Source		A Synchronized Point is Necessary
	Air	Submarine	
1	0.18	0.8	
2	0.36	1.6	
3	0.54	2.4	
4	0.72	3.2	
5	0.90	4.0	
(etc.)			

TABLE 7-2
(from *Radio Navigational Aids*)

200F.   Radio Bearing Conversion Table

Correction to be applied to radio bearing to convert to Mercator bearing

Difference of longitude

Mid. lat.	0.5°	1°	1.5°	2°	2.5°	3°	3.5°	4°	4.5°	5°	5.5°	6°	6.5°	7°	7.5°	Mid. lat.
°	°	°	°	°	°	°	°	°	°	°	°	°	°	°	°	°
4	---	---	---	---	0.1	0.1	0.1	0.1	0.2	0.2	0.2	0.2	0.2	0.2	0.3	4
5	---	0.1	0.1	.1	.1	.1	.2	.2	.2	.2	.2	.3	.3	.3	.3	5
6	---	.1	.1	.1	.1	.2	.2	.2	.2	.3	.3	.3	.3	.4	.4	6
7	---	.1	.1	.1	.2	.2	.2	.3	.3	.3	.3	.4	.4	.4	.5	7
8	---	.1	.1	.1	.2	.2	.2	.3	.3	.4	.4	.4	.5	.5	.5	8
9	---	.1	.1	.1	.2	.2	.2	.3	.3	.4	.4	.5	.5	.6	.6	9
10	---	.1	.1	.1	.2	.2	.3	.4	.4	.4	.5	.5	.6	.6	.6	10
11	---	.1	.1	.2	.2	.3	.3	.4	.4	.5	.5	.6	.6	.7	.7	11
12	.1	.1	.1	.2	.3	.3	.4	.4	.5	.5	.6	.6	.7	.7	.8	12
13	.1	.1	.2	.2	.3	.3	.4	.4	.5	.6	.6	.7	.7	.8	.8	13
14	.1	.1	.2	.2	.3	.4	.4	.5	.6	.6	.7	.7	.8	.8	.9	14
15	.1	.1	.2	.3	.3	.4	.4	.5	.6	.6	.7	.8	.8	.9	1.0	15
16	.1	.1	.2	.3	.4	.4	.5	.6	.6	.7	.8	.8	.9	1.0	1.0	16
17	.1	.2	.2	.3	.4	.4	.5	.6	.6	.7	.8	.9	1.0	1.0	1.1	17
18	.1	.2	.2	.3	.4	.5	.5	.6	.7	.8	.8	.9	1.0	1.1	1.2	18
19	.1	.2	.2	.3	.4	.5	.6	.6	.7	.8	.9	1.0	1.1	1.1	1.2	19
20	.1	.2	.2	.3	.4	.5	.6	.7	.8	.8	.9	1.0	1.1	1.2	1.3	20
21	.1	.2	.3	.4	.5	.5	.6	.7	.8	.9	1.0	1.1	1.2	1.2	1.4	21
22	.1	.2	.3	.4	.5	.6	.6	.8	.8	.9	1.0	1.1	1.2	1.3	1.4	22
23	.1	.2	.3	.4	.5	.6	.7	.8	.9	1.0	1.1	1.2	1.3	1.4	1.5	23
24	.1	.2	.3	.4	.5	.6	.7	.8	..9	1.0	1.1	1.2	1.3	1.4	1.5	24
25	.1	.2	.3	.4	.5	.6	.7	.8	1.0	1.1	1.2	1.3	1.4	1.5	1.6	25
26	.1	.2	.3	.4	.6	.6	.8	.9	1.0	1.1	1.2	1.3	1.4	1.5	1.6	26
27	.1	.2	.3	.4	.6	.7	.8	.9	1.0	1.1	1.2	1.4	1.5	1.6	1.7	27
28	.1	.2	.4	.5	.6	.7	.8	.9	1.1	1.2	1.3	1.4	1.5	1.6	1.8	28
29	.1	.2	.4	.5	.6	.7	.8	1.0	1.1	1.2	1.3	1.4	1.6	1.7	1.8	29
30	.1	.2	.4	.5	.6	.8	.9	1.0	1.1	1.2	1.4	1.5	1.6	1.8	1.9	30
31	.1	.2	.4	.5	.6	.8	.9	1.0	1.2	1.3	1.4	1.6	1.7	1.8	1.9	31
32	.1	.3	.4	.5	.7	.8	.9	1.1	1.2	1.3	1.4	1.6	1.7	1.8	2.0	32
33	.1	.3	.4	.6	.7	.8	1.0	1.1	1.2	1.4	1.5	1.6	1.8	1.9	2.1	33
34	.1	.3	.4	.6	.7	.8	1.0	1.1	1.2	1.4	1.5	1.7	1.8	2.0	2.1	34
35	.1	.3	.4	.6	.7	.9	1.0	1.2	1.3	1.4	1.6	1.7	1.9	2.0	2.2	35
36	.1	.3	.4	.6	.7	.9	1.0	1.2	1.3	1.5	1.6	1.8	1.9	2.1	2.2	36
37	.2	.3	.4	.6	.8	.9	1.1	1.2	1.4	1.5	1.6	1.8	2.0	2.1	2.2	37
38	.2	.3	.5	.6	.8	.9	1.1	1.2	1.4	1.5	1.7	1.8	2.0	2.2	2.3	38
39	.2	.3	.5	.6	.8	1.0	1.1	1.2	1.4	1.6	1.7	1.9	2.1	2.2	2.4	39
40	.2	.3	.5	.6	.8	1.0	1.1	1.3	1.4	1.6	1.8	1.9	2.1	2.2	2.4	40
41	.2	.3	.5	.6	.8	1.0	1.2	1.3	1.5	1.6	1.8	2.0	2.1	2.3	2.5	41
42	.2	.3	.5	.7	.8	1.0	1.2	1.3	1.5	1.7	1.8	2.0	2.2	2.3	2.5	42
43	.2	.3	.5	.7	.8	1.0	1.2	1.4	1.5	1.7	1.9	2.1	2.2	2.4	2.6	43
44	.2	.4	.5	.7	.9	1.1	1.2	1.4	1.6	1.7	1.9	2.1	2.2	2.4	2.6	44
45	.2	.4	.5	.7	.9	1.1	1.2	1.4	1.6	1.8	2.0	2.1	2.3	2.5	2.6	45
46	.2	.4	.5	.7	.9	1.1	1.3	1.4	1.6	1.8	2.0	2.2	2.3	2.5	2.7	46
47	.2	.4	.6	.7	.9	1.1	1.3	1.5	1.7	1.8	2.0	2.2	2.4	2.6	2.8	47
48	.2	.4	.6	.8	.9	1.1	1.3	1.5	1.7	1.8	2.1	2.2	2.4	2.6	2.8	48
49	.2	.4	.6	.8	1.0	1.1	1.3	1.5	1.7	1.9	2.1	2.3	2.5	2.6	2.8	49
50	.2	.4	.6	.8	1.0	1.1	1.3	1.5	1.7	1.9	2.1	2.3	2.5	2.7	2.9	50
51	.2	.4	.6	.8	1.0	1.2	1.4	1.6	1.8	2.0	2.1	2.3	2.5	2.7	2.9	51
52	.2	.4	.6	.8	1.0	1.2	1.4	1.6	1.8	2.0	2.2	2.4	2.6	2.8	3.0	52
53	.2	.4	.6	.8	1.0	1.2	1.4	1.6	1.8	2.0	2.2	2.4	2.6	2.8	3.0	53
54	.2	.4	.6	.8	1.0	1.2	1.4	1.6	1.8	2.0	2.2	2.4	2.6	2.8	3.0	54
55	.2	.4	.6	.8	1.0	1.2	1.4	1.6	1.8	2.1	2.2	2.4	2.7	2.9	3.1	55
56	.2	.4	.6	.8	1.0	1.2	1.4	1.7	1.9	2.1	2.3	2.5	2.7	2.9	3.1	56
57	.2	.4	.6	.8	1.1	1.2	1.5	1.7	1.9	2.1	2.3	2.5	2.7	2.9	3.2	57
58	.2	.4	.6	.8	1.1	1.3	1.5	1.7	1.9	2.1	2.3	2.6	2.8	3.0	3.2	58
59	.2	.4	.6	.8	1:1	1.3	1.5	1.7	1.9	2.2	2.4	2.6	2.8	3.0	3.2	59
60	.2	.4	.6	.9	1.1	1.3	1.5	1.7	2.0	2.2	2.4	2.6	2.8	3.0	3.2	60

Receiver (latitude)	Transmitter (direction from receiver)	Correction Sign	Receiver (latitude)	Transmitter (direction from receiver)	Correction Sign
North	Eastward	+	South	Eastward	−
North	Westward	−	South	Westward	+

In this example, from Little Gull Island light and Montauk Point Light Station, there is no synchronization. With synchronization, if this technique appeals to you, a stop watch (always an important aid) is advised in order to obtain accuracy in the seconds of time, when synchronization is present. Also, note in advance as to whether you are apt, in your particular cruise, to have available synchronized signals. As you turn the pages of *Pub. 117*, there are not too many synchronized stations.

Plotting Radio Bearing Lines. There is another possible correction to remember here. It depends upon the fact that radio waves travel in great circles (with their planes through the center of the Earth). You will probably plot these bearing lines on a Mercator chart, the only chart explained at this point in detail, because it is the most popular chart in marine navigation. A great circle course on the Mercator projection would be a *curved line* and so *not* a straight line, the easiest course to plot. Hence, the radio bearing must be corrected sometimes, so that you can plot a straight line, and the correction table is on a full page in Chapter 2 of *Pub. 117* (Table 7-2, in this text). As stated at the top, under the title, it is the *correction to be applied to radio bearing to convert to Mercator bearing*. Inspection of this table shows that the corrections are given in degrees, as might be expected, but the values depend upon the difference in Longitude between your vessel and the radio beacon or station. These values are small, only up to 0.4 degrees if the difference of Long. does not exceed 1°. Also, in higher Latitudes, the corrections are much greater than around the Equator. Up to 2° in Long. difference the correction does not exceed about 0.8°. Only for a difference of Long. of 5° does the correction become more significant, around 2.2°. Approaching Lands End Radio Station off England, for instance, a few degrees to the West in Longitude, you would certainly make these corrections to your radio bearing lines before plotting them. Nearer to the radiobeacons, much depends upon the accuracy of the particular bearing. If the null arc is wide, for instance, there is not much point in applying a correction ("Mid Lat." equals a Latitude midway between your own Latitude and the Latitude of the station). The *nearest degree* only is sufficient in entering the Radio Conversion Table in *Pub. 117* with "Mid Lat" (Table 7-2). Rules for *adding* or *subtracting* the corrections are given at the bottom of the page. Remember, also that great circles curve towards the nearest pole of the Earth, and that a radio wave follows a great circle track. A rough sketch will always tell you whether to add or subtract a correction to your radio bearing (See Fig. 7-3, exaggerated).

In North Latitude, if a boat West of radiobeacon received a signal, correction to radio bearing would be *added* in plotting a rhumb line on Mercator chart; if boat is East of radiobeacon, the correction is *subtracted* for greatest accuracy in plotting the rhumb line. (A drawing can replace the rules at the bottom of Table 7-2.) Note change in signs for South Latitude.

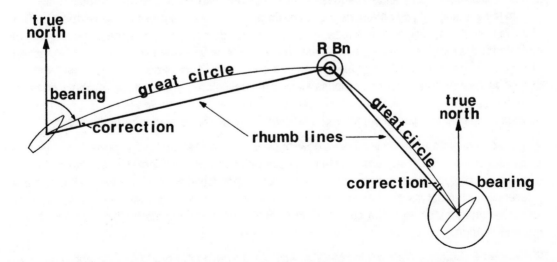

Fig. 7-3. Correction for radio bearing in plotting bearing as a straight line on a Mercator chart.

In plotting the radio bearing lops, you can use an extra Universal Plotting Sheet (really a simple Mercator chart) or make your own simple Mercator chart, if you wish to keep your main chart clean.

A Harvard class went upon their observatory roof with an RDF, a recent copy of *Radio Navigational Aids (Pub. 117A)*, and a recent aeronautical chart, since aeronautical beacons may also be used (more are available on land than in the case of nautical beacons). The accuracy of the results could be tested since the class members were at a known position. They made their own Mercator charts and plotted radio bearings thereon. The results were very good. At this point it might be mentioned that an excellent method for a lone navigator to use when recording observations is to attach a small pad to his arm with the help of a strong elastic band. This arrangement was originated by one of my Harvard students in 1973. The arm makes a convenient table and the elastic also holds the pencil. Other students constructed a small plastic arm-table which can be attached with straps and also designed and made an arm-table of plastic but with an added small light powered by batteries. Practicing techniques first on a roof is good preparation for using them at sea!

FINAL IMPORTANT FACTS about radio bearings are found in *Pub. 117*, as follows:

1. A third radio bearing line, from a third beacon, might reduce the area of your fix, and would certainly provide a check on the other two, just as three lops are always safer than two. An area common to all three lines must be your fix (area in this case).

2. In obtaining your radio direction beacon, tune sharply for best results.

3. Watch for coastal refraction or *land effect*. In the case of bearings which cut an intervening coastline at an oblique angle, or which cross high intervening land, errors of from 4° to 5° have been reported.

4. Bearings obtained from about half an hour before sunset to about half an hour after sunrise are occasionally unreliable. These are called *Sunrise, Sunset, or Night Effects* in *Pub. 117*.

5. There may sometimes be confusion about which, of the two bearings 180° apart, is the correct one. The DR position will generally be the determining factor, but if it does not, you can take a second radio bearing a short while after the first one. If the radio bearing is increasing, the radio beacon must be to starboard; if it is decreasing, the radio beacon must be to port. In some sets, a switch is provided which cuts out one half of the loop. A stronger *maximum* on one bearing can be noticed as a rule. Incorporated in many instruments is a magnetic compass (or gyro-repeater for ships) which enables you to obtain bearings without reference to the heading by your main compass. All this is another illustration of the necessity of understanding principles, so that you can adjust yourself and your techniques to any conditions with which you may want to deal.

In this instance, if you obtain magnetic bearings and have a magnetic compass rose, you can plot them by the directions of this rose. If, however, you do not have a magnetic rose, just apply variation to the magnetic bearings, to obtain true bearings, to be plotted according to the directions of a true compass rose, which is always printed on a chart. And, of course, if you start with just *compass bearings*, and your compass has large deviations, you must also apply deviation corrections, as explained in Chapter 2 of your text. *You never plot compass bearings, unless the deviations are negligible—whether you deal with visual bearings or with radio bearings.*

6. They do not exist in the United States now, but in Europe and some foreign ports, there are RDF and radar stations. RDF stations are stations equipped with special apparatus for determining the direction of radio signals transmitted by ships and other stations. Again, *Pub. 117* is the best reference for the details of all these individual stations. You must study all the details of any port which you might visit, to make sure that you have a set and equipment which is adequate for communication.

7. Chapter 6 (Stations Transmitting Medical Advice) of *Pub. 117* should be noted and remembered. Of course, boats and small yachts are not apt to carry transmitters for radio equipment, but

when William A. Robinson had appendicitis aboard his yacht SVAAP off the Galapagos, his wife Florence and cousin Dan managed to steer to Narborough and to SANTA CRUZ. The latter's radio, and communications which began with a message from a U.S. Naval Hospital in California, accomplished the rescue arrival of naval planes and naval surgeons. With the additional help of the Mackay Radio Company, Robinson was saved. Often there is more assistance at hand than the average mariner realizes. He must know about possibilities!

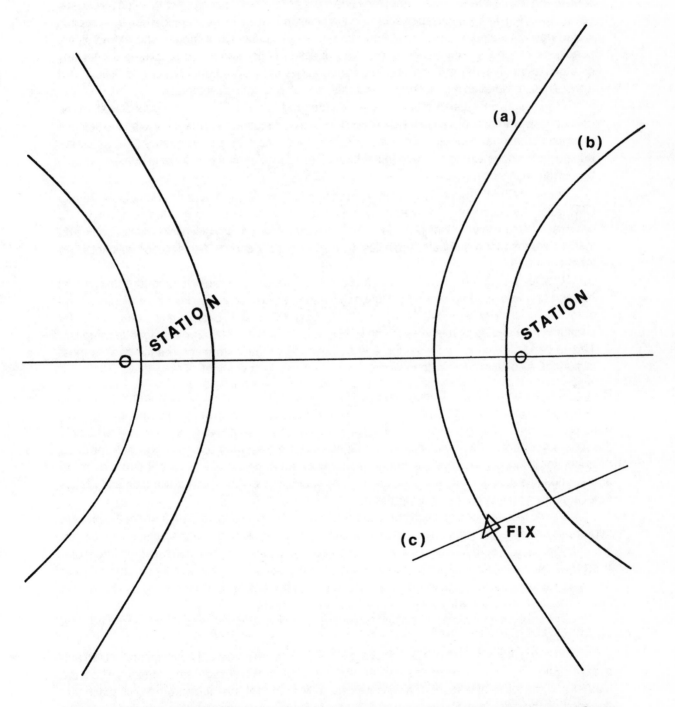

Fig. 7-4. Hyperbolas (a) and (b) with the same distance between the foci (stations from which Loran and Omega signals could be sent). Part of another hyperbola is (c) with different stations. If you found that you were on (a) and also on (c), you would be at the intersection—your fix.

8. Finally, before taking your RDF on a voyage you should check or calibrate it, since almost every instrument may have errors which can be handled if known, but of no help and even a danger if you do not know them.

One way to check for errors is to approach a calibration station or radiobeacon after reading about the proper procedure in *Pub. 117*, which warns, "It is essential that the radio direction finder be accurately calibrated in order that bearings may be corrected for deviation. Later, while the bearings are being taken, other radio antennas on board must be in the same condition as they were when the calibration was made; movable parts of the ship's superstructure such as booms, davits, wire rigging, etc., must be secured in the positions which they occupied when the direction finder was calibrated. Unusual cargoes such as large quantities of metals and extraordinary conditions of loading may cause errors. The direction finder should be recalibrated after any changes have been made in the set or its surroundings whenever there is reason to believe that the previous calibration has become inaccurate, and also at periodic intervals.

"The calibration must be made on approximately the same frequency or frequencies as will be used to take bearings, because the deviation for several frequencies is not likely to be the same. It is believed that one calibration curve is satisfactory for the normal radio frequency (285-325 kHz), but the instructions issued by the manufacturer of the particular direction finder in question should be studied in this connection."

For your Chart 116-SC Tr and the region of Long Island Sound, Eastern Point Light Station Calibration Radiobeacon, MA (#1085) was available in 1976. If you wanted to use it, you would have read first the instructions given in *Pub. 117*. *Ranges* are usually given for radiobeacons, and in this case the range is equal to ten miles. (Note that in 1977 and 1978 this station was not listed for calibration.)

Another way to check your set is to be close enough to a radiobeacon to obtain visual bearings as well as radio bearings. Obtain the latter first, so that you will not be prejudiced, and obtain them all the way around through 360°, for every 15° or so, in bearing directions. Do this by changing the heading of your vessel. The RDF is almost as important as your magnetic compass. This is certainly true in bad weather, and so checking of the instrument in each case is most important. All of this must be done *before* you set out on a long voyage!

Radio Navigation Systems. During and since World War II, many and various electronic navigation systems have been initiated and developed. Some of these systems have not lingered; others have been strengthened and improved. Every successful navigator or mariner should be able to identify the most important of these techniques, some of which he may want to use. A few are designed distinctly for transoceanic voyages, but a mariner knows that he usually takes departure near the shore, and ends a cruise near the shore. Hence, he needs to know the general situation and what is most important for his coastwise navigation.

Very brief facts for identification purposes are given in the following Table 7-3 where the present hyperbolic systems are grouped together. The underlying principle of these systems depends upon the definition of a hyperbola: *the path or locus of a point which moves so that its distance from one fixed point minus its distance from another fixed point is a constant.* If the constant is changed, but the fixed points remain the same, a different branch of the hyperbolic family is obtained, as shown in Fig. 7-4. Each branch there is associated with a certain constant.

Even if *Loran-A* is phased out, it is fairly easy to understand, and understanding Loran-A will help in understanding other electronic systems.

In the navigational hyperbolic system, Loran-A, the two fixed points are a *master* station (M) and a *slave* station (S). Loran-A is a pulse system. Think of pulses which are sent simultaneously from the master and the slave. If you are in a vessel closer to M than to S, the pulse from M will reach you sooner than the pulse from S. The *difference in time* here places you on a certain hyperbola, which is then like a lop.

As explained both in Bowditch and Dutton, a mariner must first *tune in* with the Loran-A stations.

To accomplish this he must note the three variables which are used for identification:

Frequency
Basic pulse (signal) recurrence rate
Specific pulse recurrent rate

For frequency, three channels are available:

Channel 1, at 1950 kHz   *Note:* These frequencies do not have to be
Channel 2, at 1850 kHz   remembered, since you turn switch-
Channel 3, at 1900 kHz   es which are marked 1, 2 or 3.

Three basic rates are used:

S = special   = 20 pulses per second, 50,000 microsecond intervals
L = low   = 25 pulses per second, 40,000 microsecond intervals
H = high   = 33 1/3 pulses per second, 30,000 microsecond intervals
Note: There are switches marked S, L or H.

Eight stations (0, 1, 2, 3, 4, 5, 6, 7) may use the same frequency and same basic rate but with a specific rate varying by 100 microseconds from the basic rate.

A pair of stations is identified by giving the three variables. For example, 2H4 indicates Channel 2, high basic recurrent rate, and the "4" means station pair *4*.

The reason for tuning in, by turning the right knobs of the set, is to match the signals coming from the master and the slave. By matching signals, the time difference can be read and the correct hyperbolic lop identified.

After tuning in, there are three knobs to turn, *in order to match signals*:

1. the sweep or function switch, with three positions
2. delay knob
3. drift knob

With the sweep switch in the first position, the master signal will appear on the upper line and the slave signal on the lower line of the cathode-ray tube display.

With the delay knob, move the master and slave signals to the left edge of the pedestals.

Adjust the drift knob to stop the movement or drift of these signals.

Turn the sweep switch to the number 2 position, which enlarges the left part of the pedestal.

With delay switch align the signals, one under the other.

With drift knob adjustment move both signals to the left side of the scope.

Turn the sweep switch to the number 3 position, bringing the 2 signals together on the same line.

With fine delay knob align the left edges.

During all the steps you may need some increase or decrease in the gain or balance control settings, to obtain the proper amplitude, (maximum amplitide which will not cause distortion is desired).

Read the time difference off the dial, and find for your lop, on your Loran chart, the hyperbola with the same time difference above the line, or interpolate between curves shown there.

Pub. 117 shows tables for use with the electronic systems Loran-A and C, and the Omega, but it is easier to use charts with the hyperbolas plotted when they are available. Two different hyperbolas provide a fix, if care is taken to see that the angle of intersection of the two lops is not too small (See Fig. 7-4).

TABLE 7-3
Electronic Navigation Systems

I. Hyperbolic Systems

Brief Description	Frequency	Range	Accuracy	Use
1. LORAN-A (Standard Loran)				
Single-pulse system Time difference = basis	1850 - 1950 kHz	Long Range ~ 1000 mi.	1.5 miles Ground waves 5-7 miles Sky waves	Least expensive now, but on way out during next few years according to predictions.
2. LORAN-C				
Time difference Multi-pulse Phase comparison in addition to pulse. (Automatic, within receiver)	100 kHz carrier frequency	1200 miles, Ground waves 3000 miles, Sky waves	0.1% Dist. traveled, ground waves; 3-5 miles, Sky waves	Longer Range and more expensive. Skippers who can afford it, carry it or combined A & C.
3. LORAN-D				
Pulse-type	90 - 110 kHz	~ 500 mi.	0.1 miles possible	Semi-mobile
4. DECCA				
Phase comparison British system	70 -130 kHz	~ 240 mi.	150 yards in daytime; 800 yards at night.	Operative in West Europe, Northeast U.S. and Canada, Persian Gulf and Bay of Bengal; most useful off Newfoundland in fog.
5. OMEGA				
Phase difference measurement of continuous wave radio signals	10.2 kHz 13.6 kHz 11.33 kHz	4 stations available at any point on Earth, giving a minimum of 6 possible lops.	1 mile in daytime, 2 miles at night	Planned as worldwide, all-weather system for ships, aircraft and submarines submerged or surfaced. Developed for all branches of U.S. Navy, and for wide application for civilian vessels, commercial and private.

II. Non-Hyperbolic Systems

1. Inertial navigation
2. Omnirange (also of use to mariners)
3. Navstar (Global Positioning System), (GPS), (for future)

1. Inertial Navigation

This system was developed in the United States during 1945-1955. An outstanding contributor was Professor Charles Stark Draper, former director of the MIT Instrumentation Laboratory, which became the Charles Stark Draper Laboratory. The system and its components have been developed for aircraft, ships, missiles and spacecraft. It has proved to be popular and accurate for transoceanic flying, and if you have flown overseas during the last few years, your plane probably used this system. Inertial navigation employs accelerometers to measure the acceleration, and gyroscopes to stabilize the accelerometers in a desired orientation. There is also a computer which, among many processes, integrates the acceleration components sensed in the vehicle to obtain position and velocity. The system is certainly sophisticated; an interested mariner can read a short account readily available in the *Encyclopedia Britannica*.

2. Omnirange or Omni

Omnirange navigation is sometimes referred to as VOR. The V stands for very high frequency, and the OR for the first letters of Omni and Range. It is also called OMNI for a short term, and is used generally on airplanes across the country and other areas around the world. More recently some VOR stations have been installed on the coast, to assist both air navigators and mariners. The VOR stations operate in the frequency band 108 to 118 mHz, and the system resembles a line of sight system for planes as they fly on airways from one station to another.

Omni is based on *phase* comparison between two radiated radio frequency signals. One of these signals is nondirectional, with a constant phase through 360° in azimuth. The other signal rotates, and the phase changes as it rotates around the station. At magnetic North the two signals are exactly in phase. The aircraft receiver always compares the phase of the two signals and produces a readout which has been translated into the magnetic bearing of the station from the plane. The receiver also informs the pilot as to whether the bearing is *to* or *from* the station, of which there are several hundred in the U.S. One bearing line gives a lop. Two provide a fix. In addition, distance to a VOR station can be known by use of equipment similar to radar type equipment. In actual practice the air navigator "flies by the needle," which hangs down in a perpendicular direction when all is well, but it deviates to the right or left if the plane is off course. The pilot can then correct the heading so as to make the needle hang down again.

Omni has proved to be so successful in airplanes that instruments have been adjusted for mariners to use with VOR stations along the coast. As in the planes, lops and fixes can be obtained with little effort on the part of the mariner. The only disadvantage is the range, which is approximately 25-50 miles from the coastline, where the VOR stations are situated.

3. Navstar

Navstar should not be confused with *Navsat*, which depends upon "transit" satellites and which is successfully used today on many ships. Navsat is a complex and expensive system, but very accurate, to within a few yards. However, it is too expensive and takes up too much room on a boat.

Navstar, on the other hand, holds promise for the future and may be even more accurate and less expensive. It is the latest system in navigational development, and already is in Phase I, called "concept validation." The wise mariner should be able to identify it in a few words.

Navstar also called GPS (Global Positioning System) is a joint service program managed by the U.S. Air Force, with deputies from the Navy, Army, Marines and Defence Mapping Agency. The system will consist of 24 satellites, eight in each of three planes. This arrangement insures that at least six satellites are always in view from any point on the Earth. On the average, nine satellites are in view, providing three-dimensional positioning and navigation on a worldwide basis.

In brief, all users will have at least four satellites available. Simultaneous reception of four signals permits three independent range difference equations to be formed. The latter can be used to calculate the intersection of three hyperboloids of revolution. This intersection uniquely defines the position of the user. Predictions forecast a *reasonable* cost for the mariner in several years and the greatest accuracy yet.

The last three navigation systems in Table 7-3, though not developed primarily for coastwise navigation, should be identified for the mariner who is interested in general information which might become important for him at a future time. They are non-hyperbolic systems.

PROBLEM SET 7

Example: *Imagine that you are on Block Island Sound* and that the following positions are the two radio stations (in 1979 *Pub. 117* listed for numbers 1098 and 1099):

1098   Montauk Point Light Station, NY . . . . .41°04′15″N, 71°51′27″W
1099   Little Gull Island Light Station, NY . . . . .41°12′22″N, 72°06′29″W

		Frequency	Range (miles)	psc Radio Bearing
Little Gull	J (.---)	306 kHz	15	294°
Montauk Point	Y (-.--)	286 kHz	20	208°

If you obtained the compass radio bearings of 294° for Little Gull, and 208° for Montauk Point, *Where were you*? (*Assume that your heading was 090° psc.*)

Solution: Plot the radio stations on a Mercator chart (which you have or made). Variation for the region is 14°W. For deviation use the deviation curve which you made in Chapter 2, Fig. 2-6 and obtain (with 6°E for deviation and 8°W for total error) the true bearings of the radio stations (286°; 200°). Plot the true bearings on your chart (through radio stations). Construct the sectors, 2° on each side of the bearing lines plotted. Shade the area common to both sectors, and give the position of the central point of this area.

Lat. _____Long._____

Ans: 41°09′N, 71°49.5′W (See Fig. 7-1 for a similar problem).

Chapter 8

Plane Sailing; Traverse Table

With intensive development in electronics over the past two or three decades, "sailings" have tended to recede into the background and almost be forgotten. Many a successful navigator probably has never felt the need to recall them. However, a *traverse table*, helpful in *plane sailing*, is certainly a great aid at times, even in celestial navigation when quick *reduction tables* may be missing, and so if the present text is to function as a navigation aid in many situations of coastwise navigation, a *traverse table* should be included here, with some explanation as to its use (See Table 8-1).

EXAMPLE IN PLANE SAILING

Looking at Fig. 8-1, imagine yourself sailing from A to B on a true course of 063° for 80 miles. As evident from the figure, you change your Latitude by AF (D. Lat. means difference or change in Latitude). If the position at A (departure point) equals 42°20′N, 68°40′W, after 1 mile on course 063°t, the D. Lat. is .454. (Note rule no. 3 at top of traverse table (Table 8-1), and also note that the table was entered with 63° on the right side—the only place where 63° could be found here.)

If .454 is D. Lat. for 1 mile, as stated at top of table, you can find the D. Lat. for 80 miles by multiplying .454 by 80, giving you 36.3 miles for AF. The new Latitude at B is 42°20′ + 36.3′ = 42°56.3′N. You yourself have to tell from inspection, or from plotting the situation mentally, that 36.3′ must be *added* to give the Latitude at B. You know this fact because your course of 063° is to the North and East, with Latitude increasing North, and with West Longitude decreasing as you move East.

Departure and Conversion to D.Lo. The number of *miles* East or West by which you change your position, is called *departure.* In Fig. 8-1, departure is FB in miles. One minute of Latitude is equal to one nautical mile, but one minute of Longitude is equal to one mile *only* at the Equator. As seen in

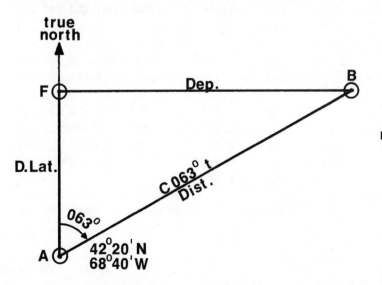

Fig. 8-1. Terms used in plane sailing—
AB = Course (063° in example)
AF = D.Lat. = Difference in Latitude
FB = Dep. = Departure
Dist. = Distance from A to B
mid-Lat. = Lm = $\dfrac{\text{Lat. at A + Lat. at B}}{2}$

Note: Inspection often gives mid-Lat. to nearest degree.

TABLE 8-1
Traverse Table

Rules: 1. If true course is on left, read column label at top.
2. If true course is on right, read column label at bottom.

(1)	(2)	(3)	(4)	(5)	(6)	(7)	(8)
True Course	D. Lat.	Dep.	D. Lat. /Dep.		Dep. to D. Lo.		
000 180 180 360	1.000	.000	Inf.	.00	1.00	Inf.	090 090 270 270
001 179 181 359	1.000	.017	57.29	.02	1.00	57.30	089 091 269 271
002 178 182 358	.999	.035	28.64	.03	1.00	28.65	088 092 268 272
003 177 183 357	.999	.052	19.08	.05	1.00	19.11	087 093 267 273
004 176 184 356	.998	.070	14.30	.07	1.00	14.34	086 094 266 274
005 175 185 355	.996	.087	11.43	.09	1.00	11.47	085 095 265 275
006 174 186 354	.995	.105	9.51	.11	1.01	9.57	084 096 264 276
007 173 187 353	.993	.122	8.14	.12	1.01	8.21	083 097 263 277
008 172 188 352	.990	.139	7.12	.14	1.01	7.19	082 098 262 278
009 171 189 351	.988	.156	6.31	.16	1.01	6.39	081 099 261 279
010 170 190 350	.985	.174	5.67	.18	1.02	5.76	080 100 260 280
011 169 191 349	.982	.191	5.14	.19	1.02	5.24	079 101 259 281
012 168 192 348	.978	.208	4.70	.21	1.02	4.81	078 102 258 282
013 167 193 347	.974	.225	4.33	.23	1.03	4.45	077 103 257 283
014 166 194 346	.970	.242	4.01	.25	1.03	4.13	076 104 256 284
015 165 195 345	.966	.259	3.73	.27	1.04	3.86	075 105 255 285
016 164 196 344	.961	.276	3.49	.29	1.04	3.63	074 106 254 286
017 163 197 343	.956	.292	3.27	.31	1.05	3.42	073 107 253 287
018 162 198 342	.951	.309	3.08	.32	1.05	3.24	072 108 252 288
019 161 199 341	.946	.326	2.90	.34	1.06	3.07	071 109 251 289
020 160 200 340	.940	.342	2.75	.36	1.06	2.92	070 110 250 290
021 159 201 339	.934	.358	2.61	.38	1.07	2.79	069 111 249 291
022 158 202 338	.927	.375	2.48	.40	1.08	2.67	068 112 248 292
023 157 203 337	.921	.391	2.36	.42	1.09	2.56	067 113 247 293
024 156 204 336	.914	.407	2.25	.45	1.09	2.46	066 114 246 294
025 155 205 335	.906	.423	2.14	.47	1.10	2.37	065 115 245 295
026 154 206 334	.899	.438	2.05	.49	1.11	2.28	064 116 244 296
027 153 207 333	.891	.454	1.96	.51	1.12	2.20	063 117 243 297
028 152 208 332	.883	.469	1.88	.53	1.13	2.13	062 118 242 298
029 151 209 331	.875	.485	1.80	.55	1.14	2.06	061 119 241 299
030 150 210 330	.866	.500	1.73	.58	1.15	2.00	060 120 240 300
031 149 211 329	.857	.515	1.66	.60	1.17	1.94	059 121 239 301
032 148 212 328	.848	.530	1.60	.62	1.18	1.89	058 122 238 302
033 147 213 327	.839	.545	1.54	.65	1.19	1.84	057 123 237 303
	Dep.	D. Lat.		D. Lat. /Dep.		Dep. to D. Lo.	True Course

TABLE 8-1
Traverse Table (continued)

3. Tabulated values are for distance = 1 nautical mile.
4. To find conversion factor for Dep. to D.Lo., enter Lat. as true course.

(1) True Course	(2) D. Lat.	(3) Dep.	(4) D. Lat. /Dep.	(5)	(6) Dep. to D. Lo.	(7)	(8)
034 146 214 326	.829	.559	1.48	.67	1.21	1.79	056 124 236 304
035 145 215 325	.819	.574	1.43	.70	1.22	1.74	055 125 235 305
036 144 216 324	.809	.588	1.38	.73	1.24	1.70	054 126 234 306
037 143 217 323	.799	.602	1.33	.75	1.25	1.66	053 127 233 307
038 142 218 322	.788	.616	1.28	.78	1.27	1.62	052 128 232 308
039 141 219 321	.777	.629	1.23	.81	1.29	1.59	051 129 231 309
040 140 220 320	.766	.643	1.19	.84	1.31	1.56	050 130 230 310
041 139 221 319	.755	.656	1.15	.87	1.33	1.52	049 131 229 311
042 138 222 318	.743	.669	1.11	.90	1.35	1.49	048 132 228 312
043 137 223 317	.731	.682	1.07	.93	1.37	1.47	047 133 227 313
044 136 224 316	.719	.695	1.04	.97	1.39	1.44	046 134 226 314
045 135 225 315	.707	.707	1.00	1.00	1.41	1.41	045 135 225 315
	Dep.	D. Lat.		D. Lat. /Dep.		Dep. to D. Lo.	True Course

Chapter 3, the expanding factor is the secant of the mid-Latitude (Lm). This factor is given in the traverse table, and you find the value which fits your case by entering the true course column with the value of the mid-Lat. In other words, the Dep. to D.Lo. column gives values for transforming Dep. to D.Lo., where D.Lo. equals the difference or change in Longitude. Conversion factor values are really values for sec Lm, as also mentioned in Chapter 3. The mariner who does not find trigonometry interesting does not have to worry about the trigonometric significance when he uses the table. (A few might enjoy seeing the relationships, as understanding the subject reduces the items which have to be remembered.)

To continue with the example, after the D. Lat. is known, the departure must be found. Another inspection of the table shows .891 as the Dep. for 1 mile (C = 63°). For 80 miles, you multiply .891 by 80 to obtain 71.3. Then you look for the conversion factor by entering the table again with the mid-Lat. Since 42°20′ is the Lat. at A, and 42°56.3′ is the Lat. at B, the mid-Lat. to the nearest degree is 43°. For mid-Lat. of 43°, enter the table as if the 43° were a course and find the conversion factor 1.37 (sec Lm). Multiplying 71.3 by 1.37 gives 97.7 for the D.Lo. Subtract this D.Lo. from 68°40′ and you have 67°02.3′W for Long. at B. In other words, you have your new Latitude and Longitude at the end of your run. Your best check would be to plot this example on a Mercator chart you could make for practice.

It should now be evident that whenever you want to find a new position, instead of plotting, you may use the traverse table, provided you do not sail more than around 500 miles, or use one to check the other. You have assumed, in this process, that you sailed on a *plane surface*, which is close to the Earth's spherical surface if the distance is not too great (less than 500 miles).

PROBLEM SET 8

PLANE SAILING

In the following problems, use the *deviation curve* (Fig. 2-6); for sailing table, use the *traverse table* in this chapter.

1) A ship at Lat. 21°43′S, Long. 15°38′W, sails 87 miles on a compass course of 151°. Variation for the region is 25°W. Find the Latitude and Longitude of the position at which she arrives. Show work here:

Solution, (partial): *Answers* given in Appendix II.

C	D	M	V	T	Dist.	D. Lat.	Dep.
151°	19°W	132°	25°W	107°	87m.	S	E

Mid-Lat. = 22°
Conversion factor = 1.08

Lat. _____ Long. _____

2) The CYGNUS, at Lat. 40°10′N, Long. 12°50′W, sails on a compass course of 202° for 67 miles. Variation for region is 11°W. What are the Latitude and Longitude at the end of the run? Show work here:

Solution (partial):

C	D	M	V	T	Dist.	D. Lat.	Dep.	D. Lo.

Lat. _____ Long. _____

If you were sailing and changing course rather frequently with various tacks, you might in this way like to keep track of your position at the end of each new heading. You might even disregard a few intermediate positions, and be interested in your position only at the end of a number of runs, as shown in Problem 3.

3) CAPRICORNUS, with a speed of 12 knots and a draft of 6 feet, takes departure at Lat. 43°37′N, Long. 69°51′W at 0921 EST, on January 27, and sails on the following legs. Find the Latitude and Longitude at point of arrival, and also the time, assuming that the 12 knot speed was maintained on all four legs:

Leg	Compass Course	Dev.	Mag. Course	Var.	True Course	Dist. n.m.	D. Lat. N	D. Lat. S	Dep. E	Dep. W
1	149°			18°W		40				
2	184°			18°W		31				
3	056°			19°W		83				
4	001°			19°W		52				
Totals:						206				

Solution:

Leg	Compass Course	Dev.	Mag. Course	Var.	True Course	Dist. n.m.	D. Lat. N	D. Lat. S	Dep. E	Dep. W
1		19°W	130°		112°			15.0′	37.1	
2		14°W	170°		152°			27.4	14.5	
3		24°E	080°		061°		40.3		72.6	
4		16°E	017°		358°		51.9			01.8
Totals:							92.2	42.4	124.2	01.8
							42.4		01.8	
							49.8		122.4	

Answers:

New Lat. = 44°26.8′N

New Long. = 67°00.9′W

Total Dist. = 206 miles

Time of Arrival = 02^h31^m January 28

$$(DL_o = 122.4 \times 1.39 = 170.1' \text{ E}$$
$$= 2°50.1' \text{E})$$

4) **Review of Currents.** Imagine that you really went on this cruise of four legs, and that other checks of your position (from Chapter 5) showed that your fix at this time was actually 44°15.5′N, 67°26.3′W. Estimate the current which has set you off during these 4 legs, during 17.2 hours.

Answer: Plot the fix and draw a line from the DR to the fix at this time. The set is the direction of the line 238°, while the drift is obtained from the length of the line (21.5 miles measured from the Latitude scale). Since the current set you off during 17.2 hours, the drift is actually 21.5 divided by 17.2 or 1.2 knots.

You must remember that all courses must be true when you enter the traverse table. Use of this table is really a kind of bookkeeping of where you are, and if you keep track in this way, it should be a part of your Log. The making of entries in the vessel's Log should be one of your major concerns as navigator. The Log, supplemented by a navigation notebook, should provide a complete narrative of the progress of your vessel. All observations and calculations should be recorded. (*Admirals in Collision* by R. Hough is a classic example of what can happen if maneuvers and positions are not written down! This 1895 disaster occurred in preparation for anchoring the vessels commanded by the Admirals. It resulted in the collision of two British warships in daylight, in peacetime, and on a perfectly calm sea.) From a well kept Log it should be possible to reconstruct step by step an entire voyage many years after it took place. And this is true of a small boat as well as of a ship.

Shackleton's famous voyage in the 22-foot boat to South Georgia Island in the worst seas of the globe testify as to the value of this procedure, as described recently in Worsley's book, *Shackleton's Boat Journey*. In addition, of course, charts are also necessary—to show dangers, hazards, rocks and reefs, and plotting is easier and safer than bookkeeping for most mariners. If you also remember the rule that *every technique should be checked by another, different technique*, it will always help you to make the best decision as to procedure.

Another column, (4) in this chapter's traverse table, can be of aid when you know where you are and where you want to go, but you want to go directly on only one leg, in a motor cruise, perhaps. Suppose you consider the same problem as is in Problem 3:

$$
\begin{array}{lll}
\text{Position at departure} = 43°37.0'N & 69°51.0'W \\
\text{Position at end} \quad = 44°26.8'N & 67°00.9'W \\
\hline
\text{D. Lat.} = \quad 49.8'N & \text{D.Lo.} = 2°50.1'E = 170.1'
\end{array}
$$

The conversion factor (columns 6 and 7) will transfer Dep. to D.Lo. Since you now have D.Lo. and want Dep., you divide by 1.39 (conversion factor found by entering the table with the mid-Lat. of 44° in this case). 170.1 divided by 1.39 gives 122.4 which is equal to the Dep. Next, you want D. Lat./Dep. or 49.8/122.4. The latter quotient = 0.407.

You look in columns 4 and 5 to find 0.407, and you find this value in column 5 (.40). Since the label of the column is at the bottom of the table, you read a true course from the right side of the table. For the value .40 you note four values for the course: 068°, 112°, 248°, and 292°. Since the second position is North and East of the first position, the course must be between 000° and 090°, and so you must select 068° from the table as your correct true course for cruising to the second position on one leg. (Your course can always be given to the *nearest degree*, as a rule.)

At this point, sufficient information has been provided for use of the traverse table, as shown in this Problem Set. Some mariners however will be interested in a few equations derived for Fig. 8-1 and the quantities represented there. In fact, this traverse table is merely a brief trigonometry table, as you can see shortly. Look at the figure and you will see that in the right triangle, ABF,

$$\text{Cos C (course)} = \frac{\text{D.Lat.}}{\text{Dist.}} \quad \text{or} \quad \underline{\text{D.Lat.} = \text{Dist.} \times \cos C}$$

$$\text{Sin C} \quad = \frac{\text{Dep.}}{\text{Dist.}} \quad \text{or} \quad \underline{\text{Dep.} = \text{Dist.} \times \sin C}$$

$$\text{If Dist.} \quad = 1 \qquad \begin{array}{l} \underline{\text{D.Lat.} = \cos C} \\ \underline{\text{Dep.} = \sin C} \end{array}$$

In other words, your traverse table gives you the sine of any angle—in the Dep. column (3), while you have the cosine of any angle in the D.Lat. column (2). All this follows just from the definitions of the sine and the cosine of an acute angle in a right triangle. You also have one more trigonometric function, to help. The cotangent of an acute angle in a right triangle equals the adjacent side divided by the opposite side, or

$$\cot C = \frac{\text{D.Lat.}}{\text{Dep.}} \text{ (where cot = cotangent).}$$

Hence, your traverse table, a small trigonometric table, can be used, as these tables are intended, for solutions of many problems. If you measure the vertical angle of a tower, for instance, you can tell your distance off by using a special table (See Appendix IV), or you can use a cotangent table such as you have in your traverse table to give your distance off from the tower (See Chapter 5).

Appendices

Appendix I

Abbreviations

B	Blue (South-seeking) magnetic pole	H, h, hrs.	Hours
Brg.	Bearing	Hdg.	Heading
		Ho	Observed (measured in degrees and corrected) height or altitude
C	Course, compass		
cel	Celestial	Hor.	Horizontal or Horizon
corr.	Correction or corrected	Hs	Height or altitude in degrees, obtained by sextant, without corrections
cos	Cosine		
cot	Cotangent	Ht	Height
CPA	Closest point of approach		
CRT	Cathode-ray tube	I.E.	Index Error (sextant)
		Inf.	Infinite
D, Dev.	Deviation		
D.A.	Danger Angle	kHz	Kilohertz
Dep.	Departure	kn	Knots (nautical miles per hour)
D.Lat.	Difference (change) of Latitude		
D.Lo.	Difference (change) of Longitude	Lat.	Latitude
		Lm	Middle- or Mid-latitude
DMAHTC	Defense Mapping Agency Hydrographic/Topographic Center	LNM	*Local Notice to Mariners*
		Long.	Longitude
DR, D.R.	Dead (Deduced) Reckoning	lop	Line of position
		M, m, Mag., mag	Magnetic
		M, m, mins.	Minutes
E	Ebb tide flow	m, mi	Miles
E, e	East	Max	Maximum
EDT	Eastern Daylight Time	mHz	Megahertz
EP	Estimated Position	MN	Magnetic North
EST	Eastern Standard Time		
ETA	Estimated Time of Arrival	N, n	North
		NM	*Notice to Mariners*
F	Flood tide flow	nm, n.m.	Nautical mile
fms	Fathoms	NOAA	National Oceanic and Atmospheric Administration
ft	Feet		
GPS	Global Positioning System	NOS	National Ocean Survey

Omni	Omnirange Navigation	W, w	West
		WOBZC 42	Magnetic Variation Chart of the World
PPI	Plan Position Indicator	WOBZP 5090	Number and identification of the Maneuvering Board
psc	Per standard compass		
pt.	Point		
Pt.Dep., Pt. of Dep.	Point of Departure		
Pub.	Publication		
		°	Degrees
R	Red (North-seeking) magnetic pole	'	Minutes of arc
		''	Seconds of arc
RBn	Radiobeacon	H, h	Hours of time
RDF	Radio direction finder	M, m	Minutes of time
Rel.Brg.	Relative Bearing	S, s	Seconds of time
R Fix	Running Fix	>	Greater than
		<	Less than
S, s	South	=	Equals
S	Speed		
SC	Small Craft (chart designation)		
sec	Secant (trigonometric function)		**Chart Symbol Categories.** (See Figs. 3-3 to 6)
sin	Sine '' ''	A	Coastline Features
stbd.	Starboard	B	Coast Features (abbreviations)
std.	Standard	C	Land (Natural Features)
		D	Control Points
T	Time	K	Lights
t, T	True (e.g. 000°t or 000°T)	L	Buoys and Beacons
tan	Tangent	M	Radio and Radar Stations
TN, tn	True North	N	Fog Signals
Tr	Training (chart designation)	O	Dangers
		P	Various Limits
V, Var	Variation	Q	Soundings
Vert.	Vertical	R	Depth Contours
VOR	Omnirange Navigation	S	Quality of Bottom
VP-OS	Universal Plotting Sheet	T	Tides and Currents

Appendix II

Answers to Problems

CHAPTER 1—PROBLEM SET 1

Answers

1) (a) 335°; (b) 155°

2) Lat. 00°32.7'N; Long. 28°01.2'W

3) $12^h37^m55^s$

4) 262°

5) (a) 312°; (b) 042°; (c) 251°; 042°

6) Lat. 14°51'S; Long. 112°37'W

CHAPTER 2—PROBLEM SET 2

Examples in Applying Variation

1. 154°	3. 232°	5. 211°	7. 180°
2. 126°	4. 294°	6. 010°	8. 287°

Answers

1) See Fig. 2-6.

2) Complete the data in the following array, assuming for your Compass the deviation curve given above. If you are in regions with variations as indicated below, use your deviation curve of Napier diagram and find, in each case, the missing values of the compass course, the magnetic course, or the true course to be plotted, as the case may be. *In each case check your arithmetic by finding the total compass error.*

	Compass Course	Dev.	Magnetic Course	Variation	True Course	Total Compass Error
1.	066°	20°E	086°	29°W	057°	9°W
2.	080°	12°E	092°	28°W	064°	16°W
3.	278°	9°W	269°	15°E	284°	6°E
4.	065°	20°E	085°	10°W	075°	10°E
5.	011°	21°E	032°	20°E	052°	41°E
6.	299°	9°W	290°	30°W	260°	39°W
7.	177°	15°W	162°	15°W	147°	30°W
8.	001°	17°E	018°	08°E	026°	25°E
9.	225°	5°W	220°	13°W	207°	18°W
10.	110°	6°W	104°	20°E	124°	14°E

Answers to within 1° or 2° of these figures should be acceptable.

3) (a) 047°; (b) 071°

4) (a) 202°; (b) 29°E

5) (a) 168°; (b)   9°E

6) (a) 225°; (b)   2°E

CHAPTER 3—PROBLEM SET 3

Answers to Chapter Text Questions

CRUISE OF VEGA. (See Figs. 5-16, 13, 15 for plotted courses)

Leg	Mag. Course	Compass Course	Lat.	Long.
1	182°	193°		
2	270°	279°		
3	105°	112°	41°15.6′N	72°04.5′W
4	064°	037°		

Answers to Problem Set

CRUISE OF ALGOL

Leg	Compass Course	Time End of Leg	Lat. End of Each Leg	Long. End of Each Leg
1	044°	0602	41°14.1′N	72°03.9′W
2	311°	0645	41°15.4′N	72°08.4′W
3	294°	0728	41°15.4′N	72°13.2′W
4	015°	0747	41°16.8′N	72°12.3′W

(plotting not shown on Chart 116-SC Tr)

CHAPTER 4—PROBLEM SET 4

Answers

TIDE PROBLEMS

1)

Time Difference		Height Difference	
High	Low	High (ft)	Low
-0^h01^m	-0^h06^m	−0.1	0.0

2)

New London		West Harbor, Fishers Island, N.Y.	
Time	Height (ft)	Time	Height (ft)
00^h11^m	2.3 High	00^h10^m	2.2 High
06 37	0.5 Low	06 31	0.5 Low
12 26	2.7 High	12 25	2.6 High
19 19	0.3 Low	19 13	0.3 Low

3) See Fig. 4-7.

4) Duration of rise = 5^h49^m
Time from nearest high = 1^h26^m
Range is 2.2 feet.
Corr. = 0.3 (Table 4-4)
Ht. at 11^h00^m = 2.4 feet. *Ans.*

5) Yes. Difference between two methods = .02 feet or 0

6) Duration of rise = 5^h54^m
Time from nearest high = 1^h25^m
Range = 2.1 feet
Corr. = 0.3 (Table 4-4)
Ht. at 11^h00^m = 2.3 feet. *Ans.*

CURRENT PROBLEMS

1)

	Time Differences	Velocity Ratios		Set
Slack Water	-0^h40^m			
Max Current:	Max F -0^h35^m	Max F	0.9	300°
	Max E -1^h40^m	Max E	0.9	135°

Reference Station: The Race, Table 4-5 in text (in *Tidal Current Tables*, p.34).

2)

	The Race		
Times	Velocities	Times	Velocities
0002	3.2 Max Ebb	1224	3.1 Max Ebb
0321	Slack; F begins	1535	Slack; F begins
0601	2.6 Max Flood	1814	2.8 Max Flood
0902	Slack; E begins	2118	Slack; E begins

3)

	Times	Velocities
Sept. 9	22^h22^m	2.9 E Max
Sept. 10	02 41	Slack; F begins
	05 26	2.3 F Max
	08 22	Slack; E begins
	10 44	2.8 E Max
	14 55	Slack; F begins
	17 39	2.5 F Max
	20 38	Slack; E begins

4) Interval between slack and desired time = 1^h33^m
Interval between slack and max = 2^h22^m
f = .9 and .9 x 2.8 = 2.5 knots = Drift at desired place. *Ans.*
Current is ebbing, and ebb direction is 135° as in problem 1 of this set.
135° = Set of Current, *Ans.*

5) Interval between slack and desired time = 3^h17^m
Interval between slack and max current = 3^h25^m
f = 1

Since max ebb velocity = 4.6 knots, the required drift at 15^h20^m = 4.6 x 1 = 4.6 knots = *Ans.* for drift.

Set = ebb direction (given at top of page for the Reference Station) = 100° for The Race = *Ans.* for set.

6) *Ans.* (Find a max and slack, one before, the other after, desired time)

The Race, Ref. Station		Black Pt. 0.8 miles S of	
Times	Velocities	Times	Velocities
13^h45^m	4.3 E Max	12^h05^m	1.7
17 02	Slack	15 37	

13^h50^m Desired Time

Interval between slack and desired times = 1^h47^m
Interval between slack and max current = 3^h32^m
f = .7

.7 x 1.7 = 1.2 = Drift of current, *Ans.*
        Set = 080°

7) Heading is 191°t; speed made good = 5.7 knots. *Ans.*

8) Four miles made good in one-half hour requires the same speed as eight miles in one hour. Hence the speed made good is 8 knots. Plot this distance in the direction 180° on the maneuvering board, and draw a vector from the end of the current vector to the end of the speed-made-good vector. The measure of the new vector is 8.3 knots, with a Heading of 188°t.

This speed of 8.3 knots may be faster than you can go conveniently, and illustrates the fact that the third type of current problem, as in number 7, is apt to be the more practical case on the water.

CHAPTER 5—PROBLEM SET 5

Answers to Chapter Text Questions

CRUISE OF TUCANA

1) (a) = 0837; (b) = 3.2 ft. (c) = 11.2 ft.

2) Slack

3) (Leg 6) 1st. Brg. = 010°; 2nd. Brg. = 103°

4) 41°17.4′N; 72°04.4′W

Answers to Problem Set. Remember: *Deviation* depends upon *heading*.

CRUISE OF ALPHECCA

1) Lat. 41°15′58′′N; Long. 72°11′58′′W

2) 1. 1.48 miles
   2. 1.48 miles
   3. 1.04 miles

3) Magnetic course = 115°; Compass course = 130°

4) Magnetic bearing of Bartlett light = 094°
   Compass bearing of Black Point tank = 015°
   Magnetic bearing of Black Point tank = 000°
   No; No; Variation and deviation are not needed in number 3 with horizontal angles

CRUISE OF TUCANA

6) a. Magnetic bearing = 028°

   b. Compass bearing = 039°

   c. Magnetic bearing of Latimer Reef light = 269°

   d. Compass bearing of Latimer Reef light = 280°

   e. Magnetic bearing of New London Ledge light = 001°

   f. Compass bearing of New London Ledge light = 010°

   g. Compass bearing of Seaflower Reef light = 103°

CHAPTER 6—PROBLEM SET 6

Answers

1) (a) em = 9.2 kn.
   (b) t = 22 minutes

2) (a) eg = 045°t
   (b) = 12^h12^m

3) (a) em = 111°t
   (b) Time for the maneuver = 2^h22^m

   Both boats should make it through the Gut, but just barely!

4) Two possibilities:
   1. em_1 = 163°t, gm_1 = 10.8 kns. Time of arrival = 1831
   2. em_2 = 048°t, gm_2 = 27.6 kns. Time of arrival = 1824
   3. At closest approach distance between K and B is 300 yards, Case 1.

5) (a) No collision
   (b) Distance 0.4 − 0.5 miles
      Time = 1109 P.M., or 2309

CHAPTER 7—PROBLEM SET 7

Answers

1) Example: Lat. 41°09′N, 71°49.5′W

CHAPTER 8—PROBLEM SET 8

Answers

1) Lat. 22° 08.4′S; Long. 14°08.2′W

2) Lat. 39°03.1′N; Long. 12°54.5′W

C	D	M	V	T	Dist.	D.Lat.	Dep	DLo
202°	8°W	194°	.11°W	183°	67	66.93S	3.48	04.5W

3)

Complete Log for CAPRICORNUS

Leg	Compass Course	Dev.	Mag. Course	Var.	True Course	Dist. n.m.	D.Lat. N	S	Dep. E	W
1	149°	19°W	130°	18°W	112°	40		15.0′	37.1	
2	184°	14°W	170°	18°W	152°	31		27.4′	14.5	
3	056°	24°E	080°	19°W	061°	83	40.3		72.6	
4	001°	16°E	017°	19°W	358°	52	51.9			01.8
Totals						206	92.2	42.4	124.2	01.8
							42.4S		01.8	
							49.8N		122.4E	

Answers:

New Lat. = 44°26.8′N
New Long. = 67°00.9′W
Total Dist. = 206 miles
Estimated time of arrival = 02ʰ31ᵐ January 28

Lm = 44°
Conversion factor = 1.39
D. Long. = 170.1′ = 2°50.1′E

4) Set = 238°

Drift = 1.2 knots

Appendix III

Bibliography and Sources of Materials

SOURCES—AGENTS

It certainly requires the least effort to go to a good sales agent authorized by the U.S. Government, for help and speed in acquiring what you want. These agents are listed in the National Oceanic and Atmospheric Administration catalogs mentioned here and also appear in the *Catalog of Nautical Charts*, numerical listing of charts and publications (Pub. 1-N-L) published by the Defense Mapping Agency Hydrographic/Topographic Center (DMAHTC), Washington, DC 20390 (successor of the old Hydrographic Office (H.O.) and later of the U.S. Naval Oceanographic Office).

Many agents are listed, with addresses within states, for the most part along the coastal regions, both West and East, and almost as many again for authorized agents in foreign countries. If you were starting your nautical life "from scratch," you could begin by looking up an agent in the telephone book under the U.S. Government, Government Printing Office, which will probably have a book store where you could purchase a few publications (such as *Nautical Almanac*) for the year. The store could tell you the number or address of commercial agents who would provide you with charts and other publications.

Your sources for all this material are the DMAHTC, National Ocean Survey (NOS), National Oceanic and Atmospheric Administration (NOAA), and the U.S. Coast Guard, but these sources usually require more time than employing the help of an authorized government agent in your region. Also, *payment is required at time of your order.*

Addresses of a few authorized sales agents:

Hub Nautical Supply Co., Inc.
200 High Street
Boston, MA 02110

James Bliss
100 Rte. 128 (at Exit 61)
Dedham, MA 02026

Captain's
1324 Second Avenue
Seattle, WA 98101

Defense Mapping Agency Hydrographic/
Topographic Center (DMAHTC)
Washington, DC 20390

New York Nautical Instrument &
Service Corp.
140 West Broadway
New York, NY 10013

Herold Boat Co.
1112 East Las Olas Blvd.
Fort Lauderdale, FL 33301

Supt. of Documents
Government Printing Office
Washington, DC 20402
Attn: Customer Service

Defense Mapping Agency
Aerospace Center
St. Louis Air Force Station
St. Louis, MO 63118

SOURCES—DMAHTC AND NOS

Your chief source of charts, and most important for the mariner practicing coastwise navigation, is the National Ocean Survey. This group publishes harbor charts, described in Chapter 3, as well as coast and general charts. The regions covered are more or less near land, while the DMAHTC usually publishes ocean charts for out of sight of land. NOS also publishes specially designed charts for use by small craft. They have SC (small craft) annexed to the usual number. *Tr* after a number indicates for training purposes, as applied to the Chart 116-SC Tr. In addition, NOS publishes catalogs freely distributed at stores of nautical agents. Again, for an emergency, use the following address:

> NOAA
> (National Oceanic & Atmospheric Administration)
> Distribution Division, C44
> National Ocean Survey
> Riverdale, MD 20840

Write for a free copy of any one of the yearly four nautical chart catalogs and for the publication of latest editions of nautical charts, all by NOS or NOAA, as follows:

Chart Catalogs, NOS or NOAA.

- Atlantic and Gulf Coasts, including Puerto Rico and Virgin Islands
- Pacific Coast, including Hawaii, Guam and Samoa Islands
- Alaska, including the Aleutian Islands
- Great Lakes and Adjacent Waterways

Each catalog lists all the published charts for that region (or regions) with the scale of the chart, so that you can tell yourself which charts you need for any particular cruise. Some sales agents do not stock both DMAHTC and NOS charts, but those chosen above, with addresses given for an emergency, stock both according to notes in the catalogs. In the catalogs there is pictorial representation of the regions, with the areas of the charts shown with boundary lines, so that selection is easy. Only one word of warning is necessary. In planning for a cruise, plan well in advance, and certainly order charts and other publications *early*, as delivery is sometimes very slow, in case the particular chart is not in stock. It may even be out of print, temporarily!

There are two DMAHTC catalogs of nautical charts which may be of particular interest to the yachtsman: (1) *Pub. 1-N-L: Numerical Listing of Charts and Publications*, and (2) *Pub. 1-N-A: Miscellaneous and Special Purpose Navigational Charts, Sheets, and Tables*. The coastwise navigator might be interested in the Loran and Omega charts and tables in *Pub. 1-N-A*.

A third, *Catalog of Nautical Charts,* shows charts which can be purchased through NOS. It contains general nautical charts of the world and coastal charts. The data in any one region pertain to *one of the nine regions* of the world, and the NOS chart numbers appear in red.

NINE REGIONS FOR CHARTS:

1. United States and Canada
2. Central and South America and Antarctica
3. Western Europe, Iceland, Greenland and the Arctic
4. Scandinavia, Baltic and USSR
5. Western Africa and the Mediterranean
6. Indian Ocean
7. Australia, Indonesia and New Zealand
8. Oceania
9. East Asia

CHART NUMBERING. Fortunately for the mariner, NOS cooperated with the DMAHTC in 1974 to begin a new national chart numbering system, with regions, subregions, etc. It has been designed to provide a uniform method of identifying charts. This system generally identifies a chart according to a geographical location, as follows:

1. One-digit number (1-9). This category pertains to charts with no scale connotation, such as symbol and flag charts.

2. Two- and three-digit numbers (10-999). This category pertains to those small-scale charts which show the major portion of an ocean basin or a large area with the first digit identifying the specific basin.

3. Four-digit numbers (5000-9999). This category includes special-type world charts and plotting sheets.

4. Five-digit numbers (11000-99999). The majority of nautical charts fall into this category. These charts cover portions of the coastline rather than significant portions of ocean basins. The five-digit numbered charts are based on the nine regions of the nautical chart index. The first of the five digits indicates the region in which the chart is shown. The second digit indicates a geographical subregion within the region, and the last three digits identify the geographical order of a chart within the subregion. For an example, the NOS chart numbered 13267 indicates a chart for Region 1 and Subregion 13 (See Appendix III—Fig. III-1). The last three digits (267) are associated with Massachusetts Bay.

The pages of these chart catalogs are somewhat bewildering to the civilian mariner, but he can remember that most of this information is for the military, with strict information about ordering charts, etc. The civilian mariner can bypass most of it, and order carefully as he would anyway, but again, remember that it is easier to go to an agent.

PUBLICATIONS AND LISTS

"Radio Navigation Aids." *Pub. 117 A,* DMAHTC, for Atlantic and Mediterranean Area, and *Pub. 117 B,* DMAHTC, for Pacific and Indian Oceans Area, provide lists of selected radio stations divided geographically so that you may readily determine which of several stations in your vicinity renders services most suited to your immediate needs (published yearly, usually). In between editions, you must make corrections yourself, with the aid of the weekly *Notice to Mariners* (See Chapter 7). This is an important publication to help you with radio bearings.

In addition to charts, you must consult the following, as mentioned in the text, but first the source of these publications should be known:

- NOS *Coast Pilot* for your Region
- *Light List* for your Region
- *Tide Tables* for your Region
- *Tidal Current Tables* if available for your Region

"NOS Coast Pilot." List of nine *NOS Coast Pilots* (1978):

1. Eastport to Cape Cod, 1978
2. Cape Cod to Sandy Hook, 1978
3. Sandy Hook to Cape Henry, 1977
4. Cape Henry to Key West, 1977
5. Gulf Coast, Puerto Rico and Virgin Islands, 1977
6. Great Lakes, 1978
7. California, Oregon, Washington and Hawaii, 1977
8. Dixon Entrance to Cape Spencer, 1969
9. Cape Spencer to Beaufort Sea, 1977

There are also U.S. *Inside Route Pilots*, as well as charts for the Intracoastal Waterway.

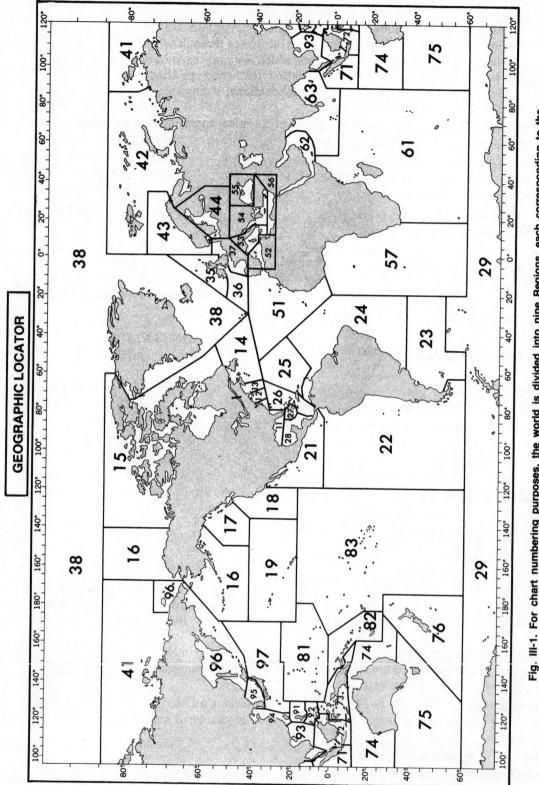

Fig. III-1. For chart numbering purposes, the world is divided into nine Regions, each corresponding to the geographic limits of one of the nine catalog Regions comprising Pub. 1-N, Catalog of Nautical Charts. Each Region is further subdivided into the numbered Subregions in the above graphic. The first two digits of all five-digit chart numbers indicate the geographic subregion to which the chart pertains. Users can locate corrections in this Notice for the charts of their immediate interest by determining the two-digit Subregion number of the pertinent geographic area, and then turn to the page or pages that list the chart numbers beginning with those two digits. (Courtesy National Ocean Survey (NOS) and Defense Mapping Agency Hydrographic/Topographic Center.)

In general, *Coast Pilots* do more than provide you with interesting reading. Their primary function is to aid you and keep you and your vessel safe amidst several dangers as you cruise. In Chapter 5, you went on a paper cruise on TUCANA, taking departure off Stonington. Along with several other remarks about Stonington, *U.S. Coast Pilot 2* gives the following information in the 1978 edition:

"There are several small craft facilities at Stonington. Berths, electricity, gasoline, diesel fuel, water, ice, storage, launching ramps, 20-ton mobile hoist, marine supplies and hull, engine and electronic repairs are available. A harbor-master is at Stonington." About Ram Island Reef, *Coast Pilot* reads: "Ram Island Reef, 1.8 miles westward of Latimer Reef light, has two detached parts: the southerly section is covered 6 1/2 feet and marked by a lighted bell buoy, and the northerly section, covered by 1 foot, is marked by a buoy. Passage between the reef and island is unsafe because of shoals." As you can see, you will never be aware of all the aids and dangers unless you read the *Coast Pilot* for your Region *before* you depart. It might well be the means of saving your life!

"Sailing Directions," DMAHTC. Very similar to Coast Pilot (but for non-U.S. waters), they cover the following areas:

1. Region of Canada, Greenland and Iceland
   Four different publications for six different regions
2. Region of Latin America and Antarctica
   Seven different areas
3. Region of British Isles
   Four different areas
4. Region of Scandinavia and Northern USSR
   Five different areas
5. Region of Western Africa
   Two different areas
6. Region of Middle East, Eastern Africa and Southern Asia
   Six different areas
7. Region of Australia and Southwest Pacific
   Nine different areas
8. Region of Central and South Pacific
   Three different areas
9. Region of Far East and Philippine Islands
   Four different areas
10. Region of Mediterranean
    Three different areas
11. Region of North Pacific Ocean
    Six different areas
12. Region of North Sea and Baltic Sea
    Six different areas

"Tide Tables." Published yearly by NOS in four different volumes (See Chapter 4); *Tide Tables* for—

- East Coast North and South America (including Greenland)
- West Coast North and South America (including Hawaiian Islands)
- Europe and West Coast of Africa (including Mediterranean Sea)
- Central and Western Pacific and Indian Oceans

Then follow *Tidal Current Tables*, companion to *Tide Tables*, as explained in Chapter 5, both are of utmost importance in coastwise navigation.

"Tidal Current Tables." There are two volumes:

   1. *Tidal Current Tables*, Atlantic Coast of North America
   2. *Tidal Current Tables*, Pacific Coast of North America and Asia

     These are published by NOS and are explained in Chapter 4, with some extracts from both *Tide* and *Tidal Current Tables*.

"Tidal Current Charts." About a dozen have been published by NOS and depict by means of arrows and figures the set and the drift of tidal current for each hour of the tidal cycle. The charts, which may be used for any year, present a comprehensive view of tidal current movement in respective waterways as a whole, and also provide a means for rapid determination, for any time, of the set and drift of the current at various points throughtout the area covered. They have been prepared for:

- Boston Harbor
- Narragansett Bay to Nantucket Sound
- Long Island Sound (Western end) and Block Island Sound
- New York Harbor
- Delaware Bay and River
- Upper Chesapeake Bay
- Charleston Harbor
- San Francisco Bay
- Puget Sound—Northern Part
- Puget Sound—Southern Part
- Narragansett Bay

"Tidal Current Diagrams." Finally, from the same NOS source there has been a more recent development of *Tidal Current Diagrams*, for two places to date:

   1. Block Island and Eastern Long Island Sound
   2. Boston Harbor

When once you become used to these diagrams, you will note they give you the set and drift of current within the area covered, more quickly than with *Tidal Current Charts* alone.

     Most *Tidal Current Charts* depend upon the annual *Tidal Current Tables* for finding the right page to turn to with your desired time. The Narragansett Bay and New York Harbor charts are used with the annual *Tide Tables*, to enable you to find the right page. The *Tidal Current Diagrams* are to be used with the *Tidal Current Charts*.

"Light Lists." There are five *Light Lists* published by the Department of Transportation, U.S. Coast Guard and sold by the U.S. Government Printing Office (Washington, DC 20402) or by sales agents as already noted. The five *Light List* volumes, published yearly are:

- Vol. 1—Atlantic Coast (St. Croix River, Maine, to Little River, South Carolina); also identified as
     CG-158
- Vol. 2—Atlantic and Gulf Coasts (Little River, South Carolina, to Rio Grande, Texas, and Antilles)
- Vol. 3—Pacific Coast and Pacific Islands
- Vol. 4—Great Lakes
- Vol. 5—Mississippi River System

Address: U.S. Coast Guard (USCG):

        First Coast Guard District
        150 Causeway Street
        Boston, MA 02114

Addresses of other districts are given on page III of *Light List*, Vol. 1, or see the beginning of this section for details on free nautical chart catalogs.

These volumes tend to be ponderous. Some mariners copy information which they might need, so they will be carrying pages rather than large books. Procedure depends very much on conditions, size of vessel, space for the mariner, etc.

Light List for foreign coasts are published by the DMAHTC for seven different areas: Greenland; parts of West and East Coasts of North and South America, Australia, Tasmania, New Zealand and the islands of the North and South Pacific Oceans; Western Pacific and Indian Oceans including the Persian Gulf and Red Sea; West Coasts of Europe and Africa, the Mediterranean Sea, Black Sea, and Azovskoye More (sea of Azov); British Isles, English Channel, and North Sea; Norway, Iceland, and Arctic Ocean, and finally, Baltic Sea, Kattegat, Belts and Sound, and Gulf of Bothnia.

"Notice to Mariners." The distribution of *Notice to Mariners* on a weekly basis is made to all U.S. Navy and Coast Guard ships and to most ships of the Merchant Marine providing a mailing address. Individuals who really need them may also receive copies. *Notice to Mariners* provides information specifically intended for *updating* the latest editions of nautical charts and publications issued or sold by the DMAHTC, NOS and the USCG.

Upon first inspection you might feel bewildered by all the changes which you think you are going to be obliged to make, for safety, on all your charts and publications, such as *Pub. 117* and *Light Lists*. However, if you stop to think about it, you are not going to sail everywhere at once. For your own interest, you probably have to keep track of a few charts, possibly around a dozen or more if you are going on a long voyage. However, your vessel is probably not of the USS FORRESTAL class, which requires more than 24,000 different charts, maps, and other navigational materials according to Dutton's *Navigation and Plotting*.

For your own cruise, once you are familiar with the present numbering system for charts and find numbers which apply to your regions, then, if you glance through all the numbers in *Notice to Mariners*, you will see that in some issues your charts will not be affected at all, and then again, in other issues, you will want to make a few changes. The important thing to remember is that you must check *each week* to see if your charts and publications are going to need changes since the date of issue of your chart or publication. The DMAHTC warns that caution should be exercised in using charts under a *red* light. If there are any vital features shown in red, orange and yellow colors, it is advisable to highlight them in some color that will show, such as blue, green, brown or purple. Avoid use of red ink or red pencil for marking.

On the first page of *NM*, it states: "Information for the *Notice to Mariners* is contributed by the following agencies: DMAHTC (Department of Defense) for waters outside the territorial limits of the United States; National Ocean Survey (NOAA, Department of Commerce), which is charged with the surveys and charting of the coasts and harbors of the United States and its territories; the U.S. Coast Guard (Department of Transportation) which is responsible for the safety of life at sea and the establishment and operation of aids to navigation; and the Corps of Engineers, U.S. Army (Department of Defense) which is charged with the improvement of rivers and harbors of the United States. In addition, important contributions are made by foreign hydrographic offices and cooperating observers of all nationalities."

Each issue of *NM* is usually divided into three main parts:

Sec. I — Chart Corrections
    Coast Pilots/Sailing Directions Corrections
    Catalog Corrections—New Charts and Pubs
    Chartlets/Depth Tabulations/Notes

Sec. II — Light List Corrections
    Radio Navigational Aids Corrections
    Other Pub. Corrections

Sec. III— Broadcast Warnings

Marine Information—Miscellaneous

For example in issue No. 15, 1978, of *NM* under Sec. 111, you can read:

> "354/78 (95). Japan, Honshu, Northwest Coast.
> Numerous logs adrift vicinity 35-09.8N., 132-20E.,
> about 260505 Z (GMT) March."

NM's index of regions, Geographic Locator (See Fig. III-1 in this Appendix) is always shown near the front of their publication.

Your accompanying chart numbered 116-SC Tr equals 12372, according to the newer system of numbering charts. You can discover this number by looking at the Geographic Locator; notice that the region of your chart is in the No. 12 Subregion. You could find the number 372 (or the whole number 12372) in the NOS *Nautical Chart Catalog 1*, for Atlantic and Gulf Coasts. Use this number 12372 when searching Sec. 1 of *Notice to Mariners* for chart corrections. You will *not* find the number 12372 in Section 1 of No. 15 for 1978, and so you can decide that no change at this time was made on this chart with respect to buoys, lights and other navigational aids or dangers known to the USCG.

You can note, in another issue of *NM*, that on chart #13260 a red buoy has been added at 44°32.1'N, 67°06.7'W, with a flashing red light, a bell, and a radar reflector. In this same issue of *NM* there is a block of "Cautions" which read, for Chart 37221, as follows:

1. Gas pipelines contain flammable natural gas under high pressure. Any ship damaging a pipe could face an immediate fire hazard. Mariners are strongly advised not to anchor or trawl near the pipelines.

2. The location of cables in the outer sea area may differ from those shown on this chart.

Advice of this nature should show the importance of searching through each *NM*! It is your chief line of communication on nautical matters, about which you should know.

"Local Notice to Mariners" (*LNM*), issued by the USCG, according to districts, appears weekly on the average. For example, in the August 17 Notice #37, 1977, a message pertaining to the Massachusetts Vineyard Sound read:

> "Vineyard Sound—Woods Hole—Great Harbor—The wreck buoy at the site of the 65 foot M/V VEGA has been discontinued.
> Approximate position: 41°31.4'N., 70°40.6'W
> Charts: 13229 (C&GS 114-SC), 13230 (C&GS 249)"

Note: The numbers in parentheses are the former U.S. Coast and Geodetic Survey numbers. The other numbers pertain to the newer system of numbering charts.

This issue also contained:

> "*Special local regulations for the 1977 America's Cup Races, Newport, R.I.....*
> "These regulations are issued to provide control over the America's Cup Races and to insure safety of life and property in the race area....Penalties up to $500 for violation of these regulations may be awarded....Enforcement will be by U.S. Coast Guard vessels and helicopters...."

Details followed, with a chart and picture of the area, with desired disposition of the spectator craft.

And finally, there are sometimes "Public Notices" of proposed changes in buoys and lights, or even about a footbridge across a river, with a description of the proposed moves, so that you may have an opportunity to approve or object, and suggest. In other words, you have a chance to express your views in writing, with sufficient warning for this purpose. You would report in writing to the USCG of your district.

A summary is now presented; a check list of a dozen chief publications (or pages therefrom), absolute necessities which you need to study or take with you, according to your space facilities and circumstances:

TABLE III-1
Publications Check List—Summary

For Previous Study and Planning

1. *Coast Pilot* (NOS) to cover region of your cruise or *Sailing Directions* (DMAHTC) for foreign waters
2. *Light List* (latest)
3. *Bowditch*; Vol. II, 1977, or latest
4. *Notice to Mariners*
5. *Local Notice to Mariners*
6. *Particularized Navigation*, Part I, *Emergency Booklet*
7. Preplotted cruise on appropriate chart—(Plot of courses to be made good)
8. *Rules of the Road* (May be obtained on request to USCG Marine Inspection Offices)
9. Chart Symbols

For Your Cruise

1. Watches
2. Charts to cover your regions
3. Pre-plotted cruise
4. *Tide Tables* for your region
5. *Current Tables* for your region
6. *Pub. 117 (Radio Aids) (A or B)*

7. Pages from *Light List*
8. *Coastwise Navigation* (this text), if you are a beginner
9. *Particularized Navigation*, Part II
10. Log Book
11. Pencils with erasers
12. Dividers
13. Parallel rulers, or substitute
14. *Pilot Chart* for the season
15. Six inch circular protractor
16. Compass
17. Pelorus
18. Binoculars
19. Radio Direction Finder (RDF)
20. Jackknife
21. Whistle on lanyard
22. Sextant with lanyard
23. Forms, to which you may have become attached
24. Star Chart from *Almanac*
25. Speed-distance Log
26. Signal mirror and flares
27. Flashlight
28. Fathometer (or lead and line)

RECOMMENDED BOOKS

Finally, there are numerous miscellaneous publications listed in the various catalogs mentioned here, and as an interested mariner you will enjoy browsing through all or many of the possibilities with which you might surround yourself. As always, you are limited by space, but remember also that you can read about many facts and conditions *before you depart*. You do not have to take everything with you!

The last advice certainly applies to several books which you may wish to read before departure. A few are so ponderous that you would probably like to have them in your home library. Half of the fun of going on a cruise is planning in advance, and deciding upon what you do and do not need. It really gives you *two* cruises or voyages. A list of nautical books and publications follows, some for reference, others for stimulus:

Titles

1. *Airborne: A Sentimental Journey,* William F. Buckley, Jr., Macmillan Publ. Co., NY, 1976
2. *Bowditch for Yachtsmen: Piloting* (selected from *American Practical Navigator*), David McKay Co., Inc., NY, 1976
3. Pub. No. 9, Bowditch: *American Practical Navigator,* (1977 edition for your library shelf), Vol. I, Text, Vol. II, Tables, Nathaniel Bowditch, Defense Mapping Agency Hydrographic/Topographic Center, Washington, DC
4. *The Lonely Sea and the Sky*, Francis Chichester, Coward-McCann, NY, 1964
5. *Cruising Under Sail*, Eric C. Hiscock, Oxford University Press, London, 1974
6. *The Riddle of the Sands*, Erskine Childers, Rupert Hart-Davis, London, 1969 (see also Burke Wilkinson's article in *Harvard Magazine* July-August 1978)
7. *Rules of the Nautical Road*, Farwell, U.S. Naval Institute, Annapolis, MD
8. *American Merchant Seaman's Manual*, (5th Edition), F. M. Cornell, and A.C. Hoffman, Cornell Maritime Press, Centreville, MD, 1964
9. *Merchant Marine Officers' Handbook*, (4th Edition), E.A. Turpin, and W.A. MacEwen, Cornell Maritime Press, Centreville, MD, 1965
10. *Shackleton's Boat Journey*, F.A. Worsley, W.W. Norton & Co., NY, 1977
11. *Sailing Theory and Practice*, C.A. Marchaj, Dodd, Mead & Co., NY, 1964
12. *Dutton's Navigation and Piloting*, G.D. Dunlap and H.H. Shufeldt, Naval Institute Press, Annapolis, MD, 1969
13. *Celestial Navigation*, Frances W. Wright, Cornell Maritime Press, Centreville, MD, 1969
14. *Particularized Navigation*, Part I, Emergency Booklet, Part II, Emergency Pamphlet, Frances W. Wright, Cornell Maritime Press, Centreville, MD, 1973
15. *Admirals in Collision*, R. Hough, Viking Press, NY, 1959
16. *SOS North Pacific*, G.R. Newell, Binfords and Mort, Portland, OR, 1955
17. *Chapman Piloting, Seamanship and Small Boat Handling* (53rd Edition) (excellent for practical matters of boat handling), Elbert S. Maloney, Motor Boating and Sailing Books, NY, 1978
18. *Navigation*, Journal of the Institute of Navigation, USA (for your future interest), Suite 832, 15th Street, N.W., Washington, DC
19. *The Journal of Navigation* (for your future interest), The Royal Geographical Society, 1 Kinsington Gore, London, SW 7 2 AT
20. *The Role of Magnetic Compasses in the Days of Gyrocompasses*, Hiroshi Suzuki, Paper presented at International Congress, 1976, Museum of Science, Boston, MA
21. *Pilot Chart*, Set for 3 months around your cruise and for appropriate ocean, DMAHTC
22. *Maneuvering Board Manual: H.O. Pub. No. 217*, U.S. Naval Oceanographic Office, DMAHTC
23. *Rules of the Road* (pamphlet which may be obtained upon request to USCG Headquarters, 400 Seventh Street, S.W., Washington, DC 20590 (Attn: Commandant CAS 2/81)
24. *Great Adventures in Small Boats*, David Klein & Mary Louise King, Collier Books, NY; Collier-Macmillan Ltd., London, printed in USA, 1967, 2nd printing
25. *Collision Course*, Alvin Moscow, G.P. Putnam's Sons, 1959

Appendix IV

Conversion Tables for Metric System

TABLE IV-1
Standard Conversion Factors

US/Customary Units to Metric/International			Metric/International Units to US/Customary		
Value	Multiply by	Find	Value	Multiply by	Find
inches	25.4	millimeters	centimeters	0.3937	inches
feet	0.3048	meters	meters	3.281	feet
yards	0.9144	meters	meters	1.094	yards
statute miles	1.609	kilometers	kilometers	0.6214	statute miles
nautical miles	1.852	kilometers	kilometers	0.5400	nautical miles
ounces (weight)	28.35	grams	grams	0.03527	ounce (weight)
pounds	0.4536	kilograms	kilograms	2.205	pounds
ounces (liquid)	30.28	milliliters	milliliters	0.03302	ounces (liquid)
quarts	0.9464	liters	liters	1.057	quarts
gallons	3.785	liters	liters	0.2642	gallon
Fahrenheit temperature	5/9 after subtracting 32	Celsius temperature	Celsius temperature	9/5 then add 32	Fahrenheit temperature
			radian	57.30	degree
degree	0.01745	radian			

TABLE IV-2 Feet to Meters		TABLE IV-3 Yards to Meters		TABLE IV-4 Fathoms to Meters	
(feet x 0.3048) = meters		(yards x 0.9144) = meters		(fathoms x 1.8288) = meters	
Feet	Meters	Yards	Meters	Fathoms	Meters
1	0.305	1	0.914	1	1.829
2	0.610	2	1.829	2	3.658
3	0.914	3	2.743	3	5.486
4	1.219	4	3.658	4	7.315
5	1.524	5	4.572	5	9.144
6	1.829	6	5.486	6	10.973
7	2.134	7	6.401	7	12.802
8	2.438	8	7.315	8	14.630
9	2.743	9	8.230	9	16.459
10	3.05	10	9.14	10	18.29
20	6.10	20	18.29	20	36.58
30	9.14	30	27.43	30	54.86
40	12.19	40	36.58	40	73.15
50	15.24	50	45.72	50	91.44
60	18.29	60	54.86	60	109.73
70	21.34	70	64.01	70	128.02
80	24.38	80	73.15	80	146.30
90	27.43	90	82.30	90	164.59
100	30.5	100	91.44	100	182.9

TABLE IV-5
Meters to Feet, Yards & Fathoms

(meters x 3.2808) = feet
(meters x 1.0936) = yards
(meters x 0.5468) = fathoms

Meters	Feet	Yards	Fathoms
1	3.281	1.094	0.547
2	6.562	2.187	1.094
3	9.842	3.281	1.640
4	13.123	4.374	2.187
5	16.404	5.468	2.734
6	19.685	6.562	3.281
7	22.966	7.655	3.828
8	26.246	8.749	4.374
9	29.527	9.842	4.921
10	32.81	10.94	5.47
20	65.62	21.87	10.94
30	98.42	32.81	16.40
40	131.23	43.74	21.87
50	164.04	54.68	27.34
60	196.85	65.62	32.81
70	229.66	76.55	38.28
80	262.46	87.49	43.74
90	295.27	98.42	49.21
100	328.1	109.4	54.7

TABLE IV-7
Nautical Miles to Kilometers

(Nautical miles x 1.852) = Kilometers

Nautical Miles (kn)	Kilometers (km/hr)
1	1.852
2	3.704
3	5.556
4	7.408
5	9.260
6	11.112
7	12.964
8	14.816
9	16.668
10	18.52
20	37.04
30	55.56
40	74.08
50	92.60
60	111.12
70	129.64
80	148.16
90	166.68
100	185.2

TABLE IV-8
Temperature

Celsius (C)—Fahrenheit (F)

C°	F°	C°	F°
−20°	− 4°	10°	50°
−19	− 2	11	52
−18	0	12	54
−17	+ 1	13	55
−16	+ 3	14	57
−15	+ 5	15	59
−14	+ 7	16	61
−13	+ 9	17	63
−12	+10	18	64
−11	+12	19	66
−10	+14	20	68
− 9	+16	21	70
− 8	+18	22	72
− 7	+19	23	73
− 6	+21	24	75
− 5	+23	25	77
− 4	+25	26	79
− 3	+27	27	81
− 2	+28	28	82
− 1	+30	29	84
0	32	30	86
1	34	31	88
2	36	32	90
3	37	33	91
4	39	34	93
5	41	35	95
6	43	36	97
7	45	37	99
8	46	38	100
9	48	100	212

TABLE IV-6
Kilometers to Nautical Miles

(km. x 0.5400) = nautical miles)
Distance or Speed

Kilometers (km/hr)	Nautical Miles (kn)
1	0.54
2	1.08
3	1.62
4	2.16
5	2.70
6	3.24
7	3.78
8	4.32
9	4.86
10	5.40
20	10.80
30	16.2
40	21.6
50	27.0
60	32.4
70	37.8
80	43.2
90	48.6
100	54.0

TABLE IV-9
Distance to Visible Horizon

Ht. of Object above Water (feet)	(meters)	Distance of Horizon (Nau. Miles)	Ht. of Object above Water (feet)	(meters)	Distance of Horizon (Nau. Miles)
5	1.5	2.6	200	61	16.2
10	3.0	3.6	300	91	19.8
15	4.6	4.4	500	152	25.6
20	6.1	5.1	1000	305	36.2
30	9.1	6.3	2000	610	51.2
40	12.2	7.2	3000	914	62.7
60	18.3	8.9	5000	1524	80.9
80	24.4	10.2	7000	2134	95.7
100	30.5	11.4	10000	3048	114.4
150	45.7	14.0			

1 nautical mile = 1.85 kilometers = 6080 ft. = 1.15 statute miles

You may want to know how far you can see—either the distance of the horizon from you or the distance of some object (such as a light, tank, spire, or mountain) from you. Formula is: Dist. (Nau. miles) = 1.15 $\sqrt{Ht.}$ (Ht. in feet) Example: If a light had a height of 200′ above the high-water line and you were swimming and could just see it on the horizon, the light would be 16.2 nautical miles away. If, however, you were at a height of 10′, you would be farther away. You would add the two distances and obtain 16.2 + 3.6 = 19.8 nautical miles. (Reprinted from and courtesy of *Particularized Navigation*.)

TABLE IV-10
Distance from Vertical Angles

Heights in feet. Values are degrees (°) and minutes (′).

Dist., nautical miles.	40	45	50	55	60	65	70	75	80	85	90	95	100	110	120	130	140
0.1	8 46	4 14	4 42	5 10	5 38	6 06	6 34	7 02	7 30	7 58	8 25	8 53	9 20	10 15	11 10	12 04	12 58
.2	1 53	2 07	2 21	2 35	2 49	3 04	3 18	3 32	3 46	4 00	4 14	4 28	4 42	5 10	5 38	6 06	6 34
.3	1 15	1 25	1 34	1 44	1 53	2 02	2 12	2 21	2 31	2 40	2 49	2 59	3 08	3 27	3 46	4 05	4 23
.4	0 57	1 04	1 11	1 18	1 25	1 32	1 39	1 46	1 53	2 00	2 07	2 14	2 21	2 35	2 49	3 04	3 18
0.5	0 45	0 51	0 57	1 02	1 08	1 14	1 19	1 25	1 30	1 36	1 42	1 47	1 53	2 04	2 16	2 27	2 38
.6	0 38	0 42	0 47	0 52	0 57	1 01	1 06	1 11	1 15	1 20	1 25	1 30	1 34	1 44	1 53	2 02	2 12
.7	0 32	0 36	0 40	0 44	0 48	0 53	0 57	1 01	1 05	1 09	1 13	1 17	1 21	1 29	1 37	1 45	1 53
.8	0 28	0 32	0 35	0 39	0 42	0 46	0 49	0 53	0 57	1 00	1 04	1 07	1 11	1 18	1 25	1 32	1 39
.9	0 25	0 28	0 31	0 35	0 38	0 41	0 44	0 47	0 50	0 53	0 57	1 00	1 03	1 09	1 15	1 22	1 28
1.0	0 23	0 25	0 28	0 31	0 34	0 37	0 40	0 42	0 45	0 48	0 51	0 54	0 57	1 02	1 08	1 14	1 19
.1	0 21	0 23	0 26	0 28	0 31	0 33	0 36	0 39	0 41	0 44	0 46	0 49	0 51	0 57	1 02	1 07	1 12
.2	0 19	0 21	0 24	0 26	0 28	0 31	0 33	0 35	0 38	0 40	0 42	0 45	0 47	0 52	0 57	1 01	1 06
.3	0 17	0 20	0 22	0 24	0 26	0 28	0 30	0 33	0 35	0 37	0 39	0 41	0 44	0 48	0 52	0 57	1 01
.4	0 16	0 18	0 20	0 22	0 24	0 26	0 28	0 30	0 32	0 34	0 36	0 38	0 40	0 44	0 48	0 53	0 57
1.5	0 15	0 17	0 19	0 21	0 23	0 25	0 26	0 28	0 30	0 32	0 34	0 36	0 38	0 41	0 45	0 49	0 53
.6	0 14	0 16	0 18	0 19	0 21	0 23	0 25	0 27	0 28	0 30	0 32	0 34	0 35	0 39	0 42	0 46	0 49
.7	0 13	0 15	0 17	0 18	0 20	0 22	0 23	0 25	0 27	0 28	0 30	0 32	0 33	0 37	0 40	0 43	0 47
.8	0 13	0 14	0 16	0 17	0 19	0 20	0 22	0 24	0 25	0 27	0 28	0 30	0 31	0 35	0 38	0 41	0 44
.9	0 12	0 13	0 15	0 16	0 18	0 19	0 21	0 22	0 24	0 25	0 27	0 28	0 30	0 33	0 36	0 39	0 42
2.0	0 11	0 13	0 14	0 16	0 17	0 18	0 20	0 21	0 23	0 24	0 25	0 27	0 28	0 31	0 34	0 37	0 40
.1	0 11	0 13	0 14	0 15	0 16	0 18	0 19	0 20	0 22	0 23	0 24	0 26	0 27	0 30	0 32	0 35	0 38
.2	0 10	0 12	0 13	0 14	0 15	0 17	0 18	0 19	0 21	0 22	0 23	0 24	0 26	0 28	0 31	0 33	0 36
.3	0 10	0 12	0 12	0 14	0 14	0 16	0 17	0 18	0 20	0 21	0 22	0 23	0 25	0 27	0 30	0 32	0 34
.4	0 10	0 11	0 12	0 13	0 14	0 15	0 17	0 18	0 19	0 20	0 21	0 22	0 24	0 26	0 28	0 31	0 33
2.5	0 9	0 11	0 11	0 12	0 13	0 15	0 16	0 17	0 18	0 19	0 20	0 21	0 23	0 25	0 27	0 29	0 32
.6	0 9	0 10	0 11	0 12	0 13	0 14	0 15	0 16	0 17	0 18	0 20	0 21	0 22	0 24	0 26	0 28	0 30
.7	0 9	0 10	0 10	0 11	0 12	0 14	0 15	0 16	0 17	0 18	0 19	0 20	0 21	0 23	0 25	0 27	0 29
.8	0 8	0 9	0 10	0 11	0 12	0 13	0 14	0 15	0 16	0 17	0 18	0 19	0 20	0 22	0 24	0 26	0 28
.9	0 8	0 9	0 10	0 10	0 11	0 13	0 14	0 15	0 16	0 17	0 18	0 19	0 20	0 21	0 23	0 25	0 27
3.0	0 8	0 9	0 9	0 10	0 10	0 12	0 13	0 14	0 15	0 16	0 17	0 18	0 19	0 21	0 23	0 25	0 26
.2							0 12	0 13	0 14	0 15	0 16	0 17	0 18	0 19	0 21	0 23	0 25
.4							0 12	0 12	0 13	0 14	0 15	0 16	0 17	0 18	0 20	0 22	0 23
.6							0 11	0 12	0 12	0 13	0 14	0 15	0 16	0 17	0 19	0 20	0 22
.8							0 10	0 11	0 12	0 13	0 13	0 14	0 15	0 16	0 18	0 19	0 21
4.0							0 10	0 11	0 11	0 12	0 13	0 13	0 14	0 16	0 17	0 18	0 20
.2										0 11	0 12	0 12	0 13	0 14	0 16	0 17	0 19
.4										0 11	0 11	0 12	0 12	0 13	0 15	0 17	0 18
.6										0 10	0 11	0 11	0 12	0 13	0 14	0 16	0 17
.8										0 10	0 11	0 11	0 12	0 13	0 14	0 15	0 17
5.0										0 10	0 10	0 11	0 11	0 12	0 14	0 15	0 16

TABLE IV-11
Speed, Time and Distance

Min-utes	Speed in knots																				Min-utes
	0.5	1.0	1.5	2.0	2.5	3.0	3.5	4.0	4.5	5.0	5.5	6.0	6.5	7.0	7.5	8.0	9.0	10.0	11.0	12.0	
	Miles	Miles	Miles	Miles	Miles	Miles	Miles	Miles	Miles	Miles	Miles	Miles	Miles	Miles	Miles	Miles	Miles	Miles	Miles	Miles	
1	0.0	0.0	0.0	0.0	0.0	0.0	0.1	0.1	0.1	0.1	0.1	0.1	0.1	0.1	0.1	0.1	0.2	0.2	0.2	0.2	1
2	0.0	0.0	0.0	0.1	0.1	0.1	0.1	0.1	0.1	0.2	0.2	0.2	0.2	0.2	0.2	0.3	0.3	0.3	0.4	0.4	2
3	0.0	0.0	0.1	0.1	0.1	0.2	0.2	0.2	0.2	0.2	0.3	0.3	0.3	0.4	0.4	0.4	0.4	0.5	0.6	0.6	3
4	0.0	0.1	0.1	0.1	0.2	0.2	0.2	0.3	0.3	0.3	0.4	0.4	0.4	0.5	0.5	0.5	0.6	0.7	0.7	0.8	4
5	0.0	0.1	0.1	0.2	0.2	0.2	0.3	0.3	0.4	0.4	0.5	0.5	0.5	0.6	0.6	0.7	0.8	0.8	0.9	1.0	5
6	0.0	0.1	0.2	0.2	0.2	0.3	0.4	0.4	0.4	0.5	0.6	0.6	0.6	0.7	0.8	0.8	0.9	1.0	1.1	1.2	6
7	0.1	0.1	0.2	0.2	0.3	0.4	0.4	0.5	0.5	0.6	0.6	0.7	0.8	0.8	0.9	0.9	1.0	1.2	1.3	1.4	7
8	0.1	0.1	0.2	0.3	0.3	0.4	0.5	0.5	0.6	0.7	0.7	0.8	0.9	0.9	1.0	1.1	1.2	1.3	1.5	1.6	8
9	0.1	0.2	0.2	0.3	0.4	0.4	0.5	0.6	0.7	0.8	0.8	0.9	1.0	1.0	1.1	1.2	1.4	1.5	1.6	1.8	9
10	0.1	0.2	0.2	0.3	0.4	0.5	0.6	0.7	0.8	0.8	0.9	1.0	1.1	1.2	1.2	1.3	1.5	1.7	1.8	2.0	10
11	0.1	0.2	0.3	0.4	0.5	0.6	0.6	0.7	0.8	0.9	1.0	1.1	1.2	1.3	1.4	1.5	1.6	1.8	2.0	2.2	11
12	0.1	0.2	0.3	0.4	0.5	0.6	0.7	0.8	0.9	1.0	1.1	1.2	1.3	1.4	1.5	1.6	1.8	2.0	2.2	2.4	12
13	0.1	0.2	0.3	0.4	0.5	0.6	0.8	0.9	1.0	1.1	1.2	1.3	1.4	1.5	1.6	1.7	2.0	2.2	2.4	2.6	13
14	0.1	0.2	0.4	0.5	0.6	0.7	0.8	0.9	1.0	1.2	1.3	1.4	1.5	1.6	1.8	1.9	2.1	2.3	2.6	2.8	14
15	0.1	0.2	0.4	0.5	0.6	0.8	0.9	1.0	1.1	1.2	1.4	1.5	1.6	1.8	1.9	2.0	2.2	2.5	2.8	3.0	15
16	0.1	0.3	0.4	0.5	0.7	0.8	0.9	1.1	1.2	1.3	1.5	1.6	1.7	1.9	2.0	2.1	2.4	2.7	2.9	3.2	16
17	0.1	0.3	0.4	0.6	0.7	0.8	1.0	1.1	1.3	1.4	1.6	1.7	1.8	2.0	2.1	2.3	2.6	2.8	3.1	3.4	17
18	0.2	0.3	0.4	0.6	0.8	0.9	1.0	1.2	1.4	1.5	1.6	1.8	2.0	2.1	2.2	2.4	2.7	3.0	3.3	3.6	18
19	0.2	0.3	0.5	0.6	0.8	1.0	1.1	1.3	1.4	1.6	1.7	1.9	2.1	2.2	2.4	2.5	2.8	3.2	3.5	3.8	19
20	0.2	0.3	0.5	0.7	0.8	1.0	1.2	1.3	1.5	1.7	1.8	2.0	2.2	2.3	2.5	2.7	3.0	3.3	3.7	4.0	20
21	0.2	0.4	0.5	0.7	0.9	1.0	1.2	1.4	1.6	1.8	1.9	2.1	2.3	2.4	2.6	2.8	3.2	3.5	3.8	4.2	21
22	0.2	0.4	0.6	0.7	0.9	1.1	1.3	1.5	1.6	1.8	2.0	2.2	2.4	2.6	2.8	2.9	3.3	3.7	4.0	4.4	22
23	0.2	0.4	0.6	0.8	1.0	1.2	1.3	1.5	1.7	1.9	2.1	2.3	2.5	2.7	2.9	3.1	3.4	3.8	4.2	4.6	23
24	0.2	0.4	0.6	0.8	1.0	1.2	1.4	1.6	1.8	2.0	2.2	2.4	2.6	2.8	3.0	3.2	3.6	4.0	4.4	4.8	24
25	0.2	0.4	0.6	0.8	1.0	1.2	1.5	1.7	1.9	2.1	2.3	2.5	2.7	2.9	3.1	3.3	3.8	4.2	4.6	5.0	25
26	0.2	0.4	0.6	0.9	1.1	1.3	1.5	1.7	2.0	2.2	2.4	2.6	2.8	3.0	3.2	3.5	3.9	4.3	4.8	5.2	26
27	0.2	0.4	0.7	0.9	1.1	1.4	1.6	1.8	2.0	2.2	2.5	2.7	2.9	3.2	3.4	3.6	4.0	4.5	5.0	5.4	27
28	0.2	0.5	0.7	0.9	1.2	1.4	1.6	1.9	2.1	2.3	2.6	2.8	3.0	3.3	3.5	3.7	4.2	4.7	5.1	5.6	28
29	0.2	0.5	0.7	1.0	1.2	1.4	1.7	1.9	2.2	2.4	2.7	2.9	3.1	3.4	3.6	3.9	4.4	4.8	5.3	5.8	29
30	0.2	0.5	0.8	1.0	1.2	1.5	1.8	2.0	2.2	2.5	2.8	3.0	3.2	3.5	3.8	4.0	4.5	5.0	5.5	6.0	30
31	0.3	0.5	0.8	1.0	1.3	1.6	1.8	2.1	2.3	2.6	2.8	3.1	3.4	3.6	3.9	4.1	4.6	5.2	5.7	6.2	31
32	0.3	0.5	0.8	1.1	1.3	1.6	1.9	2.1	2.4	2.7	2.9	3.2	3.5	3.7	4.0	4.3	4.8	5.3	5.9	6.4	32
33	0.3	0.6	0.8	1.1	1.4	1.6	1.9	2.2	2.5	2.8	3.0	3.3	3.6	3.8	4.1	4.4	5.0	5.5	6.0	6.6	33
34	0.3	0.6	0.8	1.1	1.4	1.7	2.0	2.3	2.6	2.8	3.1	3.4	3.7	4.0	4.2	4.5	5.1	5.7	6.2	6.8	34
35	0.3	0.6	0.9	1.2	1.5	1.8	2.0	2.3	2.6	2.9	3.2	3.5	3.8	4.1	4.4	4.7	5.2	5.8	6.4	7.0	35
36	0.3	0.6	0.9	1.2	1.5	1.8	2.1	2.4	2.7	3.0	3.3	3.6	3.9	4.2	4.5	4.8	5.4	6.0	6.6	7.2	36
37	0.3	0.6	0.9	1.2	1.5	1.8	2.2	2.5	2.8	3.1	3.4	3.7	4.0	4.3	4.6	4.9	5.6	6.2	6.8	7.4	37
38	0.3	0.6	1.0	1.3	1.6	1.9	2.2	2.5	2.8	3.2	3.5	3.8	4.1	4.4	4.8	5.1	5.7	6.3	7.0	7.6	38
39	0.3	0.6	1.0	1.3	1.6	2.0	2.3	2.6	2.9	3.2	3.6	3.9	4.2	4.6	4.9	5.2	5.8	6.5	7.2	7.8	39
40	0.3	0.7	1.0	1.3	1.7	2.0	2.3	2.7	3.0	3.3	3.7	4.0	4.3	4.7	5.0	5.3	6.0	6.7	7.3	8.0	40
41	0.3	0.7	1.0	1.4	1.7	2.0	2.4	2.7	3.1	3.4	3.8	4.1	4.4	4.8	5.1	5.5	6.2	6.8	7.5	8.2	41
42	0.4	0.7	1.0	1.4	1.8	2.1	2.4	2.8	3.2	3.5	3.8	4.2	4.6	4.9	5.2	5.6	6.3	7.0	7.7	8.4	42
43	0.4	0.7	1.1	1.4	1.8	2.2	2.5	2.9	3.2	3.6	3.9	4.3	4.7	5.0	5.4	5.7	6.4	7.2	7.9	8.6	43
44	0.4	0.7	1.1	1.5	1.8	2.2	2.6	2.9	3.3	3.7	4.0	4.4	4.8	5.1	5.5	5.9	6.6	7.3	8.1	8.8	44
45	0.4	0.8	1.1	1.5	1.9	2.2	2.6	3.0	3.4	3.8	4.1	4.5	4.9	5.2	5.6	6.0	6.8	7.5	8.2	9.0	45
46	0.4	0.8	1.2	1.5	1.9	2.3	2.7	3.1	3.4	3.8	4.2	4.6	5.0	5.4	5.8	6.1	6.9	7.7	8.4	9.2	46
47	0.4	0.8	1.2	1.6	2.0	2.4	2.7	3.1	3.5	3.9	4.3	4.7	5.1	5.5	5.9	6.3	7.0	7.8	8.6	9.4	47
48	0.4	0.8	1.2	1.6	2.0	2.4	2.8	3.2	3.6	4.0	4.4	4.8	5.2	5.6	6.0	6.4	7.2	8.0	8.8	9.6	48
49	0.4	0.8	1.2	1.6	2.0	2.4	2.9	3.3	3.7	4.1	4.5	4.9	5.3	5.7	6.1	6.5	7.4	8.2	9.0	9.8	49
50	0.4	0.8	1.2	1.7	2.1	2.5	2.9	3.3	3.8	4.2	4.6	5.0	5.4	5.8	6.2	6.7	7.5	8.3	9.2	10.0	50
51	0.4	0.8	1.3	1.7	2.1	2.6	3.0	3.4	3.8	4.2	4.7	5.1	5.5	6.0	6.4	6.8	7.6	8.5	9.4	10.2	51
52	0.4	0.9	1.3	1.7	2.2	2.6	3.0	3.5	3.9	4.3	4.8	5.2	5.6	6.1	6.5	6.9	7.8	8.7	9.5	10.4	52
53	0.4	0.9	1.3	1.8	2.2	2.6	3.1	3.5	4.0	4.4	4.9	5.3	5.7	6.2	6.6	7.1	8.0	8.8	9.7	10.6	53
54	0.4	0.9	1.4	1.8	2.2	2.7	3.2	3.6	4.0	4.5	5.0	5.4	5.8	6.3	6.8	7.2	8.1	9.0	9.9	10.8	54
55	0.5	0.9	1.4	1.8	2.3	2.8	3.2	3.7	4.1	4.6	5.0	5.5	6.0	6.4	6.9	7.3	8.2	9.2	10.1	11.0	55
56	0.5	0.9	1.4	1.9	2.3	2.8	3.3	3.7	4.2	4.7	5.1	5.6	6.1	6.5	7.0	7.5	8.4	9.3	10.3	11.2	56
57	0.5	1.0	1.4	1.9	2.4	2.8	3.3	3.8	4.3	4.8	5.2	5.7	6.2	6.6	7.1	7.6	8.6	9.5	10.4	11.4	57
58	0.5	1.0	1.4	1.9	2.4	2.9	3.4	3.9	4.4	4.8	5.3	5.8	6.3	6.8	7.2	7.7	8.7	9.7	10.6	11.6	58
59	0.5	1.0	1.5	2.0	2.5	3.0	3.4	3.9	4.4	4.9	5.4	5.9	6.4	6.9	7.4	7.9	8.8	9.8	10.8	11.8	59
60	0.5	1.0	1.5	2.0	2.5	3.0	3.5	4.0	4.5	5.0	5.5	6.0	6.5	7.0	7.5	8.0	9.0	10.0	11.0	12.0	60

INDEX

Index